Frank
Lloyd
Wright

REMEMBERED

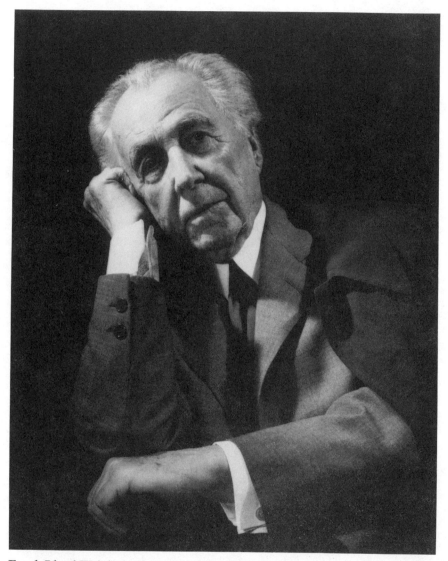

Frank Lloyd Wright in the early 1940s. (State Historical Society of Wisconsin)

Frank Lloyd Wright

REMEMBERED

Patrick J. Meehan, AIA, Editor

The Preservation Press
National Trust for Historic Preservation

The Preservation Press
National Trust for Historic Preservation
1785 Massachusetts Avenue, N.W.
Washington, D.C. 20036

The National Trust for Historic Preservation in the United
States is the only private, nonprofit organization chartered
by Congress to encourage public participation in the
preservation of sites, buildings, and objects significant in
American history and culture. Support is provided by
membership dues, endowment funds, contributions, and
grants from federal agencies, including the U.S. Department
of the Interior, under provisions of the National Historic
Preservation Act of 1966. For information about membership,
write to the Trust at the above address.

Printed in the United States of America
95 94 93 92 91   5 4 3 2 1

Library of Congress Cataloging in Publication Data
Meehan, Patrick Joseph.
  Frank Lloyd Wright remembered / Patrick J. Meehan.
    p.   cm.
  Includes bibliographical references and index.
  ISBN 0-89133-187-5
  1. Wright, Frank Lloyd, 1867-1959—Criticism and
  interpretation.   I. Title.
  NA737.W7M44   1991
  720'.92—dc20   91-3728

Designed and typeset by J. Scott Knudsen, Park City, Utah
Printed by the John D. Lucas Printing Company,
Baltimore, Maryland

∞ The paper used in this publication meets the minimum requirements of the American
National Standard for Permanence of Paper for Printed Library Mateials Z39.48–1984

To Karen, Ryan, Sean,

and the young architects of the future—

The Nature of Man

Can Be As Complex

As Nature Itself

Contents

PREFACE viii

IN HIS OWN WORDS: FRANK LLOYD WRIGHT'S PUBLIC PERSONA
1 The Shape of the City 2
2 The Shape of Miami 8
3 On the Design of the U.S. Air Force Academy 15

ARCHITECTS
4 Bruce Goff 34
5 R. Buckminster Fuller 39
6 Walter Gropius 42
7 Philip Johnson 48
8 Ludwig Mies van der Rohe 53
9 Eero Saarinen 55
10 Edward D. Stone 56

CLIENTS
11 Samuel Freeman 61
12 Loren B. Pope 65
13 Arch Oboler 76
14 Sarah Smith 88
15 Nicholas P. Daphne 97
16 James Edwards 100
17 Robert and Gloria Berger 104
18 Richard Davis 110

APPRENTICES
19 John H. Howe 116
20 William Beye Fyfe 136

21 William Wesley Peters 137

22 Marya de Czarnecka Lilien 139

23 Gordon O. Chadwick 140

24 Aaron G. Green 148

25 John Geiger 158

26 Fay Jones 162

27 Vernon D. Swaback 164

FRIENDS AND ACQUAINTANCES

28 Alan Reiach 172

29 Robert L. Ziegelman 176

30 Aline B. Saarinen 178

31 Joan W. Saltzstein 183

32 Egon Weiner 188

33 William T. Evjue 190

34 Ben Raeburn 193

35 Rev. Joseph A. Vaughan, S.J. 196

36 Louise Mendelsohn 198

37 Lewis Mumford 200

FAMILY

38 Olgivanna Lloyd Wright 213

39 Lloyd Wright 218

40 Catherine Dorothy Wright Baxter 231

41 Robert Llewellyn Wright 235

42 Anne Baxter 240

EPILOGUE 245

NOTES 246

BIBLIOGRAPHY 248

INDEX 250

PREFACE

This book presents Frank Lloyd Wright from the perspective of those who knew him best: fellow architects, clients, apprentices, acquaintances and friends, and members of his immediate family. No other book on Wright reveals his personal side from so many differing points of view or levels of intimacy.

Frank Lloyd Wright Remembered is the third transcribed volume of a predominantly oral trilogy concerning Wright that I have both edited and introduced. The first volume, *The Master Architect: Conversations with Frank Lloyd Wright,* presented 18 conversations between Wright and close friends, notable press personalities, and real estate developers. The second volume, *Truth Against the World: Frank Lloyd Wright Speaks for an Organic Architecture,* provided the first comprehensive one-volume collection of Wright's most important speeches on architecture and contemporary society.

This is my fourth book on Wright. My first, *Frank Lloyd Wright: A Research Guide to Archival Sources,* served as an introduction to the many well-known (and other lesser-known) manuscript materials on Wright available almost exclusively to the scholarly researcher.

Similar to the sources used in compiling my earlier books, those used in the preparation of *Frank Lloyd Wright Remembered* were mostly rare and obscure publications, radio broadcasts, and public speeches and discussions. A few of the reminiscences were written especially for this book.

The 42 chapters of *Frank Lloyd Wright Remembered* are divided into six parts, arranged in sequence to reveal Frank Lloyd Wright on an ever-increasing personal level. The fond, and sometimes not so fond, remembrances of 40 people are included. Through this arrangement, the complex nature of Wright's personality emerges. And what emerges, ultimately, is a personality as complex as his genius. Since many of the people quoted are now deceased, a further intent of this book is to preserve these obscure oral records in published form so they are available to a wide audience and do not become lost.

As during the conduct of my research for my earlier books on Wright, I have been fortunate in receiving considerable kind aid from others. I wish, therefore, to give thanks to the following persons for their help in providing me with materials and permissions that allowed me to complete this book: Patricia Akre, San Francisco Public Library; Jose C. Arroyo, Putman Publishing Group; William B. Babcock, Wisconsin Society of Architects/AIA; Robert M. Beckley, FAIA, College of Architecture and

Urban Planning, University of Michigan; John C. Brewer, New York Times Company; Katherine Burns, *Reader's Digest*; Carol Christiansen, Doubleday, a division of the Bantam, Doubleday, Dell Publishing Group; Richard M. Davis, M.D.; Barbara Dembski, *Milwaukee Journal*; Mr. and Mrs. James J. Edwards; John Geiger; Jack Golden, AIA, Friends of Kebyar; Randolph C. Henning, Architect, of Winston-Salem, North Carolina; John H. Howe, Architect, of Burnsville, Minnesota; Beate Johansen; Hoyt Johnson, *Scottsdale Scene Magazine*, Scottsdale, Arizona; Philip Johnson, Architect, of New York City; Gary F. Karner, Ph.D.; Rep. Gerald D. Kleczka, 4th District, Wisconsin; Meg Klinkow, Research Center, Frank Lloyd Wright Home and Studio Foundation, Oak Park, Illinois; Pamela L. Kortan, Documents Program, American Institute of Architects; Rev. Ernest O. Martin, The Wayfarer's Chapel of Rancho Palos Verdes, California; Diane Maddex, formerly of The Preservation Press, National Trust for Historic Preservation; Richard E. McCommons, *Journal of Architectural Education*; Robert S. McGonigal; Robert Meloon, *Capital Times* and Leigh A. Milner, formerly of the *Capital Times*, Madison, Wisconsin; Lewis Mumford; Sophia Mumford; Nancy Nipp, Directorate of Public Affairs, United States Air Force Academy, Colorado Springs, Colorado; Stephen E. Ostrow, Prints and Photographs Division, Library of Congress; Anne Palamaro, American Institute of Architects Library; Miriam E. Phelps, Research Librarian, *Publishers Weekly*; Loren B. Pope; Polly Povejsil, *Washington Post*; Cynthia C. Davidson-Powers, *Inland Architect*; Peter F. Schmid, Marriott Library, University of Utah; Edward Storin, *Miami Herald*; William Allin Storrer; Harvey A. Tafel, The Wayfarer's Chapel of Rancho Palos Verdes, California; Bill Thomas, Pacifica Program Service, Radio Archive, North Hollywood, California; Gavin Townwend, Architectural Drawing Collection, University of California, Santa Barbara, California; the staff of the Interlibrary Loan Office of the Golda Meir Library at the University of Wisconsin-Milwaukee; Philip B. Wargelin; Ron Wiener, Photography by Wiener; Myrna Williamson, State Historical Society of Wisconsin; Nancy V. Young, Manuscripts Division, Marriott Library, University of Utah; Robert L. Ziegelman, FAIA; and Dave Zweifel, *Capital Times*, Madison, Wisconsin.

Special thanks are due to Buckley C. Jeppson, director; Janet Walker, managing editor; and Pamela Dwight, editorial assistant, of The Preservation Press, National Trust for Historic Preservation, for making this project a reality.

PATRICK J. MEEHAN, AIA

PART I

IN HIS OWN WORDS:
FRANK LLOYD WRIGHT'S
PUBLIC PERSONA

Frank Lloyd Wright, c. 1952. (Frank Lloyd Wright
Home and Studio Foundation)

1

THE SHAPE OF THE CITY

**The modern city is the basis for
banking and prostitution and very little else.**

O*n November 26, 1956, when Frank Lloyd Wright was in his 90th year, he addressed a meeting of the American Municipal Association in St. Louis, Missouri. The address was aptly titled "The Shape of the City." It was, in part, a response to a speech by the real estate magnate William Zeckendorf, then president of Webb & Knapp. One newspaper account of the event stated:*

Dressed in a brown suit, porkpie hat and carrying a cane, Wright walked off the platform amidst a standing ovation after insulting city planning, suburban life and millionaire real estate men like William Zeckendorf, his debating opponent. . . . Wright said the modern city is the "basis for banking and prostitution and very little else." Later, at a press conference, Wright added real estate promoters to the list.

Although Wright and Zeckendorf were pitted against each other on many occasions and in various public forums, they apparently remained friends through the years. "We had an undying friendship," Zeckendorf wrote in his autobiography.

Before Wright rose to the podium, he was introduced by Robert F. Wagner, mayor of New York City and president of the American Municipal Association.

MAYOR ROBERT F. WAGNER: Now we will hear from a gentleman who is one of the world's most renowned architects, and one who has recently again made news by his proposal to build a mile-high building in Chicago. Some of you may remember his debate on television with Mr. Zeckendorf on the shape of the city, and we are delighted that he is here with us today. I am very proud to introduce to you Mr. Frank Lloyd Wright.

FRANK LLOYD WRIGHT: Ladies and gentlemen, . . . you are up against

---

Frank Lloyd Wright's speech "The Shape of the City" was originally published in the American Municipal Association's *Proceedings*, 1956.

FRANK LLOYD WRIGHT: *"I study nature and from nature comes what little wisdom I can give you. I urge you to study the nature of this problem of the city in America."* **Frank Lloyd Wright in the mid-1950s. (Jun Fujita, Chicago Historical Society)**

something that is going to require from you something from the spirit rather than the pocket, something from your humanity and good will rather than scientific planning of any kind. This is deeper than a well and wider than any church door, and, as you decide it, we live as a democracy or we go down the river with the lowest form of socialism this world has ever seen. Now it is just as simple as that.

I am what they call an engineering architect. I study nature, and from nature comes what little wisdom I can give you. I urge you to study the nature of this problem of the city in America; find out the conclusion of that octopus, that monstrosity, that little overgrown village in agony and dying of its own weight.

I am not interested in redevelopment. I hate the term *re-* as a prefix for anything. What I would like to see in America is a genuine sense of development, some grasp of the fundamental idea of what the city now means to America itself. It does not mean what it used to mean any longer.

The city once upon a time was the center of all culture available; without the city, no culture. Believe me, ladies and gentlemen, now there is no culture with the city as it is. The city is the enemy of what indigenous cultures we ourselves are entitled to by way of our Declaration of Independence. We are a republic professing democracy, believing in it—a great many of us still—without knowing how we hang on to it, but still we do, and we love the idea of individual freedom. The sovereignty of the individual has come as a light to the world—if only we lived up to our profession of it, which we do not do.

Now, what of the city of the future? Our cities are overgrown villages, like this agonized monster we call New York—garbage on the sidewalks, trucks off the railroads competing with solid-gold Cadillacs, everything mixed up in a mess. And New York is only an extravagant expression of nearly every city we've got. They would all do the same if they could.

What is the common sense in this thing? Where does good sense lie? We won't talk about good taste, because taste is always a matter of ignorance. But where are we going to put our feet to consider the nature of this thing we are in?

There is a good Welsh definition of genius that came down from King Arthur's Round Table. I am Welsh; my mother was a teacher and my father a preacher, and the whole family may have been preachers back to the days of the Reformation. Here come precious little nuggets of wisdom. What we need is American genius to the fore—and this is the Welsh definition of a genius: a man who has an eye for nature, a man who has a heart for nature, and a man who has the boldness to follow nature.

Now that is the American genius. You can set him aside if you please, but there is the quality the Declaration of Independence intended to liberate in this nation, intended to put to work. It did not mean we were to have an architecture founded upon the past when we have everything new to do a new architecture with. We have steel tension, we have glass, we have entirely new opportunities to be ourselves.

Well, that applies to the city, too. The city is utterly unplanned; no thought has ever been given to it except as a redevelopment. Why not give some thought to the affair as a development according to the nature of what we are, where we are, how we are, and what it is all about?

Have you read anything on the subject? Have you ever given your own personal attention in detail to the problems of this thing as a fact of nature?

What is the nature of this thing? What is it doing to us? Where is your teen-age problem coming from? Where is all this wasted time to and fro? Whence come all these silly designs for traffic and automobiles? There is nothing mobile about the automobile . . . except the name. It is still the old lumber wagon with an engine attached to a big platform, gnashing its teeth at you as it comes down the street. There is no sense in it, no sense at all.

Bob Moses would agree with me now. Look at the taxicabs in New York City. What are they like? Imitations of Madam's little private car, and the average load of passengers is one and a half. They talk about the traffic problem, but they had better do something besides talk about it.

The traffic problem, ladies and gentlemen: if you are going to have the car, you are not going to have the present city. You are just going to have to make up your minds to choose, which do you want? Do you want to keep your cars, or do you want to keep your city practically as it is? You have got to make up your minds. What you see in the streets is only a precursor, it is only the beginning. There is nothing down there yet compared to what is coming. That flood of traffic will be up at the level of the third story in five years' time, and nobody is doing anything about it. They are building still in New York City—take the "whiskey building" [the Seagram Building], a 50-story building. No one seems to have any sense of what constitutes the nature of the thing we are in.

Now you can put a price tag on it, as Brother Zeckendorf has just done so well. He is the man to do it. He looks to me as though he has a million dollars in his pocket right now. I know how he gets it. He gets it out of the dying city. He gets it out of the thing that we've got to die with—or else raise hell with Mr. Zeckendorf and what he represents. Those are nice gentle words, Zeck, but they are true. You can't go on with this jockeying with investment in an overgrown situation that makes no sense, and culture now is independent of this thing. With television, radio, telephone, decentralization is inevitable, and I don't mean the suburb.

We, unfortunately, when we camped down here on fresh new soil, brought over the dormitory town from England. We never got from England the great spacious love of country, the love of the green that existed and made England what she is today. We have never had it in our country. Somehow we skipped it. It has got to come back. We have got to deal with it now. We want life on the green. We don't want life on hard pavements.

I have been reproached for this mile-high, 528-story skyscraper as going back on the thesis I have just uttered. It is not. I am saying with this building that if you want to centralize, here is the way to centralize for the "brain workers": get them all together. Two of those buildings would hold all there is in New York if they put them in Central Park. One of them would be over-size for St. Louis. You cannot have your commodities in the same area and under the same circumstances as you have your thinking apparatus. Nature does not do it that way. Study the human anatomy as it stands today and get from it a plan for your city.

If I were to carry this forward even two jumps, I would be obscene. Your city is just as silly as that obscenity would be if I were to utter it. And you can imagine it; I don't have to go into details.

This is not a question for Mr. Zeckendorf. This is not a question for government. Government should never be allowed to put a finger on housing for the American people. It is not in the nature of government. Culture and government are at odds, and always will be. And when you turn your affairs of culture over to government, well, you will deserve what you get. You will get what you deserve, too.

This is an individual matter. This is a matter for the American family. The American family is the unit of our democracy, and I am not speaking of the slums. I am speaking of the better democratic American element, the American family of the upper and middle third; not mobocracy, not snobocracy, but the upper and middle third.

Now let them consider this question, let them take it under advisement. Let's have some common sense spread on it, regardless of selfish political or financial interests. Let's think of it as we would think of any sensible proposition we were up against and had to decide on to save our lives. Because, you know, Brother Zeckendorf has not referred to the atom bomb, he has not referred to the fact that concentrations of the character of the city of New York and the big cities today are just plain "murder." And isn't it interesting that no newspaper report or analysis of the bomb ever gave us the nature of the bomb? It was left to a humorous magazine to do it, and that was *The New Yorker*. You remember? *The New Yorker* told us that it was out-and-out a poison bomb of the most desolating, damnable character ever conceived by the mind of men. We've lost sight of it, but you can't lose sight of it. To me, war is now unthinkable, as the president said it was in a speech I listened to over the radio. He said that war was now suicide and was unthinkable, and it is. But has it made any difference in our thinking and our lives as we live them?

We just now heard a lot about water pollution. What about air pollution? What about smog out in Los Angeles? What about carbon monoxide on the streets of New York? You could not live there very long, unless you lived in a penthouse, without consulting a doctor. It is the same everywhere. It is a betrayal of the rights and privileges and opportunities of the individual.

I am referred to often as an individualist. Well, I plead guilty to that soft impeachment. I believe in the Declaration of Independence, and I believe in the mission of this country among nations. I think everything we have here we are betraying instead of developing and emphasizing in the spirit of our forefathers and the things they sought to see happen. And they have not happened. Why? That is a question for you to answer, not for me, although I am doing it in my little way, too.

I foresaw that the city and the country were going to marry and live happily together, and I worked out a scheme and a plan for it that some people said was communism, some said was fascism. But nobody understood what it was all about, not even Zeckendorf. I called it Broadacre City. It was the green city. The green city is now a possibility. All our advantages point to it, all the gifts of science. We need that.

Another thing we need—and Zeckendorf was talking about the railroads—we need to take those railroads (that is, the vacant land on the sides of them) away from the railroaders. They are not using it, it is no good to them. Let them have their own little railway, and put the trucks on roads on each side of the railroad . . . and leave us the roadways. All the freeways we can build won't be enough just for Pa and Ma and Aunt Hattie. We've got to do this. It will help a lot.

And another thing, we've got to talk about something besides suburbia. Suburbia is a degrading existence. It takes most of Father's time—and Mother's time, too, when she isn't busy with the children in the kitchen—going to and from the city. For what? What do you go to the city for anymore? What do you get there when you go? It is only because the "brain workers" have gathered together in the city, and you have to go and consult them. The modern city is the basis for banking and prostitution and very little else.

Just as Madam has demoralized the modern car and has a taste for the elegance which she thinks is in it (which isn't there), so these other things have happened. We have lost our grip on what should be our American genius. . . . We are selling it down the river on all sorts of pretexts, and today success is about the lowest form of excess that can be imagined. Beware of success!

Well, I could go on for a long time, but I think I've said enough.

WAGNER: Thank you very much, Mr. Wright.

WRIGHT: You are entirely welcome, Mr. Mayor.

WAGNER: You are going to say good-bye to Mr. Zeckendorf, aren't you?

WRIGHT: Goodbye, Zeck.

[*Resounding applause—a standing ovation—as Wright walks off the platform*]

2

THE SHAPE OF MIAMI

**Nature must be ashamed of these hotels that you're building
down here. Nature must be ashamed of the way this place
has been laid out, and patterned after a checkerboard, and parceled out
in little parcels where you stand on each other's toes,
face the sidewalk, your elbows in the next neighbor's ribs.**

*I*n 1984 the Miami *Herald recalled a visit Frank Lloyd Wright had paid to
the city nearly three decades earlier:*

Wright came to Miami only once, on November 3, 1955, to speak to
the Fashion Group of Miami at the Balmoral Hotel. The Fashion Group
still exists, but the Balmoral is long gone, razed to make way for the
Sheraton Bal Harbour. He arrived late, sweeping into the ballroom wearing his red-lined cape and gaucho hat. It was all theatrics, as usual, but
from the moment he arrived the crowd was his to amuse, abuse, accuse.

The speech is pure Wright—he moves from worrying about the fate of
civilization to fussing over the size of billboards. He had toured Miami
with his host, architect Alfred Browning Parker, and he had been appalled
by what he had seen—boxes on the beach, boxes on the Biscayne
Boulevard. And he said so.

Later, his wife told him that this was one of the best speeches he had
ever given. And it is a delight. It is fresh and as rambunctious today as it
was then.

In the audience were architects and designers, mostly.

He talked just less than half an hour, but that was long enough. Wright
philosophized a bit, and excoriated the architecture he had seen.

*The audience's response to Wright as he delivered the speech is set forth in the
text.*

Frank Lloyd Wright's "Straight Talk About Miami Architecture" was first published in the
Miami Herald on April 1, 1984. Accompanying it was an article by Beth Dunlap entitled "An
Original American Genius." Reprinted with permission.

FRANK LLOYD WRIGHT: We were coming in on the plane looking over this great, marvelous, and very beautiful plateau, and what do we see? Little tiny subdivisions of squares, little pigeonholes, little lots, everything divided up into little lots, little boxes on little lots, little tacky things.

And you come downtown and what's happening? Plenty of skyscrapers. You call them hotels. You can't tell whether they're hotels or office buildings or something in a cemetery.

AUDIENCE: [*Laughter*]

WRIGHT: They have no feeling, no richness, no sense of this region.

And that, I think, is happening to the country. It's not alone your misfortune.

But where you have all these exquisite, lovely, beautiful things with such charm, why don't you learn from them? Why don't you do something down here that belongs?

You have nothing in Miami that belongs to Miami, practically. Miami has a character. It has charm. It has these beautiful coral reefs, this white sand, these palms, these flowers, this beautiful growth on so slender a soil, these things that [can] grow in salt water—trees. Think of it!

You have all these marvelous natural resources, and [did] you go to school to learn what to do with them? You didn't. And why didn't you? There's no such school to go to.

Why are we so ignorant that we live in little boxes, and Realtors can sell us something that a pig would be ashamed to live in, really, if a pig could talk and protest?

And you don't protest. You buy. You're perfectly satisfied, apparently. They'll give you anything you'll take. They'll degrade you to the level of the pig if you don't look out. And you should look out.

You should have something to say. They wouldn't sell these things. This wouldn't be going on if you had been properly educated. Because you have the feeling in your hearts, I know you have. You love beauty. You love beautiful things.

You want to live in a way becoming to human beings with the spirit and a devotion to beauty, don't you? Well, why don't you? Why would you accept this sort of thing? Why would you let them put it over on you? You say, because of economic reasons.

Well, if that's what this country talks about as the highest standard of living in the world, then I think it isn't at all the highest, it's only the biggest—and quite ignorant. . . .

Nature must be ashamed of these hotels that you're building down here. Nature must be ashamed of the way this place has been laid out, and patterned after a checkerboard, and parceled out in little parcels where you stand on each other's toes, face the sidewalk, your elbows in the next neighbor's ribs.

And the whole thing, demoralization; there is no inspiration there. There is no quality, nothing for a free people in a free nation. Nor are we free.

What does freedom mean? You think that it's something that can be handed to you by a political cabal or group or a president or something official? No. It's something you are. It's something you've got under your vest, in here. It's something that you can be, but you earn it.

We haven't stressed conscience enough in connection with freedom. Because you can be as free as we're free and land in jail pretty quick . . . unless growing up [alongside freedom] is this thing we call conscience.

It seems to me that there is no conscience in our architecture. There is no conscience in this thing that is planted on Miami. Where did it come from? What is it? Have you ever analyzed it? Have you ever really looked it in the face? For what it is? Is that the best that human beings can imagine? The best they can do for humanity—pile people up in these great aggregations of boxes, these things that look like a diagram on the ground turned up edgewise for you to look at?

And that's the man on the street. He's stuck in one of those windows, one of those holes. And you create terraced slabs running horizontally together. I think they call it the International Style, but it's no style at all. I don't care what you call it, as long as you don't call it architecture.

AUDIENCE: [*Slight laughter*]

WRIGHT: Architecture begins where the animal leaves off. Just as humanity begins where the animal leaves off. Architecture begins in the spirit of man; it begins where he begins to be somebody himself in his own right, and where he begins to sense his own freedom and know his power and his freedom and exercises them in the way he lives.

What is a civilization? I don't want to talk as though I were angry. I'm not. I'm concerned, really. I'm saying the things I've said for the last 60 years, and they don't seem to be taking very much effect yet. But a little, enough to be encouraging, because we're going to have a life of the spirit in America.

We're *going* to have an architecture of our own. That is the basis of a culture. You must understand that a civilization is nothing more than a way of life. The Indians had it before we got here—and, in some ways, a better one than we seem to be able to produce.

What is culture? Culture is what makes that way of life a beautiful way of life.

What have we done about it in Miami? What have we done about it anywhere? Miami is no worse than any other part of the country except that your opportunities were greater. Except that you've had a distinctive character of your own, except that things that grew here for you had a beauty—and a character, too, you'd say—of their own.

I'm a great believer in so-called regional development. I don't believe you should have the same things in Miami that you have in the streets of New York City. I don't believe that New York is entitled to anything that Miami has naturally.

Why can't Miami be Miami? Why can't you citizens of Miami not only boast but produce something really of your own? It's all here. Now what you need to do it—this is going to be personal—are architects.

All that's the matter with Miami, of course, is the Miamians—you people. Nobody's done this thing to you; you've done it to yourselves. You've allowed it to happen to you, haven't you? Of course you have.

Now why don't you get out of it? Why don't you turn about? Go up the other way. Refuse to register in any of these hotels!

AUDIENCE: [*Laughter*]

WRIGHT: Refuse to live in any of these boxes they offer you at a cheap price. As a matter of fact, they want at least three times what they're worth. Why pay it?

No. This thing has to come from you people, come from the people, come from you, and nobody's going to do it for you. It imposes upon you all down the line. You live under a profit system, and a profit system consists of getting the sheep into condition where they can be sheared without too much fuss.

AUDIENCE: [*Loud laughter*]

WRIGHT: I guess Miami has been sheared without too much fuss.

AUDIENCE: [*Continued laughter*]

WRIGHT: You know, why do you submit?

Look at the flowers. Look at the trees. Look at the beauty of your coral reefs. Look at these outcroppings of your wonderful stone. Look what you've got!

I'm not going to point to your architects. . . . Being in love with architecture, I've found that what's the matter with architecture is the architects who have hold of it. I think all that's the matter with Miami is the citizens who have hold of it.

There was a preacher once, a very good preacher, Gerald Stanley Lee . . . who said that the only thing the matter with goodness in America was the people who had hold of it. And he was right. And we are right. . . . We've been busy down there on that little campus [at Florida Southern College in Lakeland, Florida], and it has something of these things in it. I beg you take a look at those buildings, and you'll see they respected these things

The Esplanades (1946), foreground, and the Annie Merner Pfeiffer Chapel (1938) at Florida Southern College in Lakeland, Florida. (Patrick J. Meehan)

The Annie Merner Pfeiffer Chapel (1938) at Florida Southern College. (Patrick J. Meehan)

that Florida can produce. Florida Southern is "Floridian," whether you recognize it or not.

And so Miami is not in the least Floridian.

I think *Florida* is a lovely name, isn't it? "Floridian" is something to be proud of, the flower region, the flower country—and such flowers and such forms and such inspiration are right at your door.

I'm here because of [the] so-called Fashion Group, you know.

AUDIENCE: [*Loud laughter*]

WRIGHT: Don't laugh, because in the sense that they should use the word and do use it, they don't mean just clothes. And they don't mean getting dressed up appropriately for a party—but fashioning. They should call themselves a fashioning group, designing group, shaping things, making things appropriate and not only appropriate to be worn, appropriate to be seen.

Who knows now when we're looking at a building what it is for? You don't know whether it's an office building or a hotel, and I'm willing to go further and say a church or anything else, a night club, a restaurant, a motel. There seems to be no sense of proportion, no sense of the appropriate. It's been lost somewhere down the line. Now where is it?

Well, let's bring it back. What's to hinder [you]? You. Only you, that's all. You folks are in the way. You folks are Miami, and that's the tragedy of it. We can't do anything with Miami until you change. Until you get something in your systems that you don't seem to have.

What is that? I blame it on the fact that you're educated. If you were natural, if you had the instincts that God gave you and intended you to have, I'll bet that Miami would be beautiful today. I wouldn't stand here saying *horrible,* because it wouldn't be true.

I didn't [mean] *horrible.* I [meant] something that was the equivalent, but *horrible* was the word that came out.

AUDIENCE: [*Laughter*]

WRIGHT: My own master Louis Sullivan's definition of a 'highbrow' was a man educated far beyond his capacity.

AUDIENCE: [*Laughter*]

WRIGHT: No doubt Miami has been educated far beyond its capacity. And that's what's the matter. You know too much and feel too little. This thing I'm talking about is a matter of the heart, of the spirit. It's a matter of love and a feeling for nature. . . .

This thing is fundamental, elemental, and it's a question of art and religion. Now, of course, science has smashed religion for us, practically. We don't admit it and we don't like to talk about it. We have no religion now, really. And we have no art either. Then, without art and religion, we have no soul. We have nothing for the soul to feed upon.

What are we going to do to get it? How is it going to come to us, this thing you call a culture of our own? I frequently have quoted this Frenchman who was witty. He was witty and he was correct when he said that we [Americans] were "the only great nation to have proceeded directly from barbarism to degeneracy with no culture of our own in between."

AUDIENCE: [*Loud laughter*]

WRIGHT: That [is] the opinion with which we are regarded around the world. Did you know that? . . .

We are considered to be the great nation of the substitute. An original is only good for the number of substitutes you can get out of it and sell.

Yes, salesmanship is the great American art, and we are not so good even at that—not so good. I've just seen it coming down the street, seen signs the size of one of your skyscrapers standing along the street with names on it. And I remember suggesting in Los Angeles that the way now to build is to build a great sign the size of a lot in front, move in behind it, and do business.

AUDIENCE: [*Laughter*]

WRIGHT: That would apply to most of the things you see along the street.

Well, *you* did it. That's the point you won't acknowledge. That's the point I'm here to drive home to you. You're to blame for it. You know better. If you take stock of what you really feel and know, you know better.

You want this thing I'm talking about just as much as I want it, but you don't know how to get it. . . .

If a civilization can't get something of beauty, something of concordant harmony, something admirable born, why should it ever have been?

And when a thing goes wrong for the spirit, when the human element in it suffers degradation or denial as it does in these buildings you're building, what are you going to do? Put up with it? No.

Well, now, this may all sound pessimistic. I talked . . . in New York, I guess about a week ago, to the interior decorators. I said something similar, and they were so offended they wouldn't allow the press to print anything concerning the interview. I think they were quite right. I think it ought to be concealed.

AUDIENCE: [*Loud laughter*]

WRIGHT: I don't think anything that I've said here today ought to get out.

AUDIENCE: [*Continued laughter*]

WRIGHT: But I do think you ought to take it to heart because it's an old-timer, an old campaigner, talking to you. In 62 years now I have some 647 buildings built. And every one of them has been a tribute to the spirit of man. They haven't been throwaways and they haven't been expedient. . .

So believe what I've said to you in the spirit in which I've said it. I do know something about what I'm talking about. And never have I stood up on a platform to talk to people about anything except what I myself experienced . . . but I know a bit about the thing I've done, and I'm passing it on to you for what it's worth. Good-bye.

AUDIENCE: [*Loud applause*]

3

On the Design of the
U.S. Air Force Academy

It is an imitation thing. It is not genuine modern architecture.
It is a glassified box on stilts, which is [an example of a style] practiced
abroad [that] has now become fanatic with certain of our
commercial architects. They are the ones that unfortunately
succeed to government work. A man like myself would never be thought
of in connection with a government job.

Frank Lloyd Wright prepared designs for only a few government-related projects. These projects included the embassy for the United States (Tokyo, Japan) of 1914; the Monona Terrace Civic Center project (Madison, Wisconsin) of 1938; the Cloverleaf Housing project (Pittsfield, Massachusetts) of 1942; the Pittsfield Defense Plant (Pittsfield, Massachusetts) of 1942; the San Antonio Transit project (San Antonio, Texas) of 1946; the Butterfly Bridge (Spring Green, Wisconsin) of 1947; the San Francisco Bridge (San Francisco, California) of 1949; the restaurant for Yosemite National Park (Yosemite, California) of 1954; the second Monona Terrace Civic Center project (Madison, Wisconsin) of 1954; the Spring Green Post Office (Spring Green, Wisconsin) of 1956; the Arizona State Capitol "Oasis" project (Phoenix, Arizona) of 1957; the Marin County Fair Pavilion, Amphitheater, Health and Services Building, and Children's Pavilion (San Raphael, California) of 1957; and the Marin County Civic Center and Post Office (San Raphael, California) of 1957. Not until after Wright's death in 1959 did one of his designs for a governmental entity in the United States actually get built—the Marin County Civic Center and Post Office. The construction of Wright's few designs for government-related buildings in the United States was indeed elusive. This was the case even though Wright's career spanned more than 70 years and even though his architecture was a distinctly American architecture.

So important to Wright was the design and construction of government buildings that he went out of his way to try to get such commissions. Two such government-related architectural commissions were the U.S. Air Force Academy in Colorado Springs, Colorado, and the "National Cultural Center" in Washington, D.C.

In July 1955 Wright testified at hearings before a subcommittee of the 84th Congress on the Department of the Air Force's proposed Air Force Academy and, specifically, on the government's method of selecting an architect for the project. He urged the congressional subcommittee to postpone work on the design of the academy until new plans could be prepared. The design that Wright was critical of had been prepared by the firm of Skidmore, Owings and Merrill (SOM).

Nathaniel Alexander Owings, a founding principal of SOM, reflected on the design of the Air Force Academy and Frank Lloyd Wright's involvement in his book The Spaces in Between: An Architect's Journey:

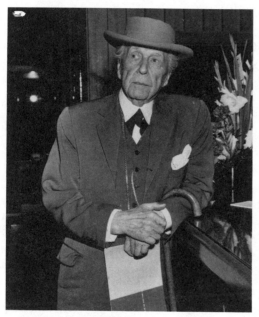

Frank Lloyd Wright on a visit to the site of the U.S. Air Force Academy near Colorado Springs, Colorado. (Frank Lloyd Wright Home and Studio Foundation)

We went after the job hard, claiming full in-house competence, refusing association with other firms. As more of our competitors began urging us to join up with them, it was clear that the word had gone out that we had the job—and even clearer when Secretary Talbott invited Skid to lunch at The Brook . . .

Shortly thereafter a ten-member board of heavily starred generals, chaired by Jim Douglas, began interviewing at length some dozen of the three-hundred-odd architect-engineer firms competing, whose brochures had apparently been large enough to remain on top of the table. The contestants' offerings varied from vague promises of what they would do if awarded the job to actual designs and models. Our own presentation consisted of a 15-foot-long, six-foot-high folding screen divided into three-foot panels, each devoted to one aspect of the total problem: research, programming, scheduling, and design of the academy. A different partner explained each section of the screen. After I had completed a summary of our proposal, I was asked by a four-star general if I proposed to design the academy in sandstone, as recommended by Frank Lloyd Wright. "General," I asked, "would you build an airplane of sandstone?"

An aerial view of the U.S. Air Force Academy. The complex was designed by the architectural firm of Skidmore, Owings and Merrill between 1956 and 1962. (Department of the Air Force)

A ground view of the U.S. Air Force Academy. Note how the buildings are imposed upon the landscape. (Gary F. Karner)

In the end, Wright's testimony fell upon deaf ears. The contract was awarded to SOM, which designed and built the U.S. Air Force Academy between 1956 and 1962. The constructed design featured teaching, residential, and administration buildings accommodating 8,000 people. The campus was set at an elevation of 6,500 feet in the Rockies. The basic exterior construction materials used by SOM were aluminum cladding and glass.

FRANK LLOYD WRIGHT: *". . .the next thing I saw was this thing, and when I saw it I was shocked, because this is an abuse of the thing which we call modern architecture."* One of the International Style buildings at the U.S. Air Force Academy and the academy's chapel. (Gary F. Karner)

REPRESENTATIVE MAHON: The committee will come to order. We are pleased to have with us this afternoon Mr. Frank Lloyd Wright, who desires to testify with reference to the requested appropriation for the Air Force Academy.

FRANK LLOYD WRIGHT: Thank you, sir.

MAHON: Mr. Wright, we have been requested to appropriate $76 million as a further expenditure for the Air Force Academy.

WRIGHT: To find out why you should spend $576 million; is that it?

MAHON: There is considerable dissatisfaction which has arisen over the proposed design of the academy. Of course, the design is not as yet fixed.

WRIGHT: Accepted.

MAHON: Accepted is right.

WRIGHT: It has been presented.

MAHON: A preliminary proposal, at least, has been presented. Are you familiar with the preliminary or with the proposal?

WRIGHT: Yes; the young editor outside there sent me the number of his paper in which it appeared, and it was very well presented. That is why I spoke up, being an old stager [*sic*] here in this thing of modern architecture. I thought if that was to represent the nation for the next 300 years or more, as modern architecture, it was time for somebody to do something. So I spoke out, and here I am.

I do not feel very comfortable here.

MAHON: Well, be perfectly at ease. We want you to be comfortable, and we want you to give us any of your ideas which will be helpful.

We are not architects, or engineers, or specialists. We are members who are charged with the responsibility of screening requests for funds.

WRIGHT: That is an admission that I admire. I was not present when this matter was first decided. I thought Mr. Talbott was a very brave and rash man to have proceeded as he did.

It seems to me that when a thing of this importance to the people and to the nation is under consideration, there is only one way of proceeding, and that is by inviting men of undoubted capacity by way of experience . . . to submit plans, and pay them for their services. You know, I have never joined the architectural profession, because they have never lived up to their so-called ethics. They will work for nothing. I think there were 700 of them reaching for this in the first place, were there not?

Anyway, it simmered down to two represented by commercial—or do you call them advertising—agencies in New York City, and myself, with no representation. When I saw how the thing was going, and that I had really signed into a competition which I had never believed in, I resigned and did not go down to sell myself to Mr. Talbott.

Well, then, the next thing I saw was this thing, and when I saw it I was shocked, because this is an abuse of the thing which we call modern architecture. I have seen it referred to in your papers as experimental architecture. Well, that is a very nice, kind name for it, because there is no soul in it; there is no feeling for humanity in it. It is, shall I say, unhuman, or inhumane. You can take your choice.

Now, the thing which I think they should have done is to have picked out, well, will we say, an old-timer like myself; and another, perhaps modernistic; and then one of the old school—three, at least, and probably five—and pay them $100,000 to take the overhead off them. Then, I think, the only fair judgment now would be to take and make a brochure out of it. Say three designs would be enough. I would be willing to put my thoughts on paper, for one. . . . Get them in and give a fair contrast.

Now, who is going to judge? The tribunal is always the question, and a tribunal in architecture is very hard to find, because it is a tribunal's blind spot. Well, culture knows nothing of architecture yet, and inasmuch as it is the basis of a culture, I could come in here wearing gold medals and with citations behind me which would cover the wall. Why? Because America at last is seen by our neighbors to have something to say for itself in the way of a culture of its own; something to exploit besides dollars. That did not get into your competition here. I mean, it did not get into your Air Force Academy.

MAHON: In specific terminology, what are some of the things which in your opinion are wrong with the proposed design? You said it had no soul, and I am inclined to agree with you.

WRIGHT: The proposed design, in the first place, ignores entirely the nature of the site. Now in good architecture, in organic architecture, the first element is to put something there that looks as though it had always been there, and always ought to be there, and if you took it away it would spoil the landscape.

REPRESENTATIVE SCRIVNER: In other words, something that fits, just naturally fits in its surroundings.

WRIGHT: Yes, sir; something becoming and something suitable and—*appropriate* is the word. It is not appropriate to the character of the American people, except a certain gang getting too big in the country altogether who are commercializing everything and who now believe that architecture also is a business. This is a big factory which did this [design]. It is one of the biggest planning factories in the country. I think they have five or six hundred draftsmen. And the two men at the head of it, what do they know about architecture? There is a boy in the back room making designs for the magazine. That is more or less a deduction, but call it a deduction, and that is the worst name for it.

MAHON: You are talking about Skidmore, Owings and Merrill?

WRIGHT: I am; and they are friends of mine, too, besides.

MAHON: Are they architects of considerable stature?

WRIGHT: Are they? I would not use that word *stature* in regard to them.

MAHON: I am asking you a serious question.

WRIGHT: They are commercial artists, and they are very successful. They know how to sell themselves, by way of their advertising agency, to the big American businessman, who knows no more about architecture than his little girl, or his son who has not yet gone to school.

MAHON: These people do commercial work, and you mean they build buildings for different concerns?

WRIGHT: They do, and they do it well, and that is why they have got so much of it to do, but it is commercial.

If you want something that represents feeling, spirit, and the future, they have not got it.

MAHON: We want some dignity in the design and something that represents feeling.

WRIGHT: Somebody said "appropriate" a little while ago, and that says the whole thing.

MAHON: But we want it to be utilitarian also. Some of the present buildings, of course, are magnificent. They, like the United States Capitol, are wholly unsuited to the job which you are supposed to do in them.

WRIGHT: Absolutely and certainly. My thesis in architecture is that those things are not incompatible. In the usefulness of the thing, and in its complete satisfaction of all the physical requirements, you will find the basis for the beauty that you are going to endow the thing with, as a rule.

MAHON: Do you have a vision as to what the academy should look like, and, if so, about how would it look?

WRIGHT: I have, and that is what hurts. I had a perfect vision of that building. I went out to the site, and I saw it, and it impressed me so much that I did not sleep at night for a long time. I have the design in the back of my head.

MAHON: Does such design involve taller buildings than these, or some flat-topped buildings?

WRIGHT: My dear Mr. Mahon, I could not describe it to you; it is woven right in with that site. The chapel is the apex of the thing, and the whole thing is wound down the side of that slope, until you get in the great field below.

REPRESENTATIVE WHITTEN: Even as a layman, it strikes one as being odd to see—and I have been in that country years ago—the mountains and beautiful lines have some flat something such as this.

WRIGHT: Yes.

WHITTEN: In an area where the mountains stand out, and a place where you would look for at least spires or something that would blend in with the surroundings, this thing made like a pancake looks out of place even to a layman.

WRIGHT: It is a factor moved into the wrong place. That was my first reaction. I think it should be something for the American people.

I want to see it appropriate. Your chapel would be the crowning feature of it on top of the mountain, and the whole thing would go up this way [Wright indicates], and out from a central avenue running up the side of the mountain, with escalators taking you up as you please. The center line would run up to the chapel on top of the hill. I am not going to give the scheme away.

REPRESENTATIVE DEANE: This thought occurs to me: How could you take a glass structure which has been created and then try to put more brick in it, or more stone in it, to take the glass effect out? It would be a worse monstrosity, would it not?

WRIGHT: Absolutely.

DEANE: How can that be done satisfactorily? I mean, unless you start from the bottom and create from the beginning?

WRIGHT: That is what you must do.

DEANE: That seems to me to be reasonable. It has been represented to us that we could take this and recast it.

WRIGHT: What is lacking is the proper feeling for the concept of the structure. It is initially wrong.

DEANE: I agree with you completely. It seems to me the chapel which they say they have not created—they just put it in there.

WRIGHT: Chapel?

DEANE: That chapel should be, as you indicated, the focal point in the whole plan.

WRIGHT: It should be the apex, the sense of the whole thing coming into some spiritual idea of life and character. The academy should be a character builder for the young people who will be in it. It should not put them on a level with the butcher, the baker, and the candlestick maker, should it?

DEANE: From your experience, what percentage of the architects of the country subscribe to that type of thinking?

WRIGHT: A very small percentage. It is novel; it is new. It is a diversion from my own thought and feeling, as you see it spread over the country today. It is not architecture. I do not think you could call it architecture. It is a commercialization and an expedient use of—an exaggeration of the use of—glass. That is what started this, the Lever Building in New York City.

SCRIVNER: In your vision, did you not see more use made of the natural stone that you have right there that would blend right in?

WRIGHT: Of course, the red stone. I would have the whole thing red stone, with a great use of the modern materials of glass and steel. But it would be harmonious. It would not be a sacrifice to a commercial idea. It would still maintain the dignity and beauty of architecture.

SCRIVNER: The name of Wright in architectural circles and elsewhere has been an outstanding name. My recollection is you used to be known as the father of modernistic architecture.

WRIGHT: It is modern.

DEANE: We understood you had a little hesitancy in coming here.

WRIGHT: I did.

DEANE: As one member of the committee, I would like to say that I am extremely grateful to you for coming, and I think that I speak for the other members.

WRIGHT: There is not an architect in the United States who would do what I am doing here now.

DEANE: It would probably be looked upon—

WRIGHT: As unprofessional and betraying a profession.

DEANE: I think that you are rendering a distinct service. Do you know Mr. [Welton] Becket of Los Angeles?

WRIGHT: I do not know him, but I know of him. I wish that something would happen to him soon. I would hate to see his things going as they are going now.

DEANE: What do you have reference to?

WRIGHT: That new hotel he has built out there. Why should not a hotel have something human and attractive in it?

DEANE: Who is Mr. [Eero] Saarinen?

WRIGHT: His father [Eliel Saarinen] wanted me to train him architecturally. That is the young boy.

DEANE: How old is he?

WRIGHT: Thirty-five or thirty-six.

DEANE: Do you know Mr. [Pietro] Belluschi, the dean of the architecture school of MIT?

WRIGHT: He is a teacher. He has done some very nice little houses, but he has had no experience as a builder.

DEANE: It is generally known that the names I have mentioned have been asked to advise with Mr. Merrill of the firm of Skidmore, Owings and Merrill. These gentlemen that I have just mentioned have been asked to sit as consultants to reassess Skidmore, Owings and Merrill's plan.

WRIGHT: I could not imagine anything that would [more readily] make a bad matter worse. There is not anything to assess. The start is wrong. The whole trend is wrong. There is nothing there to take hold of except something reprehensible to our nation.

WHITTEN: Did I understand you to say that the firm that got the contract is a big commercial planner, and it was represented by two publicity firms . . . in New York City?

WRIGHT: That is true. That is when I resigned. I gave up. I said, "What is the use of getting into a fracas of this sort?"

WHITTEN: You had no idea of what fees they paid such publicity firms?

WRIGHT: No.

WHITTEN: The record shows the amount they have already received for the plans.

WRIGHT: I think that you ought to leave them where they are with what they have. They have shot their bolt. Now I think that you should take a fresh start and pay some of us enough money to take the overhead off of us so that we would not have to spend any of our own money. I am willing to throw my time in for nothing. There would be other men who would do the same.

WHITTEN: How much money has been spent on architectural fees to date?

WRIGHT: I wonder!

WHITTEN: Your idea is that about $100,000 ought to take care of the overhead?

WRIGHT: Yes, and if a model were requested after you have seen the sketches, that should cost about $20,000. I just completed a model and that is what it cost me. My boys made it. We spent 3,500 man-hours on that model.

This is the point that I have come here to labor and defend. Architecture, after all, is the blind spot of our country. We do not know what constitutes a good building. Now we are going into it blind. We are having one of those planning factories do it. That is what we call them. There is a boy in the back room reading magazines who has a little flair for design; and then in the middle is the big boy who has club relations, and he is a good guy and he gets the thing over; and then there is the big fellow in the front office who gets the deal. The country is full of them; I have always deplored it. That is one reason why I have never joined the profession. They have given me their Gold Medal. I have never joined the profession because I believe that its dignity, its greatness, and what should lie in it for the American people now are not there. I think they are not there because everything is commercialized to such an extent. There is no poetry in it anymore. The poetic principle has left. They do not see the beauty. They do not understand what would . . . inspire the American people and the boys who go there. It should be like going to church. It could be like going into a great cathedral, only it would not be in those terms. It would be associated with nature, and the whole structure would be felt.

DEANE: Are you in a position to comment upon the cost of a proposed scheme such as has been presented, as compared to a more substantial one such as you are thinking of?

WRIGHT: I think of something of a more substantial nature because it would cost less than all this artificiality. The other has no true appropriateness.

DEANE: You can take that one step further. The maintenance, likewise, would be much more expensive?

WRIGHT: It is elemental. One does not plan programs without all that as synthesis in the mind of the architect.

WHITTEN: You might be interested in this. I thought it odd, but when questioning the witnesses here about the flat roof, I asked if it was not unusual in that area. The Assistant Secretary said it was like a telephone building in Colorado Springs.

WRIGHT: If the scheme was right, you would not think about the roof being flat. You would feel the whole thing was like a tree in the landscape; that it was natural to it and that it belonged there.

WHITTEN: If it was good enough for the local telephone company building in Colorado Springs, it was good enough.

WRIGHT: That is about the way the building looks. That is about the way it impressed me when I first saw it. It would make a good market out there somewhere on the plains near a big city, or on the outskirts of a city.

WHITTEN: This will mean a lot to the young men who go there. Actually, for each American who perhaps will have a chance to go to see the interior, there will be 1,000 who will know it only by pictures. The point I make is the outside appearance of it as a public building will be the thing that will be known to millions of American people. If you leave that out, you are depriving the American people of everything.

WRIGHT: That is why I am sitting here now talking to you gentlemen. I know that it is going to have a great effect upon the course of architecture in America, and I do not want it to go that way.

I have fought it consistently now for a great many years. I do not want to see it go clumpety-clump all the way down the backstairs, which is the commercial stairs. That is the backstairs, no matter what you say, when it comes to art.

DEANE: As I understand it, the contract has been entered into with this firm. They have people on the ground. How can you change the creative thinking of a man, or of a firm, or people that may be brought in to advertise? How could you get away from the course that it appears to be following?

WRIGHT: You cannot. It is natural that the constructive interpretation of an idea at the beginning should enlist all these forces and activate them and direct them . . . toward a coherent, comprehensive scheme.

DEANE: What can this committee do? What can the public do about this? As I see it, we are helpless.

WRIGHT: Say that it did not have sufficient benefit of the clergy and that a reconsideration has been ordered, and give it a reconsideration. That is all you can do. It is an honorable state of mind.

DEANE: If you had placed your name on a contract and then, for reasons comparable to what we are discussing here, the plans were pulled away, and someone else came into the picture, how would you feel?

WRIGHT: I would feel if I had done anything of this kind . . . that if the hand of God was not sufficient, the hand of man should rise and execute justice.

DEANE: Being a lawyer, I appreciate the validity of a contract.

WRIGHT: But do not get the contract bigger than the man.

DEANE: We wrote the law saying that there should be an Air Force Academy. We did not spell out the plans and the specifications.

WRIGHT: There was not enough depth of consideration given.

DEANE: It seems that the Congress will have to yield to the wishes of the defense establishment in arriving at the final plans, as much as we might regret it. We could refuse them money. I do not know whether that would be right or not. We need an academy. The first class has already been recruited.

WRIGHT: It is the age-old dilemma, man versus the net which he weaves for himself and finally becomes entangled in and has to be rescued from. I do not know what method of procedure could be. My thought is, leave this as it is for the time being. Postpone it. Do not abrogate it. Let it lie. Let me show you what is in my mind and what I have been talking about. Get somebody else in and do the same thing with him you do with me. Get up a little brochure and get it to every high school in the nation, not to the architects, not to the prejudices of the people as they exist. This is a democratic process, and I would let them vote to see what the consensus of opinion of the nation is regarding this thing. It is not going to be ours. We will hardly see it. They are the ones who are going to live with it. Why not make a definite appeal to their sensibilities? They are fresh. They can be manipulated, too, and will be, and the idea is not perfect, but it is as near to it as you can get.

You are in the realm of the spirit when you are in art, and when you are talking about a work of art that is where you are.

The great difficulty is to get a conception worthy of execution and to get the thing right. None of those men that you have mentioned to me could ever conceive a thing, so what is the use of monkeying along with it?

WHITTEN: Back in the days when the Capitol was built all of these modern things were not available, but in the new buildings you can adapt those things.

WRIGHT: We do it every day. There is no trouble about that, even for the old-timer. We can do it.

WHITTEN: That is the point that I made.

WRIGHT: Who would be the outstanding concern now, the Richard Hunt of today? Do they exist? I do not know.

WHITTEN: On behalf of the committee I wish to thank you. We have the mechanical problem of what we can do. But this type of expression and opinion is of value to the committee. It will be printed and will be of value to those who read it.

WRIGHT: Do not say [the problem] is mechanical; it is moral.

WHITTEN: How we can do it is a matter of mechanics. How we can get our hands again on it is another matter.

WRIGHT: You have a lawyer at the head of the table. The lawyers have succeeded in doing this, that, and the other with the law. Now the law knows neither justice nor money, so he can do anything with the law he wants to.

DEANE: The implication is we should ride herd on this and see if we can bring up something?

WRIGHT: Postpone; wait and start this other thing in motion as a codicil. Wait to see what happens. If you see something that you should have had in the first place, then you will manage to get it.

WHITTEN: If they do not have the money, it will hold them back. This is not a question of money.

We appreciate your appearance, Mr. Wright.

Later in July 1955 Wright testified before the U.S. Senate Committee on Appropriations.

FRANK LLOYD WRIGHT: I am not here to ask for the appropriation of anything except a little uncommon common sense regarding the culture of this nation. I consider the action of your subcommittee recently on appropriations to be one of the most encouraging things and a salvation clause in the history of architecture. . . .

It seems that the ways and means of communicating these commissions [for buildings] that characterize the appearance of the nation and the architecture of the nation for 300 years is somewhat remiss, commercialized, and in the hands of a small clique . . . the planning factory, the institution with 500 or 600 draftsmen, instead of the inspired individual.

I suppose the whole country is drifting toward egalitarianism quite rapidly, but it is a pity to see it enter into architecture, which is an inspired region and should be.

If we do not know a little better than we seem to in this Air Force Academy plan, I cannot say anything more for architecture along the line of modern architecture, which I represent.

I refused to enter this competition for reasons I have stated and the statement I handed to the committee. I do not think I shall bother you with it.

I have written certain things concerning the project as it stands, which are also readable, and I do not want to bother you with those.

All I ask is that some real consideration be given by Congress, by our government, to these things that usually go by default. I regard this [proposed design] as it now stands as something that went by the usual default, expediency for the expedient. It has no virtue.

Senator Chavez: As a professional man of 60 years' experience, you would like to have the plans that would meet the atmosphere and the elements of the locale, while you may not do it.

Wright: Certainly; and some inspiration, something of the spirit and not be wholly a concession to the expediency of the time. Now, how to get it? I have outlined a little plan that takes it by democratic process to the young people of this nation, those unspoiled by the average conditioning which they receive concerning the arts. That plan I have also given to the committee, and I will not waste your time now. But it seems to me encouraging when our Congress will take a vital interest in the character of the whole thing that is going to characterize us for the next 300 years.

Chavez: I want to do it. I want to keep every section of the country intact; even the aesthetic end of it. I know a building that would fit Philadelphia would not fit Colorado Springs.

Wright: That is true.

Chavez: I know the one that would fit Colorado Springs probably would not suit Seattle, Washington, or Boston.

Wright: That is a very admirable statement.

Chavez: We just happen to have a particular atmosphere, some attitude, some mountains, some blue skies, and this and that. If I understand you correctly, you want whoever draws the plans to keep those things in mind.

WRIGHT: I went to the city, was inspired by it, and thought it would be a shame to turn the average ambition loose in that magnificent opportunity where buildings and scenery and the countryside could be made one and express something noble, something worthy of our nation, something you could call American architecture.

The present effort, as we see it, on the record, is said to be a picture of a picture of a picture. A picture of what? A picture of whom? Who paid for the picture? The American people. How much? For what purpose?

I would like to know myself.

SENATOR STENNIS: Mr. Chairman, may I ask a question?

CHAVEZ: You certainly may, Senator.

STENNIS: Mr. Wright, I have not had a chance to read your statements. I went out to the city with Senator Talbott about a month ago when these plans were first disclosed. That is, these pictures that you refer to. I was impressed with the city. I was disappointed with the plans in that they were a shocking contrast to the surroundings, as I saw it.

WRIGHT: "Shocking" is the word.

STENNIS: What do you suggest? I know Secretary Talbott is very much concerned about this. I judge he has never been completely pleased with those plans.

WRIGHT: I think he ought to have it on his conscience.

STENNIS: I am sure he does. I do not join in any reflections on Secretary Talbott at all on this matter because he is very much concerned about it.

WRIGHT: There is no reflection upon anybody except the intelligence of the people of the United States in allowing a thing like this to happen continually. This is not the first time. This will not be the last time until [we devise] some better way of arriving at conclusions concerning what is characterizing the country culturally.

STENNIS: I want to get down to a concrete suggestion from you if I can. I wrote Secretary Talbott when I got back, and from the layman's standpoint I suggested that a committee of educators be called in to pass on this matter from their viewpoint, in building buildings that inspire and of a cultural background, and appearance, along with the rugged beauty of the Rocky Mountains.

That is as far as I could go.

What do you suggest?

WRIGHT: I suggest a fresh start and a paid competition, a nominal sum given to men chosen for their creative ability in the various strata of our life. We are passing away now from the old sort of thing that characterizes Washington.

STENNIS: You mean a group of architects?

WRIGHT: Say, three, selected for their capacity to put something into this besides mechanisms.

STENNIS: Three architectural concepts?

WRIGHT: Then I would suggest, as a tribunal, the young people of this nation. I would have the three designs made into brochures and sent to the principals of the high schools of the nation. Let the children—we won't call them children, I think they are referred to as teen-agers—vote on it, and you take that result and decide how it is to be executed. I would like to see some native appreciation concerning what we call architecture. It is the mother art. There is no culture without it as a basis.

Why not make it educational? Why not get something out of this fiasco for the people of the United States, and that means the young people, doesn't it?

STENNIS: As a general proposition, do you not think the architecture should blend with the surroundings of that area?

WRIGHT: It has been the ambition of my life to make it come true. I think everything I have built you will see there.

SENATOR SALTONSTALL: How were these plans conceived?

WRIGHT: I did not quite understand.

STENNIS: These pictures that are given to us, who drew these designs and how was the architecture chosen for them?

WRIGHT: I am sure I do not know.

STENNIS: You simply object to what they have done.

CHAVEZ: To the style?

WRIGHT: No; I think the thing is sort of a cliché. It is an imitation thing. It is not genuine modern architecture. It is a glassified box on stilts, which is [an example of a style] practiced abroad [that] has now become fanatic with certain of our commercial architects. They are the ones that unfortunately succeed to government work. A man like myself would never be thought of in connection with a government job.

So it all goes to the busy architect, the plan factory, the five or six hundred draftsmen. No inspiration; à la mode. When things get à la mode in the fine arts and the soul of our nation, it is time to revolt. That is why I am here. I am uncomfortable being here. I suppose I have no business here. Yet I am here. I could not take this thing myself.

CHAVEZ: I think you will find the committee most sympathetic to your general idea.

WRIGHT: Good, sir.

CHAVEZ: I do not want to have a brick building in Albuquerque for the federal building.

WRIGHT: If the thing is suitable for a poster [advertising] something on Park Avenue, it is not suitable for . . . this glorious city in Colorado, and that is what has happened to it.

In the first place, the thing on Park Avenue is not original.

CHAVEZ: I wanted to get your views, and that is why I sent you a telegram inviting you to come before us.

WRIGHT: I am honored to come. I came down here because, while they have said that I am disgruntled because I did not get the job, I am disgruntled because the thing is the way it is, regardless of any personal interest except for the cause of architecture. Whatever happens, for God's sake, let us have something superior to what now has been offered to characterize this nation for the next 300 years. We are not that low. We do have something under here, in our vests and our souls, and this does not express it. This is just about as high as a wayside market in the wrong place.

STENNIS: Mr. Chairman, as I understand, these plans have not been approved by the Secretary.

CHAVEZ: They have not.

WRIGHT: Your Honor, it would be interesting to know how much this picture of a picture of a picture has cost the people of the United States already. I think the figures should be submitted.

CHAVEZ: Do you care to have some of these associates of yours testify?

WRIGHT: I have given these documents that I referred to Mr. Sarra here, and I have said clearly what I have only here hinted at and have not had the time to say.

CHAVEZ: All right. . . .

In the late 1950s there was a movement afoot in Washington, D.C., to construct what was then termed a "National Cultural Center" in the nation's capital. Ten acres of land on the Potomac River were set aside by the United States government to accommodate the center, which was intended to house and foster the various performing arts, including theater, opera, and symphony orchestra. Wright again became publicly involved in the process of selecting an architect for a government-related building. On October 3, 1958, he actually offered his services for free if awarded the commission to design this facility. Unfortunately, Wright died before the commission was awarded. In 1962 the architect Edward Durell Stone (see Chapter 10) was selected to design the cultural center, which was eventually renamed the John F. Kennedy Center for the Performing Arts.

PART II

ARCHITECTS

Frank Lloyd Wright at his drafting table in February 1947.
(Capital Times)

4

BRUCE GOFF

Ever since I heard the name of Frank Lloyd Wright it's been very dear to me. . . . The first time I ever saw anything on Frank Lloyd Wright it was [in] the March 1908 issue of *Architectural Record;* the whole issue was devoted to his work . . . From that day on, I was a devout Wrightian.

*L*ike Wright himself, Bruce Goff (1904–82) was a true American architect. Some considered him to be a protege of Wright's, but both Wright and Goff would have said he was not. Each of Goff's buildings, projects, and decorative designs had a certain "organic" originality about it that was peculiar both to Goff and to the client for whom the design was intended.

Goff's friendship with Wright began when, at age 12, Goff wrote to Wright to request information about his recent works. Wright responded by sending the young Goff a gratis copy of his famous Wasmuth portfolio. (The portfolio, a collection of Wright's drawings published in Germany as Ausgeführte Bauten und Entwürfe von Frank Lloyd Wright, represented Wright's work to 1910.) The friendship lasted until Wright's death in 1959.

The following passages are derived from a talk Goff gave in October 1977 in Milwaukee, Wisconsin, at a conference entitled "An American Architecture: Its Roots, Growth, and Horizons." The editor was in attendance during Goff's insightful presentation to an audience of approximately 175 people. Goff's manner was relaxed and highly personable.

ON ATTENDING ARCHITECTURE SCHOOL

I had a chance to go to school when I was a young man. A wealthy family [that] had no children wanted to send me to MIT or the Beaux Arts, and they would pay my way. They said, "We know your parents aren't able to do this, and we want to help you." I asked the firm I was with if I should do it, and they said no. And some of them were school men. I didn't think I should either, but my parents were determined I should. I decided that there were only two people I could trust—[Louis] Sullivan and Wright. So I wrote to both of them. I stated the problem to Mr. Sullivan, asking what he would advise, and he wrote me back: "My Dear Young Friend, I had precisely that same kind of education you speak of and I've spent my entire

BRUCE GOFF: *"Ever since I heard the name of Frank Lloyd Wright it's been very dear to me. . . ."* **Frank Lloyd Wright and Bruce Goff (center) at the University of Oklahoma in 1954. Students are presenting Wright with the gift of a 16-inch-square handmade box. (Friends of Kebyar Archives)**

lifetime trying to live it down and I don't see what anyone would want with it." And he put his signature at the bottom. So that was good. Mr. Wright answered in a single line: "If you want to lose Bruce Goff, go to school." Well, that was all I needed. I waved those [letters] in front of my parents. They didn't know much about either one of [the men], but they knew I thought they were gods, and they agreed to let me off the hook.

So I'm still ignorant. And I think I know more and more what Mr. Wright meant [when] often he said, "I've been struggling all my life to maintain my amateur status." You'll remember when he got the AIA Gold Medal [in 1949] he said something to that effect. Not many people really realized what he meant, because most people would say, "Lord, he's no amateur, that's for sure!" But he wanted to believe he was. He wanted to believe there was still a lot to do in what he should do. Gertrude Stein [once] said, "We begin again and again," and I think that's the secret. We have to keep beginning again and again. Besides, it's exciting to see people doing that. It's like the Irishman said, "The only reason to keep on living is to see what in the hell is coming next!" I think that's a good reason.

On Meeting Wright for the First Time

[The sculptor Alfonso Iannelli] took me up to meet Mr. Wright. We got along very nicely. Mr. Wright was very kind to me, and the first thing I noticed when I looked in where his desk was, here was a portfolio [of paintings] of [Gustav] Klimt's—volume one of the Klimt work—on his desk. I had already mortgaged my soul to buy it for $90, you see, and I was so surprised to see that on his desk. I don't know why, I shouldn't have been. And I said, "Oh, I see you have the book on Klimt."

He gave me a real quick look and said, "Do you know Klimt?"

"No, I don't know him, but I'm very interested in him." I said, "Do you feel that he's had any influence on you?" You know that old question people ask you.

"Yes," he said, and then he caught himself. "Well, let's say I was refreshed by him." Mr. Wright said he met Klimt when he was in Vienna, when he'd gone over for the Wasmuth portfolio, and Klimt had invited him out to his studio. He described him to me and said, "He was the only one of those European painters worth a damn!" That was his comment then. He said, "He's marvelous. He wore a smock that he had designed himself—a very majestic man. . . . His work was just unbelievable, and I wanted every painting I saw. . . . The cheapest one was $300, and [I] didn't even have 300 cents. The best [I] could do was to get the portfolio." And I think Klimt gave him a little statue about this big. . . . Mr. Wright also described Klimt's garden. "It was just a riot of flowers." Mr. Wright said that he liked the way Klimt had planned the vines on his walls to get the same shapes he had in his paintings. Mr. Wright also commented, "Some of the rooms were painted orange, and we shared our interest in Japanese art, too."

On Wright's Architectural Influence

I got to thinking [that] with all these loyalties which I still have, and probably always will, I have a need for a loyalty to myself, too. I can't be satisfied with doing something in the feeling or manner of somebody else, as much as I admire them. I have to do what comes naturally.

One time I was showing Wright some of my work that had just been published—it was *Baukunst*, I believe. I was turning the pages and all of them that he could see his influence in he liked. "That's a good thing, Bruce, you should pursue that a little further; you've got hold of something there." All very kind remarks. Mr. Wright turned the page, saw [another house] . . . and he kind of snorted and said, "What are you trying to do, Bruce, scare somebody?

"No, no more than you ever tried, Mr. Wright." He liked that.

"Well, Bruce, I guess we do scare the hell out of them sometimes, don't we?" I don't think he really liked the design, but he was glad I would defend it; and he knew that wasn't my aim, I'm sure. I get accused of it all the time, but it's never the aim. It's the by-product a lot of times.

I think being loyal to one's self is indispensable no matter how much you admire other people. No matter who you think is the greatest architect, that's fine, you should have some ideas on the subject. But when you go to do something, you're on your own. I don't think anyone can carry on a great architect's work.

ON ANTONIO GAUDI

"Mr. Wright, what do you think of Gaudi?"

"Gaudi? Who's Gaudi?"

"Oh, [don't] you know who Gaudi is? He was a contemporary [of yours], really."

"Oh yes, he did that cathedral thing in Barcelona, didn't he?"

"Yes, that's the man."

"[Gaudi's] architecture was a *laxative*."

"Is that your considered opinion, Mr. Wright?"

"I'm afraid it is."

"You value [Louis] Sullivan's opinions, don't you?"

"Oh yes, he was a great mind, he had opinions, you know." Mr. Wright proceeded to give me a big sales pitch on Sullivan then and there.

I said, "Well, you respect his opinions? [Then] how do you square what you just said with what he said about Gaudi?"

"What did he say?"

"Well, when Gaudi's work was first shown in the *Western Architect* in April 1919, they asked members of big firms with big names in architecture today what they thought of [his work]. Of course, it was nowhere near the stage it's in now, but enough of it was up [and] you could kind of get the message. They all said practically the same thing, except one. Most of them agreed that it was the work of a lunatic, or it was insane, or it was just completely an abortion or something like that. No one had a good word to say for it at all except Sullivan. And he said, 'It is poetry symbolized in stone, and the greatest flight of the creative spirit of our time.' Those were the exact words Sullivan said. Now, Mr. Wright, how do you square that with what you said?"

"Well, Bruce, in his later years the master wasn't always responsible for some of the things he said."

When Mr. Wright said that, I said, "You watch out, or I'll tell the boys that about *you!*"

"Well, perhaps."

So that was the story. But when [a magazine] asked me to write a dedication . . . article about Frank Lloyd Wright for an issue they were bringing out, I thought they'd be interested in his opinions of some of the European architects. And I quoted the story I just told you. . . . Then, when I was in France in 1939, a number of the architects took me off to the side and said, "We read your article about Wright, and we were very curious what he meant when you referred to this Gaudi business." I said, "What do you mean?" Well, the way it comes out in translation is that his remark was [Gaudi's] architecture was a *suppository*. And they couldn't quite figure out how that squared with the building. I learned then [that] it's very dangerous to be translated—and to stay away from puns.

5

R . B U C K M I N S T E R F U L L E R

**In public, he had a histrionic sense. When he got on the stage he really
enjoyed tremendously playing a part, and he enjoyed tremendously shocking people. . . . But when you were alone with Frank Lloyd Wright, in his
own chambers, he became not only modest but really a very humble child.
He was a very beautiful human being as I knew him.**

R*Buckminster ("Bucky") Fuller—designer, inventor, engineer, mathe-
matician, architect, cartographer, philosopher, poet, cosmogonist, chore-
ographer, and visionary—was a close associate of Wright's for many
years. Fuller, who developed the famous geodesic dome, was someone whom Wright
respected—especially for his unique insights into engineering.*

*Wright had the following to say about Fuller during a discussion with
architecture students at the University of California-Berkeley on April 24,
1957: "We like Bucky. I know Bucky Fuller well. He's been one of my fans from
the beginning. We've had a little something between us, but Bucky is a scientist;
he's not an architect."*

ON WRIGHT'S KNOWLEDGE OF ENGINEERING

He knew enough about engineering . . . but he didn't practice it anymore. [He began] to realize that it would be a good idea to ask me what he
could do, because he found that I was working in every kind of advanced
technology—following through on every alloy and trying to find out how
we could increase performances. And so many of his ventures did start with
[his] asking me questions [like] . . .(he was using his own intuition):
"Could I do this?" And if he did it, quite often he'd be cautious about it
and so forth.

He became interested in a great stressed roof using the catenary
form . . . having a ridge pole and then eaves, and just draping copper sheets
and being able to solder up in the joints—would that be a practical matter?
I'd say [to him] that the copper would have such low tensile [strength], it

R. Buckminster Fuller's reminiscences were recorded in the late 1960s and were transcribed
from Bruce Radde's KPFA-FM (Berkeley, California) radio program "Frank Lloyd Wright:
The Shining Brow." Printed with permission of Pacifica Radio Archive.

Model of the St. Mark's in the Bouwerie Towers Project (1927), New York City. (State Historical Society of Wisconsin)

would pay for him to do the tensile work with steel and then put a copper skin on it. He followed that kind of advice. . . . The copper part . . . he didn't think about the low tensile capability, but it was a nice idea using the natural catenary sag . . . so the expansion and contraction was taken up in the sag.

There was really quite a lot that came into Frank's thinking. For instance, the St. Mark's in the Bouwerie Towers, which he finally built [in Oklahoma as the Price Tower], was very much from that tower structure, if you look back in the designs [of St. Mark's]. Frank began to see that result. . . . He decided then [that] I was a scientist. . . . It was not plagiarism; he was taking a forward pass in a professional way and bringing it to fruition.

The last time I visited him was at Taliesin West, and it was just before he died. Frank, on every occasion of my visiting him, would ask me if I wouldn't talk to his Fellows. The last time I was there he introduced me to his Fellows by saying, "I am an architect who is interested in science, and Buckminster is a scientist who is interested in architecture."

Frank felt that anything that I did and developed as a scientist he could have the same attitude about as any engineer or architect could have about any other scientific finding: This is something of nature, and it is employable by the architect or the engineer. [He] did not feel that he was belittling his own accomplishment as an artist in employing a technology which I developed. He did not think of me, then, as a competitive designer. I felt he was complimentary. . . . [He had] good intuitions.

ON WRIGHT'S PUBLIC APPEARANCES

In public, he had a histrionic sense. When he got on the stage he really enjoyed tremendously playing a part, and he enjoyed tremendously shocking people. He knew that they liked to be shocked. So he would try to think up something, as if anything could come in the spur of the moment, that would shock people. He would say that thing, and he didn't even stop

The Price Tower (1952) in Bartlesville, Oklahoma, was based, in part, on the never-built St. Mark's in the Bouwerie Towers Project of 1927. (Patrick J. Meehan)

to think whether it fitted into his philosophy and things he had said before. He might make statements very contradictory to his own real thinking simply because he wanted to do the shocking thing.

He was a brilliant writer and a brilliant formulator of words and thoughts, so he'd get very secure in his ways of getting this seemingly contradictory statement tied into the things he had already said. A lot of that was very elaborate. But when you were alone with Frank Lloyd Wright, in his own chambers, he became not only modest but really a very humble child. He was a very beautiful human being as I knew him.

6

WALTER GROPIUS

**His self-centeredness was irritating and at the same time disarming,
for he was hiding his hurt feelings behind a mask of haughty arrogance
which gradually became his second nature.**

T*he German architect Walter Gropius founded the famous Bauhaus School
in 1919. In 1937 Gropius emigrated to the United States and joined the
faculty of Harvard University's Graduate School of Design. In 1946 he
founded the architectural firm The Architects Collaborative. Throughout his
career, Gropius focused on and endorsed the team approach to architectural
design.*

*The team-approach philosophy, along with the Europeans' domination of
modern architectural design and practice during the early to mid-20th century
(not only abroad but also in the United States), was disconcerting to Frank
Lloyd Wright, who believed firmly in the "sovereignty of the individual." Even
more nettlesome to Wright was that many European architects of the so-called
"modern" or "International" style claimed that they had been influenced by
Wright, with whose work they were familiar through the Wasmuth portfolio.*

*Wright and Gropius met for the first time in the mid-1930s. As part of a
lecture tour Gropius was visiting Madison, Wisconsin, where Wright's design for
the first Herbert Jacobs residence was under construction (page 142). Edgar
Tafel, former apprentice to Wright, recalled the encounter in his book*
Apprentice to Genius: Years with Frank Lloyd Wright.

There was a call [at Taliesin]: "Mr. Walter Gropius is here, and he
would like very much to come out and meet you." . . . Mr. Wright was
brusque: "I'm very sorry. I'm quite busy, and I have no desire to meet or
entertain Herr Gropius. What he stands for and what I stand for are
poles apart. Our ideas could never merge. In a sense, we're professional

---

Most of Walter Gropius's reminiscences of Wright were previously published in Gropius's
Apollo in the Democracy: The Cultural Obligation of the Architect, pp. 167–70. Reprinted with
permission of Beate Johansen. The passage entitled "Architectural Individualism versus
Teamwork" was transcribed from Bruce Radde's KPFA-FM (Berkeley, California) radio
program "Frank Lloyd Wright: The World's Greatest Architect." Printed with permission of
Pacifica Radio Archive.

Frank Lloyd Wright (left) talking with Walter and Ise Gropius at the opening of the Bauhaus exhibition at the Museum of Modern Art, New York City, 1938. (Beate Johansen)

enemies—but he's an outside enemy. At least I'm staying in my own country". . . . Mr. Wright would then . . . say triumphantly, "Well, I told him!"

Just after the phone call . . . Mr. Wright announced that we were driving to Racine on Johnson Building business. . . .

So early that morning we left. . . . When we got near Madison, he said, "Go to the Jacobs house." . . . We parked the car in front, opposite the carport [of the Jacobs house]. As we drove up, out came a group of men, walking directly toward our car. They couldn't miss us. In the group was Herr Gropius.

He recognized Mr. Wright at once and came right over. One of the men greeted Wright and said, "Mr. Wright, this is Dr. Gropius." And Gropius leaned down and said through the open window, "Mr. Wright, it's a pleasure to meet you. I have always admired your work." Mr. Wright, sitting calmly in the front seat, merely turned slightly to face Gropius and said, "Herr Gropius, you're a guest of the university here. I just want to tell you that they're as snobbish here as they are at Harvard only they don't have a New England accent." Turning to me, he continued jauntily, "Well,

WALTER GROPIUS: *"When the Academy of Arts in Berlin arranged an exhibition of Frank Lloyd Wright's work in 1911, and the publishing house of Wasmuth, Berlin, subsequently published a portfolio of it, I first became attracted to his strong, .imaginative approach."* **Drawing of the Frederick G. Robie residence (1906) in Chicago, Illinois, from** *Ausgeführte Bauten und Entwürfe von Frank Lloyd Wright.* **The residence is a massive brick masonry structure with dynamic, sweeping horizontal lines and cantilevered roof eaves along a single-plane axis. The horizontal masses of the building appear to be suspended, yet are at one with the ground plane. The Robie residence is an excellent example of Wright's work in an urban setting.**

we have to get on, Edgar!" That was the signal. I put the car in gear and we were off, leaving Mr. Gropius and colleagues standing there.

Gropius himself later recalled other meetings with Wright.

Frank Lloyd Wright was very well known and respected in Europe long before he gained a reputation in the United States. When the Academy of Arts in Berlin arranged an exhibition of Frank Lloyd Wright's work in 1911, and the publishing house of Wasmuth, Berlin, subsequently published a portfolio of it, I first became attracted to his strong, imaginative approach. I still remember that I was impressed by the Larkin Building in Buffalo and by the Robie House in Chicago, both of which were close to my own thinking and feeling. Their straight-forwardness of unconventional design fascinated me, while I was less attracted by the romanticism of many of his residential buildings.

At this time I had just designed the Fagus Factory in Alfeld a. d. Leine. My acquaintance with Wright's work clarified my own approach and helped me to become more articulate in defining my own design philosophy.

When I came to the United States for the first time on a visit in 1928, almost nobody appreciated Wright's work except a few personal admirers.

It was almost impossible even to start a conversation about him, because his architectural deeds were at that time completely overshadowed by scandalous newspaper gossip about his private life. In the AIA he was considered to be an "immoral crank." However, I managed to see and photograph quite a few of his buildings in Chicago and Los Angeles, which I then used frequently for my lectures on architecture in Germany.

When I returned to the United States in 1937 to become chairman of the Department of Architecture of the Harvard Graduate School of Design, I still found such a vast ignorance about Wright's work among my students and the public that I undertook to open their eyes to his brilliant work and to his historic importance, in public lectures and in discussions in the school.

In 1940 Wright came to Boston to deliver a lecture. He accepted an invitation to my house in Lincoln, Massachusetts, and we had a few undisturbed hours of free conversation, during which he complained bitterly about the treatment he had received in his own country. He referred particularly to the fact that I had been made Chairman of the Department of Architecture at Harvard, whereas he himself had never been offered such a position of influence when he was younger. He believed seriously that I had been given in my life and career every advantage and every opportunity that anybody could wish for. He seemed quite baffled when I told him that the modern European architects, including myself, had run into much

WALTER GROPIUS:
"I still remember that I was impressed by the Larkin Building in Buffalo and by the Robie House in Chicago, both of which were close to my own thinking and feeling." The Seneca Street elevation of the Larkin Company Administration Building (1903, demolished 1949–50), Buffalo, New York. Drawing from *Ausgeführte Bauten und Entwürfe von Frank Lloyd Wright.*

greater obstacles in obtaining any commissions at all than he ever had to contend with.

His self-centeredness was irritating and at the same time disarming, for he was hiding his hurt feelings behind a mask of haughty arrogance which gradually became his second nature. The students at Harvard who had hoped to have a question and answer period with him soon found that they were only at the receiving end.

In subsequent years, Wright conducted an aggressive campaign against the so-called International Style, which he sensed to be a challenge to his own.

In 1947 I met Wright again at Princeton University at the "Bicentennial Conference on Planning Man's Physical Surroundings" and again in Mexico City. The Mexican government had invited both of us to be present at the opening of their new university. The Mexican-German architect Max Cetto, with whom I was staying, gave an evening to which he invited leading Mexican architects and also Frank Lloyd Wright. Just before Wright arrived, I talked to my colleagues about collaborative teams in our profession. When Wright entered, he sat at my side and smilingly encouraged me to go ahead. When I had finished, he said, "But, Walter, when you want to make a child you don't ask for the help of your neighbor." Thinking fast, I countered, "If the neighbor happens to be a woman, I might." Frank laughed, and this was the only time I managed to have the last word in skirmishes with the quick-witted master. This was also my last personal meeting with him.

Wright's notorious opposition to the Bauhaus had, I believe, its origin in their widely differing conceptions of the educational process. This may become evident when I compare our methods of approach in educating students. Wright, ingenious, inventive artist and full of stimulating ideas, followed his conception that a style of the century could be achieved by disseminating his own personal vocabulary of form. His school in Taliesin, Wisconsin, was meant to consolidate his own form pattern into a universal style. In 1961 I visited his school, which his widow valiantly carried on after his death. There I saw the work of several scores of students turning out, without exception, designs in the vocabulary of their great master. I did not see any independent design. The autocratic method of approach cannot be called creative, for it invites imitation; it results in training assistants, not independent artists. Surely the contact of the student with a radiating personality like Frank Lloyd Wright must have been an invaluable and unforgettable experience, but here I try to compare educational methods and goals, which must not be confounded with the artistic potency of the teacher. A great architect does not necessarily develop an effective educational method.

Already in the Bauhaus I had come to the conclusion that an autocratic, subjective approach must block the innate, budding expression of differently gifted students if the teacher, even with the best intentions, imposes the results of his own thought and work on them. We tried, therefore, on the contrary, to discourage imitation of the teacher and to help the student observe and understand physical and psychological facts and from there let him find his own way. Here, then, I differ in principle from Wright's approach to education, which strikes me as being wholly egocentric. But from this strong emphasis on his ego originated also his superb if somewhat upsetting showmanship, which, there can be no doubt, has helped to bring the course of architecture into the public consciousness.

ARCHITECTURAL INDIVIDUALISM V. TEAMWORK

Fortunately, in my early times, I saw a lot of [the work] of Frank Lloyd Wright, who interested me very much. Of course, in the philosophy of architecture I am on another limb than he is. He is very strongly an individualist, whereas I am very much in favor of teamwork. I think that the field we have to see today is so large that it's impossible in one head to have everything. And I daresay that even a genius, if he understands to develop teams around himself and lead these teams, that the spark he can give . . . will be [better] used when he has many team helpers in the whole thing than when he is all alone in an ivory tower.

7

P H I L I P   J O H N S O N

**No one understands the third dimension as well as he, the capacity of
architecture to be an experience in depth, rather than a mere facade.**

*P*hilip Johnson—one of the foremost proponents of the 20th-century
International Style of architecture—remarked in an interview conducted
in the early 1980s, "Forty years ago Wright seemed like a very old character that was of no use anymore to our International Style orthodoxy . . . I wanted
him out of the way. . . . Today I revere that man more than anybody else except
H. H. Richardson."

In truth, Johnson was not so dismissive of Wright in the 1940s. The following article from the August 1949 issue of Architectural Review (unlike most of
the reflections in this book, this piece was written while Wright was still living) is
marked by a tone of great respect for Wright and his contributions to architecture. Indeed, Johnson interprets "the movement away from the 'boxes' that
Wright attacks [as bringing] the Internationalists nearer to Wright's position
and further from their own position of 20 years ago." The evolution of the
International Style is, of course, still debatable today. And it is interesting to
note that Johnson himself, later in his architectural career, abandoned, to some
degree, the International Style for more eclectic forms still further divergent from
Wright's concept of "organic" architecture.

In my opinion, Frank Lloyd Wright is the greatest living architect, and
for many reasons. He is the founder of modern architecture as we know it in
the West, the originator of so many styles that his emulators are invariably a
decade or so behind. All younger moderns—except perhaps Le Corbusier—
acknowledge Wright's influence, though some may forget the debt in their
later years. There can be no disagreement, however, that he is the most
influential architect of our century. In the 1900s he originated the Prairie
House, with its open plan, which through the Wasmuth publication of 1910
became the prototype of so much modern design. In the 1920s he outdid
the massiveness of the Mayan with a new kind of ferro-concrete structure. In

---

Philip Johnson's reflections on Wright originally appeared in an article entitled "The
Frontiersman," *Architectural Review* (England), Vol. CVI, August 1949, pp. 105–06.
Reprinted by permission of Philip Johnson.

An exterior view of the Johnson Wax Administration Building (1936), foreground, and the Johnson Wax Research and Development Tower (1944) in Racine, Wisconsin. (Patrick J. Meehan)

The lobby of the Johnson Wax Administration Building. Note the use of the incandescent lighting and the mushroom-shaped columns. (Patrick J. Meehan)

the 1930s and 1940s he has been and still is inventing new shapes: using circles, hexagons, and triangles to articulate space in new ways.

But he is more than an inventor. No one understands the third dimension as well as he, the capacity of architecture to be an experience in depth, rather than a mere facade. His buildings can rarely be appreciated correctly except at first hand. A photograph can never relay the experience of being surrounded by one of them. Nor can a camera record the cumulative impact of moving through his organized spaces, the effect of passing through low space into high, from narrow to wide, from dark to light (Taliesin, Taliesin West [pages 139, 149, and 150], Johnson Wax Co.).

Wright is also unique in his ability to adjust buildings to natural surroundings. Whether they rise from a hill (the Pauson House, the Loeb House, Hartford Tower) or hug the slopes (Taliesin, Taliesin West, and the Jacobs House) his structures always look rooted to the soil— in his words, "organic."

It is of great importance, therefore, to listen to Wright's opinions— especially when expressed so violently—on the work of the architects whom he calls here "Internationalists," "stencilists," "functionalists." Since he refers twice to the exhibition which I organized at the Museum of Modern Art in 1932 as the agent responsible for the introduction of these foreign "isms," perhaps a few notes on the intervening years would be appropriate.

Wright would undoubtedly include in his list of "stencilists" most of the architects in our 1932 catalogue. Besides himself, there were men like Le Corbusier, Mies van der Rohe, Gropius, Oud, Mendelsohn, Aalto, Neutra, Lescaze, and Stonorov. According to Wright, these are fascist-inspired cliché artistes, many of whom design two-dimensional flat-facade buildings because they are more interested in painting than architecture. Furthermore, they do not understand nature; in fact, they are anti-nature.

There is a lot of meat in Wright's castigations, but he is wrong in attributing functionalist leanings to us at the Museum who have fought it for 20 years. There is also much doubt how many of these artists really believed in functionalism even though they sometimes give it lip service. Wright, for example, might better have remembered not only Le Corbusier's unfortunate propagandist *"machine à habiter"* but also his beautiful definition *"L'architecture, c'est, avec des materiaux bruts, établir des rapports emouvants,"* to which most architects, including Mr. Wright, would subscribe.

When he writes that International architecture is "stencilist," and able to be repeated, taught, and learned so easily that our universities have adopted it rather than Wright's own "organic" architecture, he is correct.

The glass-door–walled exterior south elevation of the second Herbert Jacobs residence (1943), Middleton, Wisconsin. (Patrick J. Meehan)

Le Corbusier, and perhaps latterly Mies van der Rohe, have indeed been too superficially adapted for teaching; Wright's principles, on the other hand, are impossible to teach in the conventional, institutional way.

Again when he cites Le Corbusier for being two-dimensional in his approach he has a point. Le Corbusier's facades are often flat, those of his followers flatter. And certainly the group as a whole has been distinguished by its extraordinary interest in painting. Le Corbusier himself is an active and accomplished practitioner of the art, but it does not necessarily follow, as Wright implies, that because he is capable of creating in two dimensions he cannot create in three. A cube is undeniably three-dimensional. To raise it on stilts only serves to emphasize that fact. Such a purist concept is, of course, a far cry from the spatial complexity of a building by Wright, but the one does not necessarily negate the value of the other.

Wright has often attacked the slick boxlike "negativities" of International work, the painted stucco, the boredom of repeated columns. But these objections have long since been met by the Internationalists themselves. They no longer use stucco, nor rely on paint. The smooth flatness is gone. Mies projects his windbraces and columns to get shadow; Le

Corbusier complicates his facades with Mondrian-shaped mullion patterns and *brise-soleils*; Gropius, Breuer, and Neutra now use native wood, pitched roofs, and deep porchlike overhangs; Aalto curves entire buildings. The movement away from the "boxes" that Wright attacks brings the Internationalists nearer to Wright's position and further from their own position of 20 years ago. How much of this enrichment is caused by a reappreciation of Wright and how much by a natural reaction against bad material and lonely cubes would be hard to say.

When Wright claims that the International movement is fascist-inspired, he uses the word in two senses. He argues first that the "provincial art elite," the trustees and visitors of the Museum of Modern Art, being rich, are fascist-inclined because rich, and, second, that because Mussolini favored the *stile razionale*, therefore modern architects admired Mussolini.

The New York rich, however, are demonstrably Republican and, as a class, are the best clients for Georgian and Elizabethan mansions in the world. But, more important, a large percentage of Wright's "foreigners" are refugees from Nazism and Fascism. It is hard to understand his argument. As a matter of fact, modern architecture has never flourished in any totalitarian country, whether communist or fascist. It is a true child of social democracy.

It is on the question of nature and its relation to architecture that Wright is clearest. "We must learn to use the word *nature* in its proper *romantic* (i.e., integral) sense," he writes (italics mine), and he is indeed romantic about nature. He has proposed elsewhere that "the tree should be the inspiration for American architecture of the Machine Age." He speaks of his new Johnson Laboratory Tower as having a taproot and branches. His greatest objection to the Internationalists is their anti-nature stand.

In his eyes Japanese and Mayan work are "organic" while Greek and Renaissance architecture are inorganic, opposed to nature. The Internationalists, he correctly points out, admire the Greeks and consequently conceive their work as a contrast to nature rather than a part of it. Like the Parthenon, their buildings are placed against nature.

Mr. Wright's preference for regarding his buildings as identified with nature has inspired him to produce the most remarkable architectural creations of our time, but does this in itself invalidate the other point of view? Rather, is not the contrast between Le Corbusier's *prisme pur* and Wright's luxuriant forms but another manifestation of the Classic-Romantic dichotomy? Does not Le Corbusier's work symbolize Mediterranean culture today: the bright tight shapes of a static civilization, against a blue sky? And does not Wright's work typify the exuberant individualism of an ever-expanding frontier?

8

LUDWIG MIES VAN DER ROHE

Wright had a great influence, but late in his life.
But his influence on the face of America is quite modest.

The great German-born architect Ludwig Mies van der Rohe first met Frank Lloyd Wright during a visit to Taliesin near Spring Green, Wisconsin, in September 1937. The two men became friends, and through the next decade they corresponded regularly, if infrequently. This correspondence ended, however, soon after Wright's attendance at an exhibition of Mies's work at the Museum of Modern Art in New York in the fall of 1947—the first major exhibition of Mies's architectural work. While at this exhibition, Wright publicly attacked Mies's architectural philosophy of "less is more" and "doing next to nothing."

Ten years later Wright mentioned Mies in a conversation with the poet Carl Sandburg:

And as for Mies—he is a very honest man and a very nice one, but he has a very scientific list to starboard and he has never gone sufficiently far left. He is still in the 19th century, doing the old steel frame that was the great contribution of the 19th-century engineers to building; he is trying to make the old box frame beautiful. He has come as near to it as anybody, but it can't be done.

At the time of Wright's death in 1959 Mies was quoted as saying, "In his undiminishing power he resembles a giant tree in a wide landscape which year after year attains a more noble crown."

In 1963 Mies spoke with Peter Blake, a noted architect, educator, and architectural historian. According to Blake:

The great man sits close to a window. There is the sound of cars. Outside the window is Chicago. The Chicago of Adler and Sullivan, Burnham and Root, William Le Baron Jenney, and now Mies van der Rohe.

Peter Blake's "A Conversation With Mies" was published in *Four Great Makers of Modern Architecture: Gropius, Le Corbusier, Mies van der Rohe, Wright*.

Mies is goaded into talk (for this man does not talk easily) by an inter-
rogator who is purposely shadowy. From time to time there is a hearty
laugh at campaigns remembered; there are simple sentences in a heavy
German accent, a man more at home with building than with words.

It is interesting to note the brevity Mies affords Wright.

PETER BLAKE: It seems to me that in some of your early buildings like
the Barcelona Pavilion, there are traces of Wright's principles. To what
extent has Wright impressed you and influenced your work?

LUDWIG MIES VAN DER ROHE: For Philip Johnson's book [i.e., Philip
Johnson's *Mies van der Rohe]*, I wrote about Wright and the influence he
had on us in Europe. Certainly I was very much impressed by the Robie
house [page 45] and by the office building in Buffalo [page 46]. Who
wouldn't be impressed? He was certainly a great genius—there is no question about that. You know, it is very difficult to go in his direction. You
sense that his architecture is based on fantasy. You have to have fantasy in
order to go in this direction, and if you have fantasy, you don't go in his
direction, you go in your own! Wright had a great influence, but late in his
life. But his influence on the face of America is quite modest.

9

E E R O   S A A R I N E N

**I think it may well be that 50 years from now we will feel
him stronger amongst us than right now.**

The American architect Eero Saarinen (1910–61) was the son of the
equally famous Finnish architect Eliel Saarinen (1873–1950). Both
architects' work owed much to Frank Lloyd Wright, and, indeed, both
men knew Wright on a personal basis. (Eero Saarinen's wife, the architectural
critic Aline B. Saarinen, describes a visit to Taliesin on page 178.)

Wright has given us the greatest inspiration about the use of space and
has also shown us the plastic form of architecture in relation to nature, in
relation to the material, and, to a certain degree, to structure. He has
shown us also the dramatization of architecture, which I think is a very
important thing.

You know, some try in their work to be influenced by Wright directly.
Now, I could never do that, and I think it's wrong. His influence on one is,
and should be, not through the form itself but much more through the philosophy . . . and, maybe, the enthusiasm behind his forms. I think it may
well be that 50 years from now we will feel him stronger amongst us than
right now. We live too close to him now. That is the way I look at Wright,
and I think of Wright as the greatest living architect.

Well, I might add one little thing: that so much of Wright's forms are
really of quite a different era. And the young architect and the student who
isn't aware of that sort of slides right into it and wrongly so.

But, boy, don't ever underestimate Wright! Wright hasn't really been
integrated into [modern] architecture yet—and I think that's the wisest
statement I've made today. I think Wright's contribution has not yet been
integrated into modern architecture.

Eero Saarinen's reminiscences, recorded in the late 1950s, were transcribed from Bruce
Radde's KPFA-FM (Berkeley, California) radio program "Frank Lloyd Wright: The World's
Greatest Architect."

1 0

E D W A R D   D .   S T O N E

No architect touches his pencil to paper today without subconsciously paying tribute to Mr. Wright.

On February 15, 1960, Edward D. Stone delivered a brief speech at the groundbreaking ceremonies for the Frank Lloyd Wright–designed Marin County Civic Center. Among the roughly 500 people in attendance, apart from citizens and officials of Marin County, were Wright's widow, Olgivanna Lloyd Wright; his son Lloyd Wright; his daughters Catherine Dorothy Wright Baxter and Iovanna Lloyd Wright; his grandson Eric Lloyd Wright; William Wesley Peters; Eugene Masselink; and Aaron Green.

Mr. Wright was my personal friend and personal hero for the past 25 years, and I'm sure that this occasion would give him great pleasure wherever he is. To the best of my knowledge, this is the first opportunity he was given to completely design a government center. It speaks well for your wisdom, in this day when material considerations, standardization of ideas, and creature comforts seem to govern our daily lives.

Fortunately, there is a great debate going on in Washington where one group maintains that we are wasting our efforts and our resources. The emphasis on creature comforts, etc., is dissipating our strength, and we are indeed a nation without a purpose. Emphasis on education, health, cultural and spiritual values, has given way to superficial luxuries. With our pioneering over and with our untold wealth, we should be turning our attention to cultural and spiritual values, and first among them would be the creation of a beautiful environment in which we can live and work.

It has been said that in periods of prosperity and overabundance we seem to be able to afford everything but beauty. It is therefore inspiring that your community had the wisdom to accept this challenge and aspire to a great civic center designed by Mr. Wright, and carried through to completion by Mrs. Wright and his faithful colleagues. I predict that it will be a place of pilgrimage for generations to come, just as today the work of Michelangelo and

Edward D. Stone's "Frank Lloyd Wright: A Tribute to a Personal Hero," was originally published in *Pacific Architect and Builder*, Vol. LXVI, March 1960, p. 20.

EDWARD D. STONE: *"I predict that it will be a place of pilgrimage for generations to come just as today the work of Michelangelo and Leonardo da Vinci provides exultation for millions of visitors to Italy."* **The pattern on the light blue roof of the Marin County Administration Building (1957) in San Raphael, California. This view shows two office wings on the building's third level as viewed from the neighboring hillside. The filigreed half-domes are almost flush with the hillside. Housed beneath the left dome is the teacher's library; beneath the right dome is the Board of Education meeting room. Both domes open out onto a hill terrace. (Patrick J. Meehan)**

Leonardo da Vinci provides exultation for millions of visitors to Italy.

In New York today we are witnessing an example of this thirst for and appreciation of great architecture. There are groups standing in line three and four abreast to visit the great Guggenheim Museum designed by Wright. With a paid admission this has been a financial bonanza for the institution. That it has been a controversial building is good. It has stimulated great interest and, as a result, has attracted visitors who have never before set foot inside a museum.

There was a time in our country when architects were content to copy monuments of the past. We're all familiar with the Greek chapel used as a bank, the Italian palazzo for a city hall, and the Renaissance dome of St. Peter's Cathedral for our state capitol buildings. This was a sad state of affairs. The creative talent of our country was repudiated, and we were renouncing our indigenous heritage.

Mr. Wright had the vision to change all of this. His principles of modern architecture at first were slow to be accepted in this country, but were immediately adopted by the Europeans who came to this country and perpetuated them. So that today, thanks to Mr. Wright, we are developing an indigenous architecture based upon his principles. No architect touches his pencil to paper today without subconsciously paying tribute to Mr. Wright.

Mr. Wright was certainly the greatest creative talent that this country ever produced and, in my opinion, the greatest architect the world has ever known. And I welcome this opportunity to pay homage to his memory.

It has been said that all great periods of history were great only because of the arts they produced. You people here in Marin County will have a great work of art, the best that our times can produce. It will be a source of inspiration and pleasure for generations to come. I salute you in your wisdom.

PART III

CLIENTS

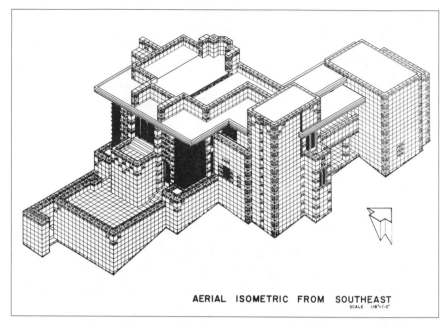

AERIAL ISOMETRIC FROM SOUTHEAST
SCALE 1/8"=1'-0"

Aerial axonometric line drawing and first-floor plan of the Samuel Freeman
residence (1924), Los Angeles. (Jeffrey B. Lentz and Robert C. Giebner,
Historic American Buildings Survey)

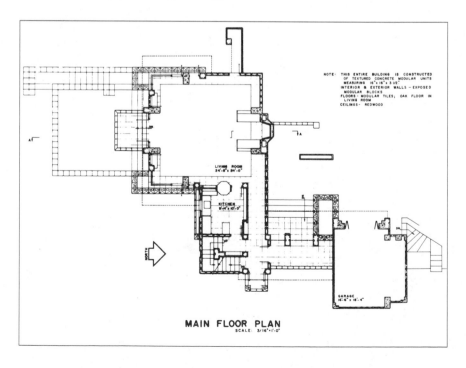

NOTE: THIS ENTIRE BUILDING IS CONSTRUCTED
OF TEXTURED CONCRETE MODULAR UNITS
MEASURING 16"x 16"x 3 1/2"
INTERIOR & EXTERIOR WALLS — EXPOSED
MODULAR BLOCKS
FLOORS- MODULAR TILES; OAK FLOOR IN
LIVING ROOM
CEILINGS- REDWOOD

MAIN FLOOR PLAN
SCALE: 3/16"=1'-0"

1 1

S A M U E L F R E E M A N

**I've heard people speak derogatorily of Mr. Wright and his financial
dealings, and I don't think there is any truth in it!
Because the last thing in this world that anybody could say about him
was that he was a man looking for dollars.**

*S*amuel Freeman was one of Frank Lloyd Wright's earliest clients in
California and one of the first clients for whom Wright designed one of his
famous textile-block–constructed houses. The Freeman residence In Los
Angeles was designed in 1924.

ON WORKING WITH WRIGHT

SAMUEL FREEMAN: In our relationship with Mr. Wright, we told him
simply the kind of life we thought we were going to live, and we left [the
design] of the house completely to him.

BRUCE RADDE: Did you make any requests as to what you wanted?
That is, for example, after he came up with the drawings, if you didn't like
something, could you change it?

FREEMAN: Frankly, I wasn't capable of judging the drawings and I
accepted them in total. I figured here was a very great man, a man who had
much to give to the world, and I felt we were very fortunate to get his services. Of course, at that time, we thought we were going to build a house
for $10,000. So we did not put any restrictions on its design or [show]
favor in the building [for] our creative ideas because we didn't have any! So
we went down and built the house and, as any type of house that deals with
new ideas and new materials, we had difficulties and disappointments. But,
all in all, considering that we were using new materials and new methods—
I think we got along very well! Of course, the costs went up but as far Mr.
Wright was concerned, he didn't profit. When the job was all done, [con-
sidering] all the aid he had given us, I think that Wright was actually out of

Samuel Freeman's reminiscences, recorded in the late 1960s, were transcribed from Bruce
Radde's KPFA-FM (Berkeley, California) radio programs "Frank Lloyd Wright: Ask the Man
Who Owns One," and "Frank Lloyd Wright: The Shining Brow." Printed with permission of
Pacifica Radio Archive.

Exterior detail of a corner window of the Samuel Freeman residence (1924). State Historical Society of Wisconsin)

pocket. I've heard people speak derogatorily of Mr. Wright and his financial dealings, and I don't think there is any truth in it! Because the last thing in this world that anybody could say about him was that he was a man looking for dollars.

We were so glad that Mr. Wright would take on this modest house that we figured if we'd stay out of it we would be better off. And to this day I think that it was a very wise decision. Because I've run into so many people contemplating building a house, and they say to me, "I know exactly what I want." I always think that if a man is going to build a house for me, he better know an awful lot more than I!

ON THE DESIGN OF THE HOUSE

The highlight of my experience is that, after living in this house since 1923, the house does not bore me. It is always interesting—when I sit in the living room or in another part of the house—there's always something alive in the place. It isn't just a cubicle, as most houses are; there are four walls decorated with various drapes and pictures and such to make the place livable. When the house was finished enough so we could move in, we did not have a stick of furniture. We sat on boxes, and the house never seemed bare. Now you could take this room [the living room] and strip everything out of it, and you wouldn't feel that you were in an empty room. This room itself is a piece of sculpture. It has a life of its own. They say that a

Interior detail of a corner window of the Samuel Freeman residence. (State Historical Society of Wisconsin)

square room is an abomination . . . that you should never build a square room [and] you must build a rectangular room. Well, this room is square, but I can't find anything about the room that's anything but interesting. . . . It has broken planes, different heights . . . the whole thing [is] like music. I've sat in this room and used it since 1923, and I'm never bored with the room. I can go to the average house and, after a few minutes, you've explored all its possibilities [and] there's nothing more for you to search or to explore; you've got it all. As long as I've lived in this house, this room was always exciting to me. It's almost alive, it's in motion.

RADDE: After living in this particular house for about 45 years, do you think you could move into a regular plaster-built house?

FREEMAN: No, if I had some choice I wouldn't want to [live in] that type of house which you describe. However, if you had no choice, you'd get used to it.

ON WRIGHT THE MAN

We found him very charming and, of course, I must say that he was always very sure of himself. My impression was that the man knew his stuff, and he knew that he knew it. . . . He was forthright, and this type of man I

Frank Lloyd Wright at Taliesin near Spring Green, Wisconsin, c. 1924. (Frank Lloyd Wright Home and Studio Foundation, Maginel Wright Barney Collection)

could always deal with very easily—never had any difficulty.

He had a very great ego, but on him it looked good. You see so many people who have a very great ego but don't have any special legitimate reason for it; it's something that they've built up because they liked it. But this man was a great man. And, as I mentioned before, his forthrightness was very pleasant. Although he might not agree with you, you couldn't dislike him for it because there was an honesty with it.

1 2

L O R E N   B .   P O P E

**The importance of Wright's architecture is that it speaks to the spirit.
It is applied research on the way, the truth, and the light. . . . My friends
began telling me I was a little giddy to think about approaching the great,
expensive, and imperious Frank Lloyd Wright. . . . I decided that no
matter how busy or important, the master would listen to someone who
wanted one of his works so much. In due time, a letter was dispatched
telling him how important was a house by him, along with a map of the
site, contours and trees—some of the specifics a client would give his
architect, all of it making an excess-postage envelope. It is very likely that
no normally sensitive ego would have been unmoved by such a panegyric.**

*In 1939 Loren B. Pope commissioned Frank Lloyd Wright to design a house
for him and his family. When the house was built the following year in Falls
Church, Virginia, Wright's apprentice Gordon O. Chadwick supervised construction (see page 140). The Popes lived in the house until 1947, when it was
sold to Robert and Marjorie Leighey.*

*In 1962 Pope learned that his former home was threatened with destruction
because it lay in the path of a proposed highway. He wrote a letter to the
Washington Post that was printed on November 21, 1962, under the headline
"Vandalism":*

Although the fact that this work of art by my friend Frank Lloyd
Wright was a home created for my family and me makes the deed that
much more painful, that is irrelevant. What is relevant is the fact that a civi-
lized society could even entertain a proposal to let a road threaten one of
the three Wright houses in Virginia, much less approve it.

The Mongols astride their wild ponies never constituted the threat to
Western culture that do these Mongoloids astride their slide rules and T-
squares. Equally chilling is a public ethos that is apparently undisturbed by
this barbarian sense of values.

"After Fifty Years," the expanded text of a talk Pope gave to the Young Adult Class of St.
Paul's Episcopal Church of Alexandria, Virginia, and delivered at the Pope-Leighey House in
the spring of 1989, copyright © Loren B. Pope 1991. Used by permission of the author.

As Mr. Wright said, America threatens to become the only society that ever went from infancy to decadence without a culture in between.

The house eventually was saved through the efforts of Marjorie Leighey, who approached the U.S. Department of the Interior and the National Trust for Historic Preservation. The National Trust agreed to provide a location for the house, to maintain it, and to permit Mrs. Leighey to continue to live in the house during her lifetime.

In the fall of 1964 the Pope-Leighey House, as it came to be called, was dismantled and moved in pieces to the site of Woodlawn Plantation, another National Trust property, in Mount Vernon, Virginia. Reassembled in 1965, the house was dedicated as a historic house museum and opened to the public. Mrs. Leighey resumed residency in 1969 until her death in 1984.

In the following two passages—recorded 25 and 50 years, respectively, after the events they describe—Pope recalls the experience of commissioning, building, and living in a Wright-designed house.

TWENTY-FIVE YEARS LATER: STILL A LOVE AFFAIR

There was a temptation to describe the reopening of the Frank Lloyd Wright house at Woodlawn Plantation as a beautification, since the modest house was taking its place across the meadow from the stately mansion as a part of our cultural and artistic heritage. That would be superfluous; in its 25 years as a home, this house had already acquired a halo. The official recognition that put it in such famous and historic company was a meet and monumentally ironic culmination of events that moved to this climax with the inevitable justice of a Greek drama.

Today it is de rigueur to regard Wright as a great master. During his life this greatest architect of modern times, a man whom British correspondent Henry Brandon aptly called "the most American," never received a commission from his own government. His one Washington project, Crystal City, was vetoed due to government zoning rules on height. Indeed, the usual story with Wright's works was one of trying to overcome the opposition of officialdom and the orthodoxy it represents. If planners and art commissioners can't recognize greatness or fear to employ it, it isn't surprising that the artist's radical ideas and forms unsettle the Establishment.

Thus, in 1940, decades after his genius had been acknowledged around the world, building inspectors in the U.S. said his dendriform columns, cantilevered roofs and terraces, and sandwich walls wouldn't stand or that floor heating wouldn't heat. Lenders, federal housing agencies, and private

An approach view from the driveway, looking south at the Loren B. Pope residence (1939) in Mount Vernon, Virginia (relocated from its original site at Falls Church in 1965). In 1940 the cost of building the house was $8,000. (Patrick J. Meehan)

The west portion of the exterior south elevation of the Loren B. Pope residence (1939), now called the Pope-Leighey House, in Mount Vernon, Virginia. (Patrick J. Meehan)

firms branded the Wright house a bad risk financially, aesthetically, and architecturally. But it was built. Then, after a quarter-century of being loved by its owners and lionized by outsiders, the events that led to making it a piece of our cultural history were triggered by a government threat to destroy a work of art to make way for a road—a devastating comment on our society's scale of values.

The genesis of this house is in the late 1930s, when a magazine article finally sparked the interest in Wright's *An Autobiography* that a friend had been vainly trying for a year to strike. I borrowed the book from the library, returned it the next day, bought my own copy, and soaked up every chapter two and three times before going on to the next one. Long before the book was finished, the light had become dazzling and I had become a true believer.

Here was a contemporary American new testament that spoke with the same clarity and daring that Emerson had a century earlier in *Nature* or in the Harvard Divinity School Address. Wright applied some basic truths expressed by Jesus, by Emerson, and by Tao to the principal art and the principal influence in our environment. He said a building, like a life, should be a free and honest expression of purpose, done with all possible disciplined skill but without sham or pretense. The building should be itself and should unaffectedly and subtly reveal its structure; materials should be used naturally and should furnish their own decoration; the building, in short, should be organic, like a tree, a cactus, a man, or anything else in nature. *Organic* was a word whose connotation Emerson had developed, and here it fit perfectly. Wright also said a house should not only be one with nature in spirit but also function as a part of it. It must not only provide shelter but also impart a sense of freedom and of unity with nature by taking the indoors out and bringing the outside in.

Compared with virtually everything ever built and most that is architect-designed, such organic architecture still is revolutionary . . . because it demonstrates Keats's maxim that "beauty is truth, truth beauty."

The conversion was fundamentally philosophical because Wright would have been a prophet had he never built a building. He had not only the moral courage but also the artistic genius to make his family motto, "Truth against the world," an aesthetic as well as an intellectual force.

In short, the importance of Wright's architecture is that it speaks to the spirit. It is applied research on the way, the truth, and the light. This is not to say that everyone likes Wright's phrasing or his applications, but this spiritual appeal is where the heart of the matter is, not in the corner window or door without a support, not in the sense of space or his ability to make it come alive, nor in any of his multitudinous innovations, brilliant or effective as they may be.

From *An Autobiography* on, my bride and I stopped buying Colonial reproductions or thinking about the picket-fenced Cape Cod we were planning to build. Instead, my friends began telling me I was a little giddy to think about approaching the great, expensive, and imperious Frank Lloyd Wright. Faith filters out fear and some error, and with the encouragement of an artist friend, Edward Rowan, I decided that, no matter how busy or important, the master would listen to someone who wanted one of his works so much. In due time, a letter was dispatched telling him how important was a house by him, along with a map of the site, contours, and trees—some of the specifics a client would give his architect, all of it making an excess-postage envelope. It is very likely that no normally sensitive ego would have been unmoved by such a panegyric.

Within three weeks I got a thin and terse reply: "Dear Loren, Of course I'm ready to give you a house. . . ." The excitement and difficulties of bringing it into being started. It's often said that building one's own house takes six months off one's life, and this venture had its full share of problems.

AFTER FIFTY YEARS

In 1939 when I wrote Frank Lloyd Wright a letter that no man with even a normal ego could say no to, and two and a half years later when we moved into this house, this country's level of consciousness had not been raised. Churches then espoused the brotherhood of man, and Virginia then practiced a limited sort of democracy, both of them apartheid-style.

And in architecture it was a similar story, for Frank Lloyd Wright was considered a flamboyant eccentric who designed strange-looking buildings, demeaned his fellow architects, and had a life of adulterous notoriety and family tragedy. Not surprisingly, many of my friends and colleagues thought I was either teched or presumptuous to want him to design my house. My father would get a rise out of me by referring to him as Harold Bell Wright (a hack writer of Western potboilers).

Wright was famous in Europe, and his Imperial Hotel in Tokyo [page 241] withstood the cataclysmic 1922 earthquake. But at home he was suspect, and largely ignored. One would never have known from reading the *New York Times*, for example, that he was a force in American architecture. I used to look in vain for any mention of him or his work.

Passionate disciple though I was, I had not screwed up my courage to approach the master. I had no idea the great man was accepting any such insignificant commissions as ours. But a friend who headed the New Deal's Public Works of Art program assured me such an artist would respond to my appeal, that he had a normal ego. The panegyric I sent him is now included in the National Trust's book on the Pope-Leighey House. Two weeks after mailing my letter, my heart leaped when I saw in my post office box the buff envelope with the red square. It said, "Dear Loren, Of course I'm ready to give you a house. We'll see you and Ed Rowan on September 14." *Euphoria* would have been a euphemism for my state; *ecstasy* would have come a little closer.

Incidentally, that is the only letter from him that I can't find. The National Trust says they don't have it either.

In 1938 *Architectural Forum* did devote an entire issue to Wright when his design for Fallingwater [page 131], one of the great buildings of all time, made it impossible not to notice him. But even a decade later, *House Beautiful* held back for a year an article—"The Love Affair of a Man and His House"—I'd sent them on our house. When the article eventually did appear, an editor's preface explained that it took a year for "us to be brave enough to print it because we were afraid it would make many readers very angry. But because we thought the subject of what a modern house means to its owners is important we are printing it." Several months later the editor said the piece had been the most popular article they'd ever published. I got fan mail long afterward.

Nevertheless, we could find no financing agency that would touch this stark-looking configuration of horizontal, flat-roofed rectangles set on a concrete mat over six inches of stone, with the heating pipes under the concrete, walls just over three inches thick with no studs, and, furthermore, with an eleven-and-a-half-foot ceiling. The retired diplomat who ran the savings and loan company in East Falls Church warned me, "Loren, this house will be a white elephant." His view was the conventional wisdom. Engineers said the heating system wouldn't work, the house would collapse under the first heavy snow, and the concrete floor would sweat.

Builders also kept us at arm's length. They'd heard stories about Wright changing the plans or making contractors tear out work not to his liking. Consequently, the lowest bid we got on a house estimated to cost $5,000 was $12,500. For a copy editor making $50 week, it might as well have been $125,000.

Obviously, both problems were solved. My employer, the *Evening Star*, loaned us $5,700, to be paid back at $12 a week out of my pay envelope. And we had the blessed good fortune to find Howard Rickert, the consummate craftsman—who, incidentally, disassembled the house in 1965 . . .

and rebuilt it in Mount Vernon, Virginia. But we had to hire him and his crew by the day, without the safety net of a contract.

Don't put your handkerchiefs away just yet: On top of Wright's fee of ten percent, we had to give Taliesin apprentice Gordon Chadwick room and board and pay him $25 a week—half of what I was making. As you might imagine, I wondered at times whether I'd accepted an open-ended invitation to bankruptcy. My fingernails stayed short. When the house was about half-completed, and Wright had been engaged to design the Crystal City project in Washington, D.C., he said, "Loren, this house is costing you too much; forget about the rest of the fee." Crystal City was doomed by the city's zoning regulations on height, but Wright's expansive gesture held.

(I have to interject the story of Gordon's first meeting with Wright. He arrived at Taliesin on a spring Saturday when all the members of the Fellowship were picnicking down by a stream. In due time, after he'd been given his plate, the great man came around. He shook Gordon's hand and asked him what he'd been doing. "I just graduated from Princeton," Gordon responded. "Just wasted four years," said Wright. "That's where I heard about you," said Gordon, picking up the marbles.)

Construction started in May 1940, and we moved in the winter of 1941. In between was a series of adventures: first, Gordon's finding of Rickert, the only builder who understood the project. "This," he said of the set of plans, "is a logical house." As construction proceeded, he enlarged on that verdict: "This is the most logical house I ever built." Finding materials was another project. There was not a stock item anywhere. The wood—cypress—was shipped from Florida and was all milled to order. Prices often went up 30 percent between the time we inquired and the time we ordered. As an example of the cabinetwork character of the house: the boards were plowed out at the ends where they met doors so as to lap over and de-emphasize the opening and accentuate the horizontal. Corners were mitered rather than butted. The screw slots were all horizontal. The plate glass was salvage to save money. Some was quarter-inch thick, some three-eighths, which meant each door sash was a new problem. And when humidity was high it was very clear whether in the glass's previous life its lettering had proclaimed a drugstore or a shoe shop.

The carport of the house is a dramatic cantilever, and Gordon expended a great deal of mental sweat solving the problem of framing, even with a steel beam. He mailed Wright a drawing outlining his concerns, and several days later it came back with Wright's notation: "Gordon, I don't see your problem." Similarly, Gordon had to solve a lot of other details that architects often leave to the help; and he did a masterfully sensitive job, as the finished house attests. However, Gordon said Wright did spend a good deal of time working on the house plans, singing to himself, "This house for Loren Pope must have charm. This house for Loren Pope must have charm."

When a house that's an architectural freedom rider is being hand-built, piece by handcrafted piece, and you have no contract, construction doesn't proceed; it drags, in excruciating slow motion. Then, when you yield to the entreaties of a friend who has no topic for her column and let her write about the house on condition she doesn't even tell what county it's in, and she does, a plague of visitors slows things even more.

The *Evening Star* did have to lend me some more money, but we had a work of art, all furnished, for not much more than the price of any old house. . . . I would guess the house cost somewhere between $7,000 and $8,000. Not being much of a bookkeeper, that's about as close as I can come.

On one of Mr. Wright's visits after the house was completed, I explained that Gordon had designed the fireplace grate to lift the fire a foot off the floor because the fireplace smoked. Mr. Wright said the grate was nice, but "overdesigned, a problem we all have." Then we walked through the house to the end bedroom where the perforated boards on the end wall were vertical rather than horizontal, as they were in all the clerestory windows. Mr. Wright said, "It is a mistake to introduce a second motif; it takes great skill to handle it." I observed that I thought Gordon had done pretty well. (The gift shop now at the house sells Pope-Leighey House T-shirts picturing in dramatic colors that second motif.)

On another occasion when Mr. Wright visited the house I had started to lay the brick patio outside the dining area, using a 30-inch mason's level. The results hadn't been perfect, and Mr. Wright said, "Loren, use a string." I did. It worked.

What was the house like to live in? It was a soaring experience of living in a work of art. (I have to explain that the [original] orientation was slightly different from this [Woodlawn Plantation orientation], which made the living area a good deal lighter and brighter.) First, it appealed to me as an expression of principle. It is honest, and, being honest, it is eloquent and it is quiet. The materials that do the work also furnish the decoration with their own soft charm. The house is free and open and gives a sense of unbounded yet sheltered space and release as the outdoors and the leaves and branches above are one with it or complement and extend it.

Coming home tired after working on a half-dozen wartime editions a day, or two shifts on Saturday by reason of a Sunday paper, I could feel the dissolving of tensions as I walked in and came down those few steps into this high space. It gave a cathedral sense of release. The tawny horizontal patterns of the cypress imparted a feeling of repose. It was like living with a great and quiet soul. It did not intrude but was always there for comfort. To me it was an implicit sermon on truth and beauty.

You think I'm going to avoid mention of that tiny kitchen, don't you? No, I have no choice. It *was* too small, but it sufficed for those days when I didn't have a copper pan to my name. We did a lot of entertaining, but don't press me for details; I simply don't remember how dinner for six guests got prepared in that space. Also, I had to build a shed out back to hold things such as a wheelbarrow and tools.

Seven years later [in December 1946] we sold the house for $17,000 to the eager buyer—one of many—who we thought would most appreciate it. As you'll see in a moment, we chose well. We could have asked more. It all goes to show what faith will do.

Why did we leave it? In the days of afternoon newspapers, the demagogues and the witch hunters who made their charges in congressional hearings in the morning got full play. But the rebuttals that followed were buried under the next day's overtaking events. I felt that newspapers were failing to inform, and that my professional role was something like sticking my finger in a cup of water and looking for the impression when I pulled it out. I was a constant reader of *The New Yorker's* E. B. White, who had just bought a farm in Maine. I had been raising pigs to beat the wartime meat shortage. So the solution seemed to be to farm, write on the side, and have a Wright pleasure palace in the country. Virginia hams were to pay for it. That was the dream.

When we put the house up for sale, one tiny classified ad brought a swarm of a hundred or so prospective buyers. As the real estate agent said, "The buying public is way ahead of the lending public."

Leaving the house was a wrench. On the last day I sat on the fireplace hob and wept. My five-year-old son came up and said, "Daddy, I don't want to leave our cozy little home."

Mr. Wright did come out to the farm and, of course, spotted the perfect site for a new house—across a stream on a far slope. Even aside from the expense of bridging that stream, the cost of a Wright house on a farming and freelance-writing income was pure fantasy. Besides, I soon went to the *New York Times*, and Mr. Wright didn't live long enough.

Mr. Wright's visit to the farm was in 1956 or 1957, when he was in his late eighties. On our route was a weeping willow tree I had long considered the most beautiful tree I'd ever seen. As we approached it, Mr. Wright sucked in his breath, grabbed my right wrist, and exclaimed, "Loren! You've got to get me a slip of that!" You may have heard a similar story that I was once told by some forgotten source. Mr. Wright was buying a tree, and the nurseryman protested that it wasn't a fast grower and that Mr. Wright was eighty years old. Mr. Wright is quoted as retorting to the nurseryman, "Then we'd better plant it today!"

I occasionally had nightmares that I'd never have another Wright house.

I've saved for last my best Wright remembrance. In the early fifties I had to go to New York on short notice, and I asked the office secretary to reserve me a room at the Plaza, where Mr. Wright was staying while the Guggenheim Museum was being built. She had to accept a much more lavish room than would have been customary. Conrad Hilton had recently bought the hotel and put his stamp on it. Opening the door to my room, I walked into what seemed like an acre of French gray carpeting, French gray walls with crystal light fixtures, and much plate-glass mirror.

The next day when I'd finished my work I called Mr. Wright and he said to come on down to his room. There was no French gray anywhere. On the parquet wood floor of the hall was an elegant Oriental runner. In the great living room facing Central Park was another Oriental rug. The walls up to the wainscoting were a black hopsacking sort of material, with gilded walls above. The ceiling was white with a great gold sunburst from which hung the chandelier. There were low, Taliesin-style, black-lacquered tables (made of plywood, I divined) with Chinese red edges; an enormous wood couch in one corner with a giant bearskin rug flowing over it onto the floor; an easel with a rendering Wright had done for a projected Belmont Park racetrack grandstand; and, of course, flowers.

"My God, Mr. Wright!" I said, "This sure doesn't look like my room."

"Well, Loren," he said, "this guy Hilton's been running around the world buying up those dogs, and he didn't know how to treat an elegant hotel. So a few weeks ago I called in some of the boys from Taliesin and we de-Hiltonized it."

Now, five decades later, Wright's artistic deification is a fact. The literature on him grows apace. Even a Wright-designed lamp or window will bring nearly half a million dollars. Throngs of tourists queue up to see the Wright exhibit house in front of the Smithsonian [part of the traveling "In the Realm of Ideas" exhibition, 1988–91]. Wright preservationists are nearly as rabid as right-to-lifers. The National Trust saved this one, thanks to Marjorie Leighey, who gave her $31,500 condemnation award toward the $48,000 cost of moving the house here [to Woodlawn Plantation]. And now the Trust is about to spend a quarter-million dollars to move it a hundred feet off the unstable marine clay it now sits on.

What is so different about this house now that it has been beatified?

What is so different about what Wright had to say half a century ago on how free people should live? By 1940, when he'd been practicing and preaching for more than a half a century, why had only 217 people in a nation of 150,000,000 sought a home that, as one client, Mrs. Avery Coonley, said, revealed "the countenance of principle?" This wasn't some strange new music that could explain a cultural lag. And it wasn't because Wright was hard to get; he accepted every job that came along. In fact, two years after we'd moved in I received a letter from Gordon saying, "If you've got any money, send it. Things are bad here. Mr. Wright is stone broke." And believe it or not, it couldn't have been much more than a year earlier when Mr. Wright and I were having lunch together, as we did when he came to town, that he had boasted, "Loren, I think we'll make a half million dollars this year."

To me what Wright has to say today is the same message that thrilled me 50 years ago, the one that blocked out fear of risks, uncertainties, or the opinions of others.

What he had to say to me was a combination of Emerson, Tao, Christ, and Keats. I had never had an art history course, and about all I knew about architecture was that the buildings we live in influence us deeply and that I didn't like the buildings we lived in. Keats said beauty is truth and truth is beauty. Wright's buildings let materials be their own ornament. Form followed function, which helped make them organic, like a tree, a cactus, or a man. The outdoors and the indoors flowed into each other as one living space. To me they exemplified Keats's statement. It was the blinding light.

I was a zealot. Today, however, I'm glad I don't know how many listeners' eyes I caused to glaze over. Finding out may be one of my hells.

In the summer of 1990 I was asked to speak to the docents at the Pope-Leighey house, of whom there are about 30. One of them, Jerry McCoy, publishes a Wright flyer for admirers of the Pope-Leighey house and of Wright's work in general. After the talk, I was agog at the fervent dedication of these volunteers, as evinced in their discussions on improving their presentations and in their respect for the house almost as a holy place. I said, "When I was living in this house 50 years ago I had no idea that I'd be instrumental in starting a new religion."

1 3

ARCH OBOLER

"There are three stages in a man's career. I will speak of mine.
First, they discover you and everything you do is wonderful. They hold
you in the cup of their hand and print glowing words about you.
Then you move into the second stage, when they start to look for feet of
clay. They can no longer write how great you are because they have
already done that. Now they are out to debunk you. And things that you
do are no good. They're lesser than what you did before, and you're
not up to the promise that you had, and so on. . . . If you live long enough,
you live through that and you become an old master." He said,
with a twinkle in his eye, "I am an old master."

—quoting Frank Lloyd Wright

A rch Oboler commissioned several residence designs by Frank Lloyd Wright
in the early 1940s. In the course of Wright's preparation of these designs,
the two men became friends. The reader will note that Oboler's recollection of certain events differs significantly from the interpretation offered later in
this book by Wright's apprentice Gordon O. Chadwick (page 144).

It was raining in Southern California—one of those God's-tipped-the-
bucket downpours we used to have back in 1940, before smog and spiral-
ing tax rates dehydrated the climate. At an authoritative knock I opened the
door of our rented house a crack. Through the sluicing rain I saw a soaked
black Inverness cape and a water-streaming gray porkpie hat. Came a sten-
torian pronouncement: "I am Frank Lloyd Wright. You wrote me. May I
come in?"

Those simple words signaled the beginning of a drastic change in the
life of the Oboler family.

The untitled portion of Arch Oboler's reminiscences originally appeared in the February 1958
issue of *Reader's Digest*. Copyright © 1958 by The Reader's Digest Association, Inc.
Reprinted with permission. Arch Oboler's other reminiscences were transcribed from three of
Bruce Radde's KPFA-FM (Berkeley, California) radio programs from the late 1960s, "Frank
Lloyd Wright: Ask the Man Who Owns One," "Frank Lloyd Wright: The World's Greatest
Architect," and "Frank Lloyd Wright: The Outspoken Philosopher." Printed with permission
of Pacifica Radio Archive.

Gatehouse for the Arch Oboler residence (1940), Malibu, California. The gatehouse is situated high in the Santa Monica Mountains. (Patrick J. Meehan)

Detailed view of the gatehouse for Arch Oboler (1940), Malibu California. (State Historical Society of Wisconsin)

Distant view of the retreat for Arch Oboler (1941), Malibu, California. Like the gatehouse, the retreat is situated in the Santa Monica Mountains. (Patrick J. Meehan)

Years before, in my boyhood neighborhood in South Side Chicago, I had discovered a house which I thought was the most beautiful I had ever seen. This building was considered the neighborhood blight; its clean horizontal lines of wood and brick exasperated the owners of the surrounding multistoried, gingerbreaded homes. But as I grew older and the conventional houses grew uglier, the horizontal house, thanks to its simple loveliness of line and the harmony of its materials to its location, grew younger and more beautiful until it became our neighborhood's pride. And so had the revolutionary designer of the house grown in esteem, the world-famous architect Frank Lloyd Wright.

When the day came that I could build my own home, I wanted that architect. In the intervening years I had been amply forewarned about the man. This was a character, the printed word told me, who strode through his world with rapier tongue and flailing Malacca cane, striking down conventionalism, hesitant clients, and architectural committees with impartial gusto. Nevertheless, I wrote to Mr. Wright, then in his early seventies, asking if it would be possible for him to design a California home for us.

Now, unexpectedly, he was here, eyes twinkling in leonine head as he met Mrs. Oboler and obviously approved. He proceeded to rapid-fire questions at us, prefaced with the statement, "I don't build houses for *houses*, I build them for *human beings*."

From his probing it was obvious he was trying to find out what sort of human beings we were.

"So you are a writer!" he said. "What do you write?" I told him I wrote plays for radio.

"Are they good plays? I build good houses!"

The fact that we had settled in the lower end of California was definitely not in our favor. "I suppose you'll want to build in that Beverly Hills!" he snorted. "Cardboard cracker boxes anointed with pink stucco!"

We assured him that the neverland of the cinema stars was not for us. We wanted the country, the mountains.

Mr. Wright grinned. "At least you've got that much sense!" Then his face lost its laughter. "You know, of course, the banks won't advance you a dime on one of my designs."

I told him we would finance the house ourselves. Mr. Wright brightened. "And how much are you prepared to spend?"

I told him.

He sighed deeply and shook his head. "It will take at least twice that much," he informed us.

Eleanor and I looked at each other. I got her telepathic nod, and took the plunge. "That will be all right," I said.

Hours after Mr. Wright had left, my wife and I turned to each other simultaneously. "Do you realize . . ." we both began. Before discussing a single detail of our proposed house, Frank Lloyd Wright had doubled the price!

(This man knew that over the years hundreds of his finest plans lay entombed in preliminary drawings—homes as exquisite as dream-remembered castles, glass-curtained skyscrapers prophetic of a time yet unborn, their bright hope destroyed by the harsh realities of economics. And so that our dream, too, might not end with a sheaf of drawings, he tried to dissuade us with the bitter truth.)

After a weeks-long search, we found our mountaintop. It was late afternoon. The rugged backbones of the mountains purpled down to the great blue-green sweep of the ocean, with a backdrop of sunset almost overpowering in its intensity. I watched as Mr. Wright stood on the cliff edge, outlined against the sky like a stern god from Olympus. I waited for him to speak.

And then his words came, strangely soft: "This is where we will build. And when I die, there will be something of me, because of you, on this mountain."

Then he sort of clutched at me and I thought, "This is too sentimental too soon, but I will go along with it for his sake." So I murmured an appropriate response and clutched right back.

Later I learned that Mr. Wright had described that scene to friends—the beautiful homesite, the dramatic sunset. Seeking to "meet each client on his own emotional level," he had decided that what client Oboler wanted was a sense of the eternal in relation to the building in the mountains. So (as Mr. Wright put it), reluctantly, because such sentimentality was foreign to his nature, he had made the speech for my sake, and had clutched me to his bosom!

(He would have been a great actor-director-producer, this man. For the sense of the dramatic is there, not only in his person but in his creations. From Fallingwater [page 131], the house perched over a stream at Bear Run, Pennsylvania, to the copper-and-plate-glass sheath of the Price skyscraper [page 41] on the Oklahoma flats, his is the brightest poetry of architectural literature.)

When the plans were completed, Mr. Wright had a word of advice: "During the actual building of your house, get out of town!"

Where clients wasted money, he went on to say, was in being around to make inconsequential changes in the original blueprints, to the great financial joy of the cost-plus contractor. Particularly when he himself would be too far away to protect the lambs from the slaughter.

The two lambs stockpiled all the materials on the building site as per the blueprints and took a boat for New York via the Panama Canal on a long overdue vacation. I was draped over the ship's rail watching the first of the locks gurgle like a king-size bathtub when the ship's radio operator handed me a message. It was from the contractor. "Mr. Wright has changed mind. Wants building made out of pine. Please instruct as to disposition four thousand dollars redwood already purchased."

Eleanor watched the anger-ripped radiogram fly overboard and listened to me dictate a vigorous reply that the original plans said redwood and I wanted redwood! "Remember, dear," she soothed, "and I quote: 'Where clients waste money is in being around to make inconsequential changes in the original blueprints. Get out of town!' "

(The years have taught us one axiomatic truth: Never disagree with the man about the details of his own architecture. For here he is magnificently Wright. Sixteen years of corrosive salt-laden winds have driven up our mountainside. Now we know that for that site the wood should have been pine.)

Back in California, we rushed anxiously to the mountain. The front elevation of the house was up in all its redwooded glory. That self-hypnosis of well-being peculiar to people viewing the birth of their first house swept over me—until I wandered out into the meadow behind. There, recumbent among the California poppies, lay what seemed to me an exact duplicate of the entire front end of the building!

The contractor dodged my first wild onrush with practiced skill. After they had finished the original framing, he told me, Mr. Wright had come by and redesigned the front end on the spot. And when the contractor had protested, "But we have it finished, Mr. Wright!" the master had spoken three words sweet to art but bitter to the exchequer: "Rip it out!"

The first section of the main building was done at expensive last, and we had moved in. The guesthouse nearby was finished. We were entertaining out guests with a barbecue when suddenly a long caravan of low-slung imported cars curved into our driveway and stopped in a draftsman's precise line.

Out of the first car stepped the unmistakable, majestic figure of our architect. From the other small cars came 20 intense young men, his students. The master recognized our presence with a quick wave of hand, stalked forward, aimed his Malacca cane at the brand-new redwood fence that jutted out from the side of the house, and roared, "Rip it out!"

I smiled knowingly at Mrs. O. This was Mr. Wright's joking reference to the front-end-of-our-house debacle. The smile froze on my face as 20 sets of eager muscles leaped and shoved. With a crackling and crunching of timbers, the fence was down!

I found voice. "But Mr. Wright! We—we just finished that fence! You—you designed it yourself! It's on the blueprints! It cost a fortune!"

Mr. Wright transfixed me with an imperious glance. "Dear friend," he demanded, "doesn't it look better without it?" I, with my checkbook still bleeding, had to admit that it did.

"Then we are in complete agreement!" Doffing his cape, he beckoned his disciples to join the Obolers and guests at the barbecue.

(He will destroy months of work on the drawing board, waive badly needed fees, turn his back on entire projects unless the work is good and true. He knows, from his experience of this amazing span of years, that the dollar is ephemeral but that the years of building are long.)

That afternoon had another surprise. Mr. Wright strode up the hillside, followed by the long line of students. He returned shortly with the announcement that someone had made a blasted blunder. Instead of hanging our redwood-and-stone guesthouse atop the nearby mountainside, the contractor had placed it smack-dab *on top of* the mountain.

"But—but it looks all right," I stuttered hastily, visualizing those 20 pairs of arms wielding house-wrecking crowbars and pickaxes.

"I designed it so you would have the house *and* the mountain," the great man thundered. "Now you've just got a house *on* a mountain. But I'll fix it—and it won't cost you a cent!" A squad of his students would camp out for a few days, he explained, and right the architectural wrong.

For 30 working days ten young men labored mightily, erecting a tremendous native-stone-and-concrete wall just off the peak of the mountain. Soon the little cantilevered guesthouse appeared to hang rather than sit. But ten gargantuan-appetited apprentices appeared three times a day for 30 days! I recall entering a steaming kitchen on the 28th day. A weary small wife glared at me over a Himalaya of pots and pans. She spoke with deadly emphasis. "I am not complaining," she said. "After all, it isn't costing us a cent!"

(As I write this, I can see the guesthouse peeping through an embryo cumulus cloud, and the mountaintop changed without desecration of bulldozer. Stone and cement blended the man-made structure to the very nature of the mountain, and the house and the place are one.)

It was raining again in California, the first rain since we had moved into the house. A fire crackled in the fireplace, and a cocker spaniel was snoring on the hearth. As I sat down to enjoy the drumming of the drops on my very own roof, the telephone rang. A feminine voice greeted me.

"Are you the Mr. Oboler who is having a house built by Frank Lloyd Wright?"

When I said I was, the woman burst into tears.

She, too, was a Frank Lloyd Wright client, she told me. "I have been standing over the baby's crib with dishpans catching the water that's leaking in! Mr. Wright experimented on us with plywood. Mr. Oboler, I called to warn you!"

I mumbled words of sympathy and hung up. I looked up smugly at my own high, lovely, matched-redwood, impenetrable ceiling—and a drop of water hit me squarely on the nose!

(The flying squad of young apprentices descended and curbed the sprinkler tendencies of the experimental roofs. Since that time the building industry has widely copied the use of those plywood panels, as so many other of the maligned Wright innovations have been copied—from hollow-stemmed piers and wraparound windows to radiant heating and kitchens wedded to living rooms; from carports and built-in furniture to ornamentation integrated within the materials themselves to continuity of interior surfaces, bringing the outdoors within and making the landscape a part of the living room.)

A year ago I sat in the house Mr. Wright had built for us, and my heart was low. I had written my first play for Broadway, a prophetic play in blank verse about the coming race for outer space, but the New York critics had vigorously attacked both the writing and the content. As a result, the production had closed. After two years of work my message had reached only a few thousand people.

Suddenly I remembered Frank Lloyd Wright's words years before when, sitting in front of that very fire, I had asked him how he had endured those long years of unremitting attacks on his own prophetic works. Mr. Wright had smiled.

"The history of every artist is this," he said. "At first people discover you, and everything you do is wondrous. Then they begin to look for your feet of clay, and everything you do is berated. But if you live long enough you become an old master." Then his eyes twinkled. "Now I am an old master."

MORE ON DISCOVERING AND FINDING WRIGHT

It was in Chicago that I actually got interested in Mr. Wright. I was living near the University of Chicago, and there was a building there that I thought was the most beautiful in the world. I was one of the few who thought it was beautiful because the rest of the neighborhood thought it was a blight. It was the Robie House [page 45]. [It] rolled horizontal and built into the background of that Hyde Park–world sort of house that stood out like a sore thumb against the [houses] of that time—the early 1900s sort of the imitation of what people were building back in the turn-of-the-century houses—the gingerbread porches and the scrollwork and all that. The neighborhood thought that the Robie House was a terrible thing; it should never have been there. Had the climate been as it is now, someone would have thrown a Molotov cocktail, but Mr. Molotov hadn't made his invention yet. So, as a boy, I liked to walk around that house and say that someday, someday I want to have either this house or something like it. I had no concept of the man. Years went by and, of course, I found out it was Frank Lloyd Wright. And as the years went by, of course, that house became more and more important to the neighborhood. The imitative gingerbread houses, the boxes with scrollwork, decayed and were torn down, but the Robie House got more and more beautiful and more and more accepted. I got older, too, and one day found that I had earned enough to buy a house and went looking for Mr. Wright—about 27 to 28 years ago.

I wrote him a letter and . . . I told him about the Robie House and I heard nothing from the man, not a word—weeks went by. By this time I was in Los Angeles, in Hollywood. One day at our rented apartment, in the midst of a torrential rain, there was a knock at the door—a very important knock. I thought that it must be either God or a bill collector. I opened the door and there in the rain stood a man in a cape, with a white mane of hair (his only protection from the elements), and he said, "I am Frank Lloyd Wright, you wrote me." In he came. And that began a friendship (and it was a friendship) that lasted until the day of his death. At that time he was in his early seventies . . . no, he was in his late sixties. He seemed horribly aged to me at the time, but in five minutes I discovered he was the youngest man I'd ever met.

MORE ON FINDING THE SITE FOR THE HOUSE

Mr. Wright always fit the design to the temperament of his clients. He knew that I was a playwright, a dramatist, so to speak and therefore he wanted to design me a dramatic house. I'd been born in the canyons of Chicago and wanted a mountain house. After a great deal of exploring with Mr. Wright, driving around day after day through southern California, we found in the Santa Monica Mountains this absolutely virgin mountain peak. There wasn't a habitation within five miles, and that was the place where I wanted the house—on the top—and that is the one that Mr. Wright designed [for].

There is an amazing story about that location. We arrived at a cliff that looked out over a canyon toward that mountaintop just at sunset. It was a fantastic panorama—misty, Japanesy clouds, tinged by the setting sun; the sun itself falling off into the ocean; the endless serrations of the mountain range falling away from this mountaintop to the ocean. It was a fantastic scene and situation. Mr. Wright suddenly put his arm around me and, pointing to the mountaintop beyond, he said, "Arch Oboler, did you realize that when I am dead and gone, a part of me will hang from that cliff side?" And he started clutching me. I thought it was a little bathetic but I went along with it. I said, "Yes, Mr. Wright, a part of you will be there. And when I die, a part of me."

Well, the next morning I got a telephone call from an actor by the name of Charles Laughton. Dear Charles said on the telephone to me, "Arch, old boy, I was at a dinner party last night and guess who the guest of honor was?"

"Who was the guest of honor?"

"Your friend, Mr. Wright. And, Arch, old boy, he told us the most amusing story. Someone said to Mr. Wright, 'How do you handle clients? How do you get along with them? Particularly the temperamental ones?' He said, 'I get along with them very well. . . . You see, I speak to them in their own terms.' He said, 'For example, this afternoon I was out with Arch Oboler. You know he's very emotional, dramatic, and so I put my arm around him. . . .' " And he told the story. In other words, dear Mr. Wright was, as we say in show biz, "hamming it up."

ON THE EAGLEFEATHER DESIGN

I would simply say that Mr. Wright had a very short temper and a very short shrift for stupidity. I bet those clients who had problems with Mr. Wright were clients who had problems. We never did. I would make suggestions and listen to Mr. Wright and he would make suggestions. It was in the manner of give and take. I quickly learned not to argue with him in areas of basic design. Our areas of discussion were those that every client has with an architect . . . but never basic design, because I liked very much what he did. The Eaglefeather design—the house he originally designed for the top of the mountain—was never built because we ran into a war [World War II], and we couldn't get the necessary steel. The only steel available to me from the rationing board was, to use their own words, "in a submarine sunk off the coast."

When, after the war, I went to Mr. Wright and told him that I no longer wanted to build on the mountaintop but rather on the plateau below, his reaction was most interesting. He wasn't perturbed at all that I was rejecting the design. In fact, I looked him in the eye and said, "To tell the truth, Mr. Wright, I never did like the design." What I said in substance was that there were big mountain peaks around and that I didn't particularly want a house that tried to be imitative of a mountain peak. We knew each other well by that time, and he took it very quietly and said, "Why in hell didn't you come to me years ago and tell me you didn't like it?"

ON WRIGHT AND MONEY

I got a phone call from him. He said he was over at the Biltmore Hotel here in Los Angeles and [asked] would I come and visit him. So I went over and he said, "Arch, we're in dire need at the Fellowship. We need money. We're in an all-time low. We don't even have groceries. Dear boy, could you advance me something on my work?" Well, my own finances were a little low at the time, and I had paid him in full to that point for all the work he had done. But I pulled a deep breath and took out my checkbook and gave him a good part of the balance of my account, which was $500.

About two weeks later . . . I went out rock hunting. Mrs. Oboler was with me; we were driving down to Phoenix, passing Taliesin. I said, "Let's stop in and say hello to the Wrights." This was in the days long before Taliesin had big signs of admission, visiting hours, gates, and all the rest of it. We drove in and we were greeted very nicely by Mr. Wright and Mrs. Wright. Mr. Wright was [all set] for a siesta, which he always took. I think it's one of the reasons that he was able to maintain such a high level of energy, because he knew when to stop. He said, "Arch, come on into the bedroom while I lie down and I'll talk to you."

So he went into his room and he lay down on his bed. . . . On a table nearby there were a couple of vases. Now, I am no antiquarian, but I recognized immediately that these were Egyptian and very old and very beautiful; they were tiny little things. I said, "Frank, these are absolutely beautiful!"

"Aren't they really!"

"Yes, I've never seen these before."

"No, no. I just got them. Don't you remember when I was down in Hollywood? I passed through Beverly Hills and I met this chap and I bought them."

Surreptitiously, I turned [them] over, and on the base was written "$500."

Well, what is the point of the story? That Mr. Wright took my money and used it for another purpose? Hardly. Mr. Wright could no more resist beauty than, shall we say, a lady of the evening can resist a check. He loved beauty, and there was no price on beauty. He would go hungry rather than miss getting this very beautiful vase. Of course, one might say, what about the Fellowship? Well, the Fellowship always managed to eat!

MORE ON "THE OLD MASTER"

Time magazine had taken one of my works and devoted three columns to tearing apart, not the work, but me personally. I was very young at the time, and I was terribly unhappy because only a month or two before *Time* magazine had said . . . very, very many nice things which I really wasn't that much [deserving] of. Wounded and hurt, I drove to Taliesin. I met with Mr. Wright and told him the sad story of what this national publication had done to me. He looked at me and he said, "Arch, I'm going to tell you something. There are three stages in a man's career. I will speak of mine. First, they discover you and everything you do is wonderful. They hold you in the cup of their hand and print glowing words about you. Then you move into the second stage, when they start to look for feet of clay. They can no longer write how great you are because they have already done that. Now they are out to debunk you. And things that you do are no good. They're lesser than you did before, and you're not up to the promise that you had, and so on. . . . If you live long enough, you live through that and you become an old master." He said, with a twinkle in his eye, "I am an old master."

Frank Lloyd Wright was an old master. But in being an old master to the day of his death he was the youngest human being I ever met, because he had that great quality of realizing that you live in the day, that you live fully in that day, that you give of yourself and your art in that day, not in yesterday, not in tomorrow but in that day, that what happens to you personally, if you're truly an artist, has nothing to do with your art. You just accept it as part of the living process and go beyond it. But, most importantly, Mr. Wright had the quality of realizing that . . . life is a gift, that it is a wonder that the accident of creation is so fantastically beautiful, that we should use and revere every moment of life and look at it every day afresh, with young eyes. And so Frank Lloyd Wright, when he died in his nineties, was a young genius.

"WHAT HAPPENS WHEN YOU DIE, MR. WRIGHT?"

I once asked him, "What happens when you die, Mr. Wright?"—we got to know each other well enough so he spoke of death as well as life. And, incidentally, as time went on he insisted that I call him Frank. Well, since there was a great deal of difference in our ages, and beyond that I truly felt and feel that this was the only genius that I met in all my life, each time that I had to call the great man "Frank" the word kind of stuck in my throat . . . it almost seemed sacrilegious. I had asked him the question about the future of his work, and all the animation and the fun he had in his face—he always had a sparkle in his eye when we talked because I quickly learned that what he liked about me was my "tongue-in-cheek" attitude about things. In this case, as I say, the fun went out of his face. He thought awhile and said, "I really don't know, I really don't know." Because he knew what I meant was not a continuation of his style of work but a continuation of his genius. And I knew before I asked the question that genius cannot be taught. It is not hereditary. I think the sum total of Mr. Wright's answer to me was that all the people he had taught had gotten pieces of his genius, but there really wasn't a genius among them.

14

SARAH SMITH

**Neither one of us will ever forget that first beautiful meeting
we had with Mr. Wright. . . . Frank Lloyd Wright was just the most
humble person. His humility was so great, so different from
what one heard about in the press.**

M*elvyn Maxwell Smith was a high school social studies teacher who first
learned about Frank Lloyd Wright in an art and architecture survey
course at Wayne State University in Detroit. Sarah Smith was an ele-
mentary school teacher. When the Smiths first visited Taliesin on a vacation trip
in 1941, they discussed with Wright the possibility of his designing a house for
them. The outbreak of World War II forced postponement of any further discussions until Melvyn Smith's return from the service. In 1946 Frank Lloyd Wright
designed the house that the Smiths subsequently built in Bloomfield Hills,
Michigan.*

*The Smith House is an excellent example of Frank Lloyd Wright's Usonian
ideal. Like other Usonian houses, it is laid out using a 2' x 4' grid. The house
has a board-and-batten wall system of cypress wood panels screwed, not nailed,
together and is heated with a hot-water radiant-heat system embedded in the
concrete floor slab.*

*In 1984 John Donoian interviewed Sarah Smith as part of a research pro-
ject for a course at Tulane University.*

JOHN DONOIAN: When did you first consider commissioning Frank
Lloyd Wright to design a home for you?

SARAH SMITH: When Smithy and I met, I had never heard of Frank
Lloyd Wright. Smithy told me all about Wright and said the girl that he
would marry must want to live in a Frank Lloyd Wright home. Well, I was
the type of girl that would have loved to live in a cabin someplace on top of
a mountain. I did not care about a plush type of home. All I wanted was
one great big room with a large fireplace and a stone floor. That fit in just

John Donoian and Dennis Doordan's "A Magnificent Adventure: An Interview with Mrs.
Sarah (Melvyn) Maxwell Smith about the Smith House by Frank Lloyd Wright" was
originally published in the *Journal of Architectural Education*, Vol. 39, No. 4, Summer 1986,
pp. 7–10. Reprinted with permission.

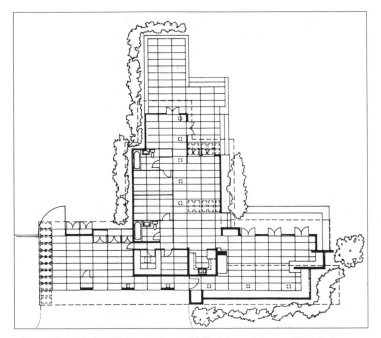

Floor plan of the Melvyn Maxwell Smith residence (1946) in Bloomfield Hills, Michigan. Plan drawn by John Donoian. (*Journal of Architectural Education*)

great with a Frank Lloyd Wright home. Smithy and I were married on March 21, 1940.

The following summer [1941], we took a beautiful trip west. We came to a place called the Dells, in Wisconsin. Spring Green—that is the summer home of Wright's studio—was not too far away. Smithy said, "Look at the map here. Oh, wonderful, why don't we go over and see Taliesin?" Well, we did. The people at Taliesin had their own time, and they were getting ready for dinner. We just walked right in towards the drafting room. A young man came up, greeted us, and he heard Smithy say to me, "One day we are going to have a Frank Lloyd Wright home."

"Are you interested in building a Frank Lloyd Wright home?"

"Oh yes, not right this minute, but we are going to have a Frank Lloyd Wright home someday."

"Would you like to see and talk to Frank Lloyd Wright about your plans?"

Smithy and I were just about bowled over. "Well, if it would be possible."

"Just a moment, and I'll see if you can't have an interview with Frank Lloyd Wright." The young man jumped into his jeep and drove off. Smithy and I were absolutely overcome. In a short while he was back again. "Mr. Wright will see you."

We jumped into the jeep, and when we got to the studio, there was Frank Lloyd Wright standing there, impeccably dressed, from his white hair down to his white shoes. He greeted us both very warmly. "Come, come in, do you have any babies?" He was already starting his interview.

"Oh, no, you see we have only been married just a little over a year." We walked in, and what an interview we had! He told us to find a site that nobody else wanted. He said to look for land that had some drop to it. He told us to take a topographical picture of the site and send it to him, and he would design our home. Smithy said, "We don't have any money. We are going to have to save for this. I see that you built a home for the Jacobses for $5,000."

Mr. Wright said, "Yes, I did."

"Well if they can have a home for $5,000, I think we can afford a home for $5,000, too."

Mr. Wright had quite a glint in his eye. He smiled at us both and said, "Well, that's one of the big problems in the architectural world, to build a home inexpensively enough so that people can afford it. It may cost you more than $5,000 now, for that was several years ago."

Smithy said, "$8,000?"

"Well, maybe, we'll just work it out." Then he asked us about our interests. We talked to him about the things we loved. Of course, Smithy and I were both great lovers of nature. Mr. Wright asked if we were planning to have a family, and we said yes, we were. We loved people and we wanted to entertain people in our home. We loved music, we loved the arts. Mr. Wright listened. We knew he knew just exactly what type of home to design for us. What a beautiful interview! I will never forget it. Neither one of us will ever forget that first beautiful meeting we had with Mr. Wright.

DONOIAN: Sarah, how were you able to find this site? Did he help you with the selection of this site, or did you make it on your own?

SMITH: Well, the minute Smithy got out of the service after the war, he started looking. Believe me, he looked and looked and looked. And he was led to find this site on Pon Valley Road in Bloomfield Hills. How my husband could see this site of all of the other sites, only God knows. Maybe God did know where he wanted us to be, because we were near a lake, and we were also near Cranbrook Educational Community. Our area looked like a wilderness then. There were a lot of trees, marshes, overgrown with greenery. I know this real estate agent was led to show us this land. Smithy had an eye for beauty, he had perception. He was able to see design when it wasn't

MRS. MELVYN MAXWELL SMITH: *". . .we were all really intoxicated with all that beauty."* An exterior view of the Gregor Affleck residence (1940) in Bloomfield Hills, Michigan. The house is sited on a sloping natural ravine. Wright designed a second house for the Afflecks in 1952, but the house was never constructed. (Patrick J. Meehan)

there. What an imagination he had. Mr. Wright didn't have anything to do with picking the site. He just told us to go and find something that nobody else wanted, and Smithy did. It's important to note that the land had a slight hill on it—just what Mr. Wright wanted us to have on our property. So Smithy immediately wired Mr. Wright. "I have found the land, and I have the 'Wright' land, and all that we need is the 'Wright' architect." He received a telegram back. Mr. Wright said, "Come right away."

This was over the Labor Day weekend, and Smithy had just a few days to spare. He immediately got a flight out. He took to Spring Green the material that was necessary for the planning of our home. They were so busy at Taliesin that weekend. Mr. Wright really did not even give Smithy the time of day, so to speak. That weekend so much was going on, and Smithy thought, "Good Heavens, he is not even going to say anything about my plans." But Monday morning Mr. Wright gathered his Fellowship around him. He said to the group, "Mr. Smith has given us a challenge. He has given us a commission to design his home."

DONOIAN: Was there any problem with how the house would be situated on the property?

SMITH: Oh, no problem whatsoever. Frank Lloyd Wright sited it perfectly. He situated the house into the hill so that the sun "poured" into the house in the wintertime—but not in the summertime.

DONOIAN: How soon did he come up with the design?

SMITH: I can't give you exactly the time, but I am sure it was close to Christmas of 1946. Smithy did ask in September when he would receive the plans. Mr. Wright said, "When the spirit moves me!" One day, while we were waiting for the plans to arrive, we took a drive to see the Affleck home. [The Gregor Affleck residence in Bloomfield Hills, Michigan, had been designed by Frank Lloyd Wright in 1940.]

With us was a young gentleman named Larry Kunin. Now, Mr. Kunin had been a boy scout with Smithy in their youth, and he was very important in the building of our home. I'll talk about that in a little while. When Mr. Affleck greeted us and invited us in, I fell in love with the lighting of his home. It was so extraordinary and so different. Of course, we immediately became friends. When we returned from that visit, we were all really intoxicated with all that beauty. It was soon after that we did receive the plans.

DONOIAN: Did Frank Lloyd Wright design any of the furnishing?

SMITH: Oh, yes, he designed all the furniture in the house. Like, for instance, people have chifforobes in their bedrooms. We didn't have to put in chifforobes and dressers, etc. We had many built-in things.

In the living room we have this lounge where we can seat 25 to 30 people; it all depends on the dimensions of the individuals. We can have 40 people in that living room, and it wouldn't be crowded. All of the hassocks, the dining room table and chairs, anything that is wood in the house was designed by Frank Lloyd Wright.

This home was designed for us, Mr. and Mrs. Melvyn Maxwell Smith. The proportions of the house are very interesting. Smithy would often go into the garden room and put his hand on the ceiling and he would say how great he felt, just as though he were a king! He could touch the low ceilings of his home. Now, of course, the ceilings were not all the same. They differed in height. In half of the living room we had a low ceiling and the other half just soared way, way up . . . so there was a variation to the heights in the house. Here's another interesting thought: Mr. Wright didn't think bedrooms should be very large; they were just to sleep in. So our bedrooms were moderate in size, they weren't huge. However, Mr. Wright knew that we wanted to entertain, so he gave us a great-sized living room, and right off the living room was the dining room. Often in Mr. Wright's smaller homes you didn't have a separate dining room; you would have a large living room, and part of that living room would be set up as a dining room. But in our home we did have a lovely dining room.

Another thing is the lighting. Mr. Wright planned all flush lighting. I just fell in love with his lighting, and in our home we have such interesting lighting effects. Just by turning on certain lights it gave us such a romantic atmosphere. Even with all the lights off in the house, at night when the moon came up and we had a full moon, oh, what a beautiful, beautiful feeling it was to look out on the water and see the moon coming into the home with its reflection. It was just beautiful.

DONOIAN: Did Frank Lloyd Wright urge special touches in the design of your home? What were they and how did they come about?

SMITH: Well, let me start with this. Smithy looked the design over, got prices, and said, "Sarah, you and I can't build this home. We do not have the money for it." It was just impossible. So he went back to Mr. Wright and said, "Mr. Wright, I cannot afford to build this house, I do not have the money."

"Smith, you can build this house. You go home and you study these plans and know these plans so that you can hire people who are interested in Frank Lloyd Wright architecture. You will be able to find people to work very reasonably. You can contract that house yourself . . . *you* can build that house." He gave Smithy much confidence, and Smithy came home.

Smithy studied those plans from 1946 to almost 1949. He would stay up sometimes until two and three in the morning studying the plans. When we went back to Taliesin in 1949, Smithy said, "Mr. Wright, I am ready to build the home. But I have made a few changes in the plans. If you disapprove, though, Mr. Wright, we'll just forget about the changes I made."

Mr. Wright took the plans. Smithy was sitting to his left, I was sitting to his right, and Mr. Wright sat there looking at the changes. Mr. Wright kept tapping his pencil, tapping it and tapping it. After a while he looked up at me and said, "Your husband would make a fine architect." Smithy said right then and there he felt he had received his degree in architecture. Mr. Wright called Jack Howe to come and take the plans and make the changes my husband suggested.

DONOIAN: Did Frank Lloyd Wright have any supervisory role in the building or did he leave it up to Mr. Smith and you to take care of the construction?

SMITH: He had nothing to do with the construction of the building, but he said to Smithy, "If you run into trouble, I will send one of my apprentices over to help you." Smithy did not run into trouble until the very end . . . and one of the disciples of Frank Lloyd Wright, Jack Howe, came and lived with us for two weeks and they settled the problem. I can't

An exterior view of the Melvyn Maxwell Smith residence (1946) in Bloomfield Hills, Michigan. This house, a Usonian design, is constructed of brick and cypress veneer. (Patrick J. Meehan)

tell you exactly what the problem was. It had something to do with the roof.

Larry Kunin and Smithy worked together on supplies for the house. Larry was in the sweeping compound business, and he had contacts in the lumber business. We finally ended up with Larry being able to get us a ridiculously cheap price for cypress. Everybody we contacted was able to do something for us. It was just amazing. The next thing we had to do was find people who would work for Smithy at a very low price. Larry was instrumental in getting Smithy two very fine people, Peter Turczyn and Steve Kovass, to work at something like two dollars per hour. These two very fine people had friends and relatives who also helped in the building of the home. They worked mostly at night because they had regular jobs during the day. The electrician, a brother of one of these men, would come at night and would stay until maybe twelve or one o'clock. The same thing happened with the plumber. What a dedicated group of people. A fine cabinetworker, George Woods, was absolutely terrific, and, of course, again, asked a minimum wage. Smithy had a brother-in-law in the cabinet manufacturing business who was a very great help because he was able to take the cypress and cut it all to size— and there wasn't a charge for that. He was also able to get all the screws and hardware. By the way, the Frank Lloyd Wright house, we might say in jest, was a "screwy" house because it was put together with screws. The hardware, of course, was all brass. Every single door in this home is piano-hinged.

An exterior view of the William Palmer residence (1950) in Ann Arbor, Michigan. This house blends with the natural topography of its site. Construction is brick and cypress. (Patrick J. Meehan)

It was amazing how the house was built. There were many people who would walk through during construction. It was very amusing listening to people trying to figure out which room was a bedroom and what room was the kitchen, and invariably they would get it all wrong. Great hordes of people would come walking through, especially during the weekend. Smithy was always very cordial to anyone who stepped into this home. He had such patience with people. It was just beautiful to see his relationship with anybody who admired Frank Lloyd Wright homes.

DONOIAN: Frank Lloyd Wright had a reputation for being arrogant. How did he treat you?

SMITH: Oh, Frank Lloyd Wright was just the most humble person. His humility was so great, so different from what one heard about in the press. He came to our home several times.

One time, when he came to Detroit to lecture to senior citizens, Mary Palmer, Elizabeth Affleck, and I got together and said let's have a luncheon for Mr. Wright. I said that we could have it at our home. Mary and Bill Palmer at that time were building their Frank Lloyd Wright home in Ann Arbor, and she wanted to invite her builder and some of the workers. Well, we had quite a group by the time we were through. Of course, Mr. Wright was delighted to come. We set up the buffet on this table in our living room. We invited Mr. Wright to be first at the buffet. He served himself and sat down on the lounge. No one went near him. Somehow or other people are afraid to approach geniuses. You rather stand in the background; you are sort of awed. Mr. Wright's voice came out loud and clear: "Isn't anybody going to sit near me?" Well, the minute he said that people approached him and he was certainly well-surrounded by other guests.

I sat down and had the greatest conversation with him. I talked with him and we got [onto the subject of] time. He told me he could tell the time by the shadows on [the] wall. He could tell the seasons and anything about time just with the shadows. You know, you used to hear about his arrogance and about his not being able to get along with the press. But really knowing that man—he was so beautiful, so wonderful, so easy to talk to. I enjoyed every minute that I was with him.

When Mr. Wright came here, he was so pleased with what Smithy had done with the house. Smithy followed Mr. Wright's plan to the nth degree. Mr. Wright said to Smithy, "You deserve one of my plaques." You see that plaque as you enter the house. He took the plaque, it was a little dusty, and he wiped it off on his trousers and gave it to Smithy. He did not give a signature plaque to many of his homes. So you see, Frank Lloyd Wright thought a great deal of this house. He called it his "little gem."

I can tell you it has been a magnificent adventure to live in this house, "My Haven" (the name of our home). Smithy often quoted Emerson: "Nothing can be done without enthusiasm." Smithy was the most enthusiastic man I have ever known. The courage and determination Smithy expressed in building our home were some of the qualities that made this venture a successful one.

Mrs. Melvyn Maxwell Smith: *"When Mr. Wright came here, he was so pleased with what Smithy had done with the house. . . .Mr. Wright said to Smithy, 'You deserve one of my plaques.' "* Frank Lloyd Wright's famous red-square tile symbol, signed "FLLW," attached to the exterior wall near the main entrance to the Melvyn Maxwell Smith residence (1946). (Patrick J. Meehan)

1 5

NICHOLAS P. DAPHNE

**[The building] would have been a monument to San Francisco
because San Francisco is such an artistic city. The art would have been a
great thing for visitors. . . . Many, many times my wife and I talked about
this. . . . God, I wish sometimes that we had had it built.**

M*any of Wright's designs for clients were never constructed. One such
unbuilt project is Wright's 1948 design for the Nicholas P. Daphne
Funeral Chapels in San Francisco. Shortly after Wright designed the
chapels, he was quoted as saying:*

Nicholas P. Daphne called me after midnight a year or so ago to say
that because he had bought the finest lot in San Francisco he wanted the
best architect in the world to build a mortuary on it. Nick asked me if I'd
ever built one. I said no, and I thought that was my best qualification for
doing one. So he gave me the job. Of course, I had to "research" a good
deal, and that nearly got me down. I would come back home now and then
wondering if I felt as well as I should. But Nick had a way of referring to
the deceased, always, as "the merchandise," and that would cheer me up. I
pulled through. . . .

The plan of the whole was an attempt to take some of the curse off the
customary undertaker's official proceeding. I didn't expect to make even the
funeral of one's enemies exactly cheerful, but I did think I could give the
obsequies some beauty without destroying their integrity. . . .

The period of mourning has been somewhat shortened and a colorful
happy environment [provided] abundant with music; dignified, sound-
proofed, well-lit space and reasonable segregation for each occasion has
been provided. Every possible convenience designed to make the place
helpful to the bereaved is here incorporated. The emphasis is here laid not
on Death but on Life.

Nicholas P. Daphne's reminiscences, recorded in the late 1960s, were transcribed from Bruce
Radde's KPFA-FM (Berkeley, California) radio program "Frank Lloyd Wright: Ask the Man
Who Owns One." Printed with permission of Pacifica Radio Archive.

In May 1949, at the Southern Conference on Hospital Planning in Biloxi, Mississippi, Wright again briefly talked of the Daphne commission. This time, however, Wright struck a different tone with regard to both the project and his client:

With us everything is merchandise. I have been planning a mortuary, of all things, and listened to the promulgator of the enterprise referring to the corpse as the "merchandise" . . . I'm not wasting my time designing a mortuary, because I have discovered that the proprietor of the merchandise wanted a gravedigger, not an architect.

Wright carried the designs only as far as presentation drawings.

In 1948 Wright also designed a house for Daphne to be built in San Francisco. Although the design was carried through the working drawings stage, the house was never constructed. Two decades later Daphne recalled working with Wright on the mortuary project.

I heard a lot about Mr. Wright. I wanted to build a mortuary in this country, especially in San Francisco, that had practical ideas, [was] convenient to the public. I [sought] some of the finest architects in this country. I studied different plans and the different designs of different types of artists and architects and finally decided it was Frank Lloyd Wright I wanted. So about eleven o'clock at night I picked up the phone in my home and I called him back in Wisconsin. He often remarked about that, because it was about three o'clock in the morning when he got my message that I wanted to get together and have him design a mortuary for me. . . .

I think I called for him at the airport and I brought him here to the site—this one on Church Street in San Francisco . . . at the time this property was a big hill of green serpentine rock. I know I was driving his car, he sat to my right in the front seat, and as we crossed . . . [this] street Mr. Wright said to me, "What is this building over here?" pointing at the U.S. Mint, a square granite building. . . . He said, "We'll make the mint look like a moth, and the moth look like a mint!"

I had often told him that I wanted a mortuary with no steps for entering. For old people, to attend funerals is a lot, and I didn't want steps. There was a lot of perennial legwork done with Mr. Wright; I showed him about three or four mortuaries around the area. I followed him again when he was with his son, Mr. Lloyd Wright. I followed him in Los Angeles; we attended two or three other mortuaries there. Another comment he made to me that I never forgot: "I think I know the funeral business by now, I don't have to eat it!"

I said, "Mr. Wright, I still [need] a very fine, organized plan that's practical to work with. I'm not worried about your design, it's having a plan that will work for the funeral business. I don't question your beautifulness of construction and colors and things, but I still have to have some of these bugs [worked] out before I go ahead with the plans." One was [that] he gave me steps, and one was that the showroom or display room for caskets was very, very small—instead of maybe showing 25 or 30 caskets, Frank Lloyd Wright only showed about seven or eight. Another thing is he left the somber rooms out—the visitation rooms—the small rooms . . . for one-night visiting before the remains go into the chapel. I went to Mr. Wright, and he refused to make these changes. He was pretty fixed. I think that this was one of the problems that Mr. Wright had in his lifetime. He knew himself [that his designs were] great, but contractors could not do his jobs when even the working drawings were finished. The working drawings were not complete where contractors could really bid on them. They said there were too many spaces [that] were open, they'd have to be decided on the scene; too time-consuming to make decisions; again, there were changes on the blueprint at the construction stage, and this would then result in bills [that] were high for the owner.

I wanted a building—the building itself and the improvements on my land—to be simply $250,000 to $300,000 of construction. In those days that would be like a million dollars now. So when we brought those plans out for preliminary cost findings for the construction, when it was finally given out, the contractors came back and said it was going to cost about three-quarters of a million dollars. Of course, I know . . . it always runs over, and I figured it was someplace like a million [dollars] it would have cost then. I couldn't afford it. So I backed off for the time being.

I know my feelings back then were sort of a little businessmanlike. But I would say if Mr. Wright had competent draftsmen who knew the construction business, who could take his ideas and really put them on paper, more of his buildings would have been built. They would have been an honor to him and his country, because he was the father of architecture in the United States and maybe the world in his time. . . . No businessman can endure four times [the cost] of what he asks for. . . . [The mortuary] would have been a monument to San Francisco because San Francisco is such an artistic city. The art would have been a great thing for visitors. . . . Many, many times my wife and I talked about this. . . . God, I wish sometimes that we had had it built.

16

JAMES EDWARDS

**Mr. Wright was great to work with. He treated us very well
all of the time—our relationship was superb.**

The *Mr. and Mrs. James Edwards residence in Okemos, Michigan, was
designed by Wright in 1949.*

Mrs. Edwards—Dolores—who was rather deeply interested in architecture, gave me an article titled "The Love Affair of a Man and His House," which was published in *House Beautiful* just after World War II. She asked for my reaction to the article. At the time, we were vacationing in an old family log cabin house in northern Michigan. We never had a house of our own and looked forward to the time of designing and building something for us to start off in.

I read the article and told her, "I'd like to call Mr. Wright in Spring Green, Wisconsin." The next day I did. Mr. Wright was traveling at the time, and I reached Mr. Wright's secretary, Gene Masselink, instead. Mr. Masselink had come from Grand Rapids. After Mr. Masselink listened for some time, he said, "Put it all down in a letter, and let's see what Mr. Wright thinks."

Well, I wrote and wrote, putting all of our plans down, and got the letter in the mail to Mr. Wright. Nothing came back—and I mean nothing. No mild answer and no comment one way or another. Finally, after about six weeks, a letter came with Mr. Wright's red square on the outside—his red square standing for integrity—and this is all it said:

> My dear Mr. Edwards:
> All right—let's see what I can do.
> FLW

That was the only contact we ever had regarding his acceptance to design our house—nothing more written and nothing more verbally. We told him we could spend $16,000. However, we finally paid him more money than we originally agreed because our house cost more. After we

The James Edwards residence (1949) in Okemos, Michigan. Construction is brick and cypress. The roof is clad with asphalt shingles. The house stands on the side of a hill in a wooded area. (Patrick J. Meehan)

sent him the additional money, he wrote back that it was the only time in his memory that he had a client forward a check without substantial proof that extra money was needed, and he thanked us for it.

After the go-ahead letter came from Mr. Wright, Mrs. Edwards and I went to Taliesin to be on hand for a substantial Sunday morning breakfast with other clients and all the architects and architects-in-training. During our visit Mr. Wright introduced us to a client whose house would cost about $500,000—remember, this was about 1948. When Dolores got Mr. Wright to one side later in the morning, she said to him, "Mr. Wright, how can you do a house for $16,000 for us when clients are here planning a house for $500,000?" Mr. Wright replied, "Mrs. Edwards, I have to have these large projects so I can afford to do the jobs for the young people that I enjoy doing so much." Mr. Wright was great to work with. He treated us very well all of the time—our relationship was superb.

We stopped one night at Taliesin West on our way to California and had dinner with Mr. and Mrs. Wright. Mrs. Wright had the responsibility for her daughter's introduction reception, and she kept this subject front and center that evening. Mr. Wright, however, knowing that I worked with the Oldsmobile division of General Motors, gave me his idea for the design of a New York cab, which was "narrow, high, and a little shorter than standard—the driver could see better and could wiggle through the cars." Mr. Wright's dining chair was an old one from the Taliesin West kitchen—the woven cane bottom long since gone, a big hole now in the chair bottom. Mr. Wright got up, found a pillow, stuffed it in the hole, and sat on it for a while. He'd get up occasionally and rearrange the pillow, and by this method he got through dinner.

We had trouble raising the money to build the house—banker friends got it for us. Moneylenders were unlimited in their ability to guard the vault—with nothing of value in their "artistic" sense. There was nothing more serious than a lumberyard house design for them. Fortunately, our friends turned the whole thing around for us.

Dolores was our family contractor. During her contracting activities she drove a handsome Oldsmobile convertible which had originally been made for the Oldsmobile division to display upcoming features. She was an excellent contractor. She would park the car out of sight around the corner in order to work with subcontractors on their bid and make sure that things were being done correctly. Dolores saved us a lot of money during construction. In one instance, she got $1,000 off the radiant hot-water heating system, which was installed in the floor, by driving to the next little town for a better price.

Dolores could hardly wait for the flush miter glass to be delivered and installed. The owner of the yard where the glass was purchased came out to do the installation. Our interest was high with no thought of failure. The glass was perfect—a three-way miter in the quarter-inch glass.

While the house was under construction, water poured off the roof onto the terrace when it rained, because no scuppers or downspouts had been provided. The water ran down the steps into the 40-foot-long living room. Mrs. Edwards took the huge rug and pad up the steps to the dining room—got them out of the way, because the wood in the fireplace floated out to the living room floor. Some problem! We fixed it by putting scuppers in the next day.

We had a lot of fun building the whole program ourselves.

One day I called Mr. Wright about something, and it took a long time for him to come to the phone. When we were all through with my part of the phone call he said, "What do you think of the offset I put in the wall supporting the living room and terrace?" I said, "It's great." Mr. Wright thought it did a lot for the wall, and it did—a great strength characteristic.

During construction Mr. Wright's chief engineer, William Wesley Peters, came to review the progress and approved the work.

We had a deluge of people come (as Mrs. Edwards expected), interested in seeing the house under construction.

One Sunday morning while up on the roof nailing down shingles, I looked behind me and saw a man standing there. I said hello. He said he just wanted to see the house, and then he moved along and down to the ground.

One night I took our German shepherd out for a little fresh air, and she held still for a moment. I could see two little figures in the dark walking slowly toward us, and I, holding the dog, waited until they were almost near and called to them, asking what it was they wanted. They asked, "Are you Mr. Edwards?" I said, "Yes." They said they were part of the group at Taliesin and had been given a car by Mr. Wright. They were touring around to see the houses designed by Mr. Wright that were available. They were Orientals (probably Chinese) and they came up to me. After much pleading on my part, they came in and saw the house. We found they had not had dinner (it was about midnight). They were planning on staying someplace along the highway. Good Lord! So we got out our own food and asked them to stay for the night, and they did. In the next hour or two we were entertained in the living room of our house by the most beautiful Oriental dancing you could imagine. They wrote their names in one of our Frank Lloyd Wright books. Early the next morning we got up to get their breakfast and found they had gone—they left a note, but there was no chance for us to see this great couple again.

We were sorry not to be able to live in our house longer than a year and a half. We went to Texas with General Motors. However, we were glad to have the opportunity to live in a Frank Lloyd Wright–designed house. The last day we were there, as vans came into the yard to move us out, people came in by the busload from some university in St. Louis to see the structure. It was a house thrilling to build and gracious to live in, but, for a family, it would soon be too small and too much a work of art.

ROBERT AND GLORIA
BERGER

I remember I had to ask him three times: "Does that mean you are going to design a house for me?" And he said yes and sort of laughed.

T*he Mr. and Mrs. Robert Berger residence in San Anselmo, California, was designed in 1950. Wright designed the house using a diamond-shaped module as the basis for generating the floor plan. The house was also designed so that Mr. Berger, a mathematics teacher, could do the actual construction work himself.*

ON BECOMING INTERESTED IN WRIGHT

ROBERT BERGER: I was trained as an engineer. I finished my training at Cal after the war [World War II]. That's when I started to teach. Of course, like any engineer, since they can draw lines and can compute, everyone thinks they can design a home. And a lot of people do. However, it's been my experience that most engineers essentially end up designing a box. I was dissatisfied with the box. Every time I would start with the design, I'd end up with a box. I'd get unhappy. I would pick up one of the new architectural magazines, like *Architectural Forum*, which at that time ran a lot of designs of the latest and best in architecture. Every time I'd see one of these I'd get more and more frustrated with what I was designing.

But, finally, in 1948 *Architectural Forum* ran a whole issue devoted to Frank Lloyd Wright, and I just fell head over heels in love with the type of housing he was designing. Frank Lloyd Wright to me at that time was a far distant person—a world-famous personality—and the idea of having him design a house for me just never occurred. I continued to draw and had friends draw for me. In fact, I insulted a few friends by letting them know that I didn't like what they designed for me. I didn't like what *I* was designing!

Mr. and Mrs. Robert Berger's reminiscences, recorded in the late 1960s, were transcribed from Bruce Radde's KPFA-FM (Berkeley, California) radio program "Frank Lloyd Wright: Ask the Man Who Owns One." Printed with permission of Pacifica Radio Archive.

Exterior view near the entrance drive of the Robert Berger residence (1950) in San Anselmo, California. Wright based his design for the house on a triangular module. The house is constructed of desert rubblestone and wood. (Patrick J. Meehan)

Wood, glass, and native stone are integrated into an organic whole in the Robert Berger residence (1950). Special wood panels use a pattern reflecting other design attributes of the residence and accommodate built-in glass for natural interior lighting. (Patrick J. Meehan)

ON HIRING WRIGHT

ROBERT BERGER: I remember distinctly coming home for lunch one day and having a cup of coffee with my wife. I suddenly put the cup of coffee down and said, "You know what I'm going to do? I'm going to ask Frank Lloyd Wright to design my house." My wife kind of laughed. That afternoon, when I went back to the school [where I was teaching], I immediately walked over to the library and went to *Who's Who in America* and looked up Frank Lloyd Wright and got his address: Paradise Valley in Arizona. I immediately wrote a handwritten letter, essentially telling him that I wanted him to design a house and that I wanted to build it myself. I knew that the longer I kept that letter in my hand the more I would talk myself out of writing to this famous person. So I got the letter in the mail just as fast as I could. In a very short while I got back a letter from Eugene Masselink, Mr. Wright's secretary, saying that Mr. Wright wanted the prospectus sent to him and essentially saying that I was to send a topo map [i.e., a topographic map of the proposed site of the house], and that was it.

After a length of time—this was around April 1950—I received papers ordering me back to Aberdeen Proving Grounds for the summer. I was in the reserves at that time. While I was at Aberdeen, I wrote to Mr. Wright again. I told him that I was coming through Chicago on my way home in the latter part of August and asked whether it would be possible to drop up and see him at Spring Green. I took a train to Madison, a bus from Madison to Spring Green, and then I phoned out to the Wright house and asked them to send someone down to pick me up. They took me to Mr. Wright's home, and I remember distinctly looking at the model of the Guggenheim Museum when Mr. Wright came in.

He was smaller than I expected. We sat down and he apologized: "I'm sorry, I haven't read your letter yet." He said very, very softly and very quietly that he had well over thirty buildings on the drawing boards at that time. I thought to myself, "Oh, here it comes—he's going to turn me down." And very, very softly and very quietly he said, "However, I think that I can work you in." I remember I had to ask him three times, "Does that mean you are going to design a house for me?" And he said yes and sort of laughed. I turned around and walked away after the interview was over, and just as I passed out of his sight, I said: "Mr. Wright, you *are* going to design a house for me?"

ON THE REQUIREMENTS FOR THE DESIGN OF THE HOUSE

ROBERT BERGER: The requirements were rather few: a house easy to build, low in cost, expandable, how many children we had—I think we asked for two bedrooms and a playroom, a place for a sewing machine for my wife, and essentially that was all.

In starting this I was, in a way, rebelling against my engineering training. I had never been trained to design beauty—to this day I cannot design beauty. I can design for utility, but I have no feeling for beauty. I was determined that I wanted beauty first, utility second, and I was going to have a person who I knew could give me the beauty design the house. I was going to leave it completely in his hands, and I have done so. When it comes to the inner construction of the house, I will play around with that to my heart's content. When it comes to the furniture, I will do what I want to as far as the construction is concerned—how the stuff is put together. But as far as the appearance is concerned, I will have nothing whatsoever to do with this. To this day, if I need any details whatsoever I will go to the Wright Foundation, which is taken care of by Aaron Green in San Francisco. I will have nothing to do with the beauty of the house. We ask Aaron for details of anything that we see in the house. As I said, when I comes to construction—how many pieces of steel, how many screws, whether the screws go here, or whether it's nailed or screwed or however it's put together—I'll do that. As a result there are, lately, few blueprints. Most of the construction is done from sketches, and I translate these sketches directly into the finished product without going through any blueprints.

These were essentially the requirements. I was so happy at getting something beautiful that I just didn't want to tell Mr. Wright in any way, shape, or form what to give me. This is probably the heaviest house in Marin County. I think I calculated at one time that I poured close to 750 tons of concrete. I probably lifted a couple million pounds. It's a very heavy, very massive house. It takes a long time to build. Aaron [Green] himself has said Mr. Wright kind of double-crossed me as far as the requirement "easy to build" is concerned.

ON FINISHING THE HOUSE

ROBERT BERGER: I have a photograph of myself with hair, a brand new pipe, a brand new pair of khakis, and a brand new shovel taken on April 1, 1953. That was the first shovelful of earth—that's when we broke ground, and I've been at it ever since. The house is not finished yet. I would say it's about 98–99 percent finished; the rest of the house is just minor details. We're very comfortable and very, very happy with it. That's perhaps why I've slowed down a little bit in building.

I, of course, when I started the house, had a dream. I wanted something that was beautiful first and utilitarian second. I found that the utility followed right along with the beauty, but to get to the beauty . . . it's hard to talk about it. It's a very emotional thing. I'm absolutely crazy about the house. It's almost like my own child. I have sat here . . . and I've seen those rocks in the fireplace probably for the last fifteen years—I've lived in the house for about twelve years—and every time I look at them they look different. It's just a constant—the constant idea of beauty in the house. I feel as if I am surrounded by it. Sometimes [I] wake up at night and I'll walk around; sometimes I'll go out onto the terrace and look back at the house. I just can't walk around the house without seeing beauty. It's exceeded my fondest dreams. Because of this experience, I really feel sorry for people who live in a house that they are using strictly as a shelter from the elements. It's such a thrill to be feeling a work of art; actually living it. It's almost like a living thing. I'm just overjoyed with the place. My wife, of course, is mad at me because I never really want to go anywhere—I just want to stay home. I like to sit here on the couch and just look around.

Wright Designs a Doghouse

ROBERT BERGER: Jim, my son, was asking me to design a doghouse. We had a dog who was kind of miserable outside, and Jim wanted a doghouse. He was twelve at the time. He came to me and, of course, I didn't want to design the doghouse. I knew nothing about artistic doghouses. Some friends who were Wright students happened to be visiting us one day. . . . Jim came in and started talking about designing the doghouse. I turned to my friend and asked if he could design it, and my friend said, "Well, why don't you have him write to Mr. Wright?" And I said, "That's it! Jimmy, write a letter to Mr. Wright and ask him to design your doghouse." So Jim wrote this charming little 12-year-old's letter [with] misspelled words, poor grammar, and all the rest of it, stating how high the dog was, how old he was in dog life, his name was Eddy, etc., etc. He asked Mr. Wright to design a doghouse to go with the house he designed for our family. The answer to this was one of the few letters that we received signed by Mr. Wright himself. It was a charming letter telling Jimmy that this was a real opportunity for him but that he was too busy at the present time to properly concentrate on it and that, if Jim would write him in November, he would possibly have something for him then. So on November 1 Jim sat down and wrote a letter: "Dear Mr. Wright: You told me to write in November, so I am writing. Please design me a doghouse." In about two to three weeks in come two blueprints of this gorgeous doghouse—shingle roof, mahogany sides, a perfect match to the house. It's quite an unusual thing to have a Frank Lloyd Wright doghouse!

ON THE DESIGN OF THE KITCHEN

GLORIA BERGER: When you look around you see lots of beauty. I'd say it's an easy house to keep up, with the exception of the floors—the chill traps [*sic*] quite a bit. There are no walls to wash because of the rockwork. There's a lot of cupboard space. Mr. Wright used to utilize the "galley," which he called it and which we call the "hallway," with the cupboards all the way down the side of the wall so I have lots of storage and bookcases which you don't find in the average home. [My friends] . . . would like a lot of the storage space, too, but I don't think they're exactly envious, because they know the work we've put into the house. But they admire it very much. My new friends might be inclined to be more envious, but a lot of them know how much work has gone into it.

BRUCE RADDE: Mr. Wright conceived this house—as he did many of his homes in recent years, certainly—essentially as a one-room dwelling; that is, the living space apart from the bedroom wing for your children. The living room, the dining room, and the kitchen are all very closely integrated. Do you find this to be an advantage or a disadvantage in keeping house, entertaining, and so on?

GLORIA BERGER: Well, it's definitely an advantage when you entertain. While everybody is in the living room or at the dining table I'm right in the middle of everything. Of course, my children are older now, and I find the fact that it's all one room is a little harder than when they were little because they're up so late. It has advantages in that you're able to know what's going on around [the house].

RADDE: Mr. Wright often designed houses with the kitchen located in the very center. Indeed, in your house the kitchen is a kind of island in the center of the house—an octagonal mass of stone which forms a kind of anchor for the whole building. . . . Do you find this at all difficult, depressive perhaps, because there are no outside windows?

GLORIA BERGER: No! Oh, no! No, no! I love that! I do have a friend who says, "I couldn't stand it because there's no window to look out of." My feeling is that I'd rather have a cupboard where the window would be, especially since there is such a beautiful room, and there's a skylight above that gives me all the light that I need. As far as looking out a window, I just turn around and look out the living room windows and I can see all the view that I want. When I go into the kitchen, I go in to work; I don't go in to admire the outdoors. But my kitchen is a beautiful room in itself. I don't feel closed in at all.

RADDE: It's a rather small kitchen. How does it work functionally?

GLORIA BERGER: It works beautifully. Everything is handy to get to.

18

RICHARD DAVIS

**For me [Mr. Wright] was a warm and understanding friend
who was interested in what I was doing with my family, career, and
future. He was always available when I telephoned or dropped by
Taliesin with the kids . . . on many occasions.**

In 1950 Dr. and Mrs. Richard Davis commissioned Wright to design a residence for them for a site in Marion, Indiana. The residence was eventually built in 1953. A few years later Richard Davis worked with Wright again on Wright's preliminary hospital designs for the Davis Medical Foundation in Marion, Indiana.

It is unfortunate that we never were able to arrive at a satisfactory solution with Mr. Wright. The technical problems of a hospital in the very complicated medical- and surgical-care situations of then and certainly today are highly specialized. Mr. Wright was not pliable enough, at that time in his career, in the "function" of this project to even get started.

In the discussions with him and our main consultant, who was devoted to Mr. Wright and was also the leading hospital authority at the time—Dr. Carl Walters, of Harvard and the Peter Bent Brigham Hospital in Boston—it was most apparent that "form" was not related to "function" in his thinking. The clinic buildings that [Wright] did do . . . are, of course, superb. But there is a big difference between ambulatory care and the secondary and tertiary care that takes place in a hospital.

Mr. Wright had a chronic gallbladder problem and spent a lot of time at Mayo Clinic (St. Mary's Hospital) and in the White Gleaming Cornell Medical Center in New York while he was building the Guggenheim, and, incidentally, my house.

When I first met him in 1950, I was Dr. C. W. Mayo's assistant surgeon. We were all set to take out Mr. Wright's diseased gall bladder at Mayo. The night before [his scheduled surgery] he told me to forget it. He felt much better and had much too much work at Taliesin to do.

He canceled, but had problems from then on. I kept reminding him over the next few years that we should take his gallbladder out, but he nev-

The Richard Davis residence (1950) in Marion, Indiana. The tepee-like, almost monumental structural form houses the massive concrete-block fireplace and living room. Construction is painted concrete block.(Patrick J. Meehan)

er had time for that. He did, however, develop very clear ideas on what the hospital room and environment should look like.

Our preliminary design that he did looked like a high-speed photograph of a drop of water hitting a plate. It was a half-circle center with spokes radiating out to the pods, which were the rooms, all surrounded by glass and gardens. The horizontal flow of this structure for support areas, etc., was all secondary. It would have been a perfect nursing home setting but couldn't function as a specialized hospital.

This hospital project was given to Eero Saarinen, who was in Bloomfield Hills, Michigan. He had just completed the General Motors Technical Center and was eager to do the new hospital design. He was very aware of the technical problems of the changing medical field. This was combined with superb talents in what Mr. Wright called "organic" architecture plus the fabulous new products that John Dinkeloo was rapidly becoming an expert in developing and using. John Dinkeloo was assigned to our project.

Unfortunately, Eero's office became very busy with several projects that were pending at the time he accepted ours. They took priority over the hospital, which was well on its way. The St. Louis Arch, the London embassy, and married students' quarters at the University of Chicago all came into his office the same week.

He transferred us to his good friend Harry Weese of Chicago, but left John Dinkeloo on the project as a consultant. Working with Harry Weese and John Dinkeloo was also a privilege. The hospital prototype was developed and exhibited at the AIA hospital convention in Atlantic City in 1958. It won first prize. It was on permanent exhibit at the Octagon Building in Washington, D.C., for several years.

Although it was never built, it did start the trend for single rooms in a nursing tower over a two- or three-story podium for emergency room, X-ray, and other support facilities. It also included an outpatient group practice clinic building and a motel type facility for same-day ambulatory medical or surgical care that could also be used for ambulatory presurgical or medical care requiring one or two days' admission.

This design was most cost-effective and is even today leading the way for the current health-delivery systems. It also pioneered the progressive concept of intensive care units, coronary care units, intermediate care, and then ambulatory units. The patient moved through the high-intensive nursing units to discharge, with each unit being staffed to fit the need. This, too, proves to be very cost-effective, providing excellent patient care, and certainly fits the current needs . . . 30 years after our presentation of the concept, which was interpreted as revolutionary at the time. It was published in several books and journals, including the *Architectural Record* in November 1958, as a "progressive hospital design."

On the Design of the Davis Residence

With respect to my Frank Lloyd Wright–designed residence . . . the contractor quit after the block work was done. He was supposed to build the roof sections in a cradle support, starting with the lower roof and then bringing the steep upper roof down to meet it. After it was all tied together, they took out the cradle holding the lower roof, and the balance of the upper roof at the clerestory junctions with the lower roof supported the entire structure. The contractor thought it would fall down, so he quit. When we finally took the cradle down, a transit was fixed on a pencil dot under the clerestory. It moved up the width of the dot.

It was first beginning to snow when the contractor quit. Mr. Wright, who was in Scottsdale, said, "Wait till spring. Keep your subs [subcontractors]. Put a phone on the tree. I will send you one of our architects, and you and I will build it section by section." This I did, and one year later we moved in. I called Mr. Wright at 6:30 every Monday morning at his breakfast time. Gene Masselink was his secretary, and between the two of them and Allen Davidson, who was our personal supervisor, we did it.

Mr. Wright gave us the plans for the "teen-age wing" to be added later. We had one child and [my wife was] pregnant at the time Mr. Wright did the plans in 1950. We started with, as he said, "one in the cabin." We later had two more [children], and that is when we added the "teen-age wing." It comes out along the driveway. We finished it in 1961, after he died, but it was just as he planned.

The entire house plus plank roofing is in clear Tidewater cypress. The interior has all been matched as to color and grain. The counters and cabinets are cypress plywood with mahogany centers.

At the time we built it, you could still get cypress boards 12 feet by 20 feet, and we could select and match. By the time we put on the "wing" we had to take what we got, and we used the unacceptable boards elsewhere.

There were several problems that we had. There were several [architectural elements] that were not there [during construction]. For instance, the 40-foot center was up. The 8-foot-by-6-foot fireplace was built with flu up the 40 feet. When the house was finally enclosed, the fireplace smoked like it had no chimney, which it did have. I took pictures of the construction to Taliesin, where Mr. Wright referred it to Wes Peters. There was no smoke shelf, no dampers, and they had built 24-inch-by-26-inch liners in two separate stacks 40 feet high. Wes said, "Take out the bottom, create a smoke shelf and space (10 feet by 8 feet), no damper, and it will work." It took one week. They tore it all out and put a man up in the area to build the shelf and "room." The fireplace lining was rebuilt. It all worked fine.

For me [Mr. Wright] was a warm and understanding friend who was interested in what I was doing with my family, career, and future. He was always available when I telephoned or dropped by Taliesin with the kids on the way from Indiana to Rochester, Minnesota, on many occasions.

One of my favorite pictures, which hangs in my office now, is of my two oldest children, at ages five and seven years, with Mr. Wright. We were in his studio just to say hello and be on our way. I asked if I could take a picture of him with the kids. He not only said yes but sat at his desk, put the kids to his left, and told me to focus and then hold the shutter open until he said close. The room was not too bright, but the windows were at the children's back. I did what he said. The negative is so light you can hardly see the image. A professional photographer developed and printed it for me. It is a work of art. A wonderful picture of Mr. Wright—left hand on chin, right hand on chair arm as he looks to the left, leaning just a bit to talk to the kids, whom he moved close so that there is a straight line of closely grouped heads in a full-length picture. He could do no wrong.

PART IV

APPRENTICES

1 9

JOHN H. HOWE

**In coming to Taliesin what we were required to bring
was no credentials, no diploma from any institution of learning,
no books, just a willing spirit, a saw and a hammer,
a T-square and triangles.**

*John H. Howe became interested in the work of Frank Lloyd Wright while he
was a high school student in Evanston, Illinois. Following his graduation
from high school, Howe enrolled as a charter member of the Taliesin
Fellowship in September 1932.*

In 1982 Howe recalled the events that led him to Taliesin:

My mother's family were friends of the Lloyd Joneses, and my mother
went to high school at the Hillside Home School. I was born and raised in
Evanston. We lived in a neighborhood of Walter Burley Griffin houses and
houses that Mr. Wright did. He'd send Walter Burley Griffin to help
mother's uncle remodel there—they were sort of Victorian houses which
tried to be horizontal but didn't quite succeed. . . .

When I was 19 years old, my aunt took me to hear the Art Institute [of
Chicago] lectures, and that's where I met Mr. Wright for the first time.
Then Charlie Morgan, who was Mr. Wright's Chicago associate at the time,
came to lecture at Evanston High School. He did a chalk talk on architecture. . . . Charlie told me that Mr. Wright had started the Taliesin
Fellowship. It was my senior year in high school and I thought that I was
doomed to go to the Armour Institute of Technology—a place that would
shrivel any architectural interest. So I was "snatched from the jaws of
defeat," as Mr. Wright would always say, by Charlie. He made arrange-
ments for me to drive up to Taliesin with him and talk with Mr. Wright,
and Mr. Wright accepted me into the Fellowship. . . .

I had only $300—this was right in the middle of the Depression—that
I had earned setting up pins at the Evanston Country Club bowling alley.
Mr. Wright said, "Okay, good, fine." And it turns out to be the case that
of the people who came to Taliesin at that time very few of us had any
money. Mr. Wright just took us on faith. Of course, Mr. Wright wasn't
making much money in those days. The only income he had was [from]

John H. Howe (right) with Frank Lloyd Wright at Taliesin in Wisconsin, c. 1932–34. (State Historical Society of Wisconsin)

his lectures. And he would drive! He would drive all the way to Ann Arbor, Michigan, in his wonderful Cord car to give a lecture for which he got [only] $150.

Howe became Wright's chief draftsman in 1937 and held that position until 1959. Following Wright's death, Howe remained at Taliesin for another five years as a member of the Taliesin Associated Architects. From 1964 to 1967 Howe worked in the San Francisco office of architect Aaron Green, another former Wright apprentice (see Chapter 24).

Howe's remembrances of Wright are presented here in two sections: the first section, "The Land Is the Beginning of Architecture," is in the form of an essay, based in part on an extemporaneous talk that Howe gave in October 1977 at a conference on "An American Architecture: Its Roots, Growth, and Horizons" and updated in 1989 especially for publication in this book; the second section, conference was in Milwaukee, Wisconsin, beginning on page 133, consists of transcriptions of Howe's remarks at a panel discussion, "I Remember Frank Lloyd Wright," held on May 11, 1982, at Unity Church in Oak Park, Illinois.

The first section's essay not only presents a glimpse of Frank Lloyd Wright the man, but also describes Howe's thoughts on architectural design based upon his close association with Wright. Wright indeed had a profound influence upon Howe and his later architectural work.

Taliesin Fellows and Wright family members take a lunch break outdoors at Taliesin in Wisconsin, c. 1934. Among those pictured are Frank Lloyd Wright, his sister Maginel Wright Barney (on his right), Olgivanna Lloyd Wright (on his left), and apprentice John H. Howe (far right). (State Historical Society of Wisconsin)

THE LAND IS THE BEGINNING OF ARCHITECTURE

I

Frank Lloyd Wright was born from the soil of middle America. Mies van der Rohe, Walter Gropius, Marcel Breuer, and the others we think of as modern master architects were all of European birth.

Mr. Wright often said, "The land is the beginning of architecture." In beginning my own architectural practice after leaving Taliesin in 1964, I took this as my "trademark." Mr. Wright also spoke of his own work as "out of the ground into the light." By the "ground" he was referring to the ethic, or principle of what he called "organic architecture." By "into the light" he was referring to buildings built according to this ethic.

The older I get, the more grateful I feel for this architectural ethic which he has given me. I find it provides both a keel and a rudder in my own work, and I wish for it to provide the same for other architects.

In associating with other architects who have been "educated" by the academic architectural schools, I have found that these architects tend to flounder, not knowing which direction to take or where to look for the solution to a design problem. They look in the current periodicals to see what other architects have done; or they have in mind some preconceived notion or sculptural form, the interior of which might somehow be made to accommodate the purposes of the building in question. It doesn't occur to them to look within the problem itself for the solution. It was Mr. Wright's teacher Louis Sullivan who first told him, "The solution to any problem lies within the problem itself."

Organic architecture is an architecture of unity, where all parts are related to the whole and must be integrated into the whole. Therefore, the architect must proceed from the general to the particular; never the other way around. Organic architecture is an architecture of change or growth; it must be such to be organic. The ethic, however, remains constant; this means that all parts are integrated into one whole, as the branches are to a tree.

Most succinctly stated, the ethic or principles of organic architecture are that a building, or group of buildings, should be suitable to, and in the nature of (1) the site or environment, (2) the use, (3) the building materials, and (4) the construction process. In following these principles we not only establish our continuity with the roots of American architecture but also hold a key to the future.

We need to affirm architecture as primarily an *art*—although it also is a science, a profession, even a business to some extent. But if it isn't an *art*, it is nothing. In architecture a poetic sense is needed to accompany the practical sense, to provide comforts to the spirit as well as the creature comforts. For instance, the computer is useful as a tool but should not be expected to replace the mind and hand of the artist.

In building these days we have to use ready-made components, and this requires more ingenuity and imagination than previously. During the years I worked with Mr. Wright, everything that went into a building was designed and specially made for the building. The Johnson Wax buildings [page 49] were prime examples of this, as was the [Annunciation] Greek Orthodox Church in Wauwatosa [Wisconsin]. This was equally true regarding all the houses Mr. Wright designed.

It is now 1989, 25 years since my wife and I left Taliesin, but I feel that my work constitutes a continuity with that done at Taliesin during Mr. Wright's lifetime. I wish other architects might have the wonderful experience that I had, or any of us had in associating with Mr. Wright.

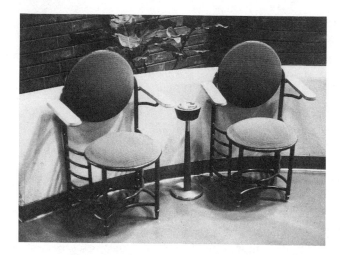

Chairs specially designed for the Johnson Wax Administration Building (1936) in Racine, Wisconsin. The chairs were painted Wright's "Cherokee" red. (Patrick J. Meehan)

In the final years of the 20th century one cannot expect to build as one did in the middle portion of the century. The building trades are no longer equipped to build as they once did. . . . To the architect who follows the principles of organic architecture, this presents an added challenge.

II

In today's culture all of the arts have become brutalized. Nervousness and dissonance have replaced the kind of innate harmony that Mr. Wright's work achieved. All of the masters of modern architecture are gone, so we're left at the mercy of the "post-modernists," the "deconstructivists," etc. Almost everyone seems to be doing the trendy thing, and caprice has replaced principle as the basis for architectural design. Design by committee or team has often replaced the creativity and imagination of the individual.

Throughout time we have seen that the enduring creative force, particularly in architecture and the other arts, is usually that of a single individual, rather than a group. This individual is spokesman or form-giver for the finest his era can produce, as Mr. Wright was. But he surpasses his era, projecting into the future. Though such an individual always has imitators, he also has followers who learn from him, understand the principles behind his work, and endeavor to give new expression to these principles. The imitators, on the other hand, always promote a "style" whose forms become clichés. In the search for new expression true followers realize that the solution to any problem must come from within the problem itself, not from copying what someone else has done.

I believe that the only valid criterion for evaluating architecture, or

perhaps any art, is one based upon an understanding of fundamental principles. One must consider the materials, the use, the users, and above all the
process by which the creation is executed. This is what Mr. Wright called
nature study: What is the nature of the material or materials? What is the
nature of the use? What is the nature of the user? And what is the process by
which this creation is to be built or made? Organic architecture is the result
of such "nature study" by the architect. In the study of nature he looks for
inner forces honestly expressed, leading to growth and resulting in beauty.

Regarding nature study Mr. Wright wrote:

> We are led to observe a characteristic habit of growth and resultant
> nature of structure. This structure proceeds from the general to the par-
> ticular in a most inevitable way, arriving at the blossom to proclaim to
> man its lines and form, the nature of the structure that bore it. It is an
> organic thing. Law and order are the basis of its finished grace and
> beauty. That which through the ages appears to us as beautiful does
> not ignore in its fiber the elements of law and order. It will appear
> from study of the forms or styles which mankind has considered beau-
> tiful that those which live longest are those which in greatest measure
> fulfill these conditions. Beauty in its essence is, for us, as mysterious as
> life. All attempts to say what it is are as foolish as cutting out the head
> of a drum to find whence comes the sound. But we may study with
> profit these truths of form and structure, facts of form as related to
> function, material traits of line determining character, laws of structure
> inherent in all natural growth.

We all have a sense of proportion and appreciation of grace in varying
degree, whether innate or cultivated. This is a deeper thing than good taste
and has been at the heart of all cultures. Cultivation of the senses, if done
with knowledge and understanding, results in culture. Unfortunately,
human sensitivity is usually driven deep inside by the so-called realities of
daily life and a lack of environment in which to grow. Inner growth has
been postponed to a vague tomorrow, and a ready-made shallow "good
taste" substituted. One falls in line with what is popular with the herd.

As traditional building techniques and materials become more costly
and unavailable, new techniques and materials present an ever-increasing
challenge to architects who wish to follow the principles of organic architecture. However, one must use these new materials and techniques in a
humane way; buildings *are* for people. As I stated, we live in a brutal time,
when all forms of art reflect the brutality of life and tend to be nervous
and noisy, seeking image rather than substance. The poetic and sensitive

qualities are regarded as out-of-date, and dissonance has replaced harmony. Too often architects, in striving to be honest, expose structural members, ductwork, etc., in the crudest possible manner. This might be called "let-it-all-hang-out architecture." If architecture and art are not aesthetic expressions, what on earth are they?

The architecture and sculpture of ancient civilizations are appreciated more later because they were high expressions of the human spirit and were based upon fundamental, timeless principles. Fundamental good design has always outlived the vagaries which know no discipline, not having the discipline of form, usage, or material.

Certainly the creation of art must be conscious; it cannot be merely accidental, the result of unplanned actions or caprice. In much of the metal sculpture we have today the "sculptor" takes found materials, welds them all together, says, "Look what I have created," and ships the result to a modern art museum.

Also, there is much misunderstanding about simplicity. Today dullness and sterility are mistaken for simplicity. Great architects achieve genuine simplicity as a result of the integrity of their work. Richness or ornament, if integral, need not compromise that fundamental simplicity. Indeed, such can be as blossoms on a tree.

III

I am not an architectural historian, but I had the delightful experience for many years, starting in 1932, of participating in architectural history as it was being made. I was one of about 20 charter members of the Taliesin Fellowship, and had recently graduated from the high school of Evanston, Illinois. Mr. Wright had been my idol, and here I was at Taliesin, very excited and learning architecture. I think almost all of the charter members were raised in cities or suburbs, so this living on a farm was a new experience for us.

We helped quarry stone for the new Fellowship buildings, and we burned the local limestone to make lime for plaster. We had a sawmill on the hillside above the old Hillside Home School buildings, and we helped cut the timber for the additions and alterations to these buildings. So we were really learning architecture from the ground up.

This was during the Great Depression, and the only income we had was from Mr. Wright's lecture fees. (With Gene Masselink at the wheel they would drive across three states to lecture for a few hundred dollars.) We grew most of our own food (especially tomatoes) and canned it. In those days Taliesin had an icehouse and a root cellar in which to keep food.

An exterior view of Taliesin III (1925), near Spring Green, Wisconsin. Note the corn growing in the farm field in the foreground. (Patrick J. Meehan)

The loggia (far left), Frank Lloyd Wright's bedroom (center and right), and his bedroom terrace (far right) at Taliesin III (1925). (Patrick J. Meehan)

Part of the Taliesin Fellowship Complex (1933) near Spring Green, Wisconsin. This particular building was formerly the Hillside Home School, designed by Wright at the turn of the century. (Patrick J. Meehan)

An exterior view of the drafting studio of the Taliesin Fellowship Complex (1933) in Wisconsin. (Patrick J. Meehan)

John H. Howe (far left in rear) in the Hillside Home School drafting room, c. 1932–34. Note the various project drawings hanging on the wall and the significant number of long-playing phonograph records in the foreground. The T-square hanging in the central portion of the photograph has "Iovanna" lettered on it. (State Historical Society of Wisconsin)

In joining the Taliesin Fellowship, apprentices were required to bring a hammer, a saw, and a good spirit. All work was to be considered creative, not menial, whether one was working in the drafting room or in the kitchen. (Incidentally, Mr. Wright often swept the walks early in the morning.)

All work was assigned by rotation, on weekly lists, to make things as equitable as possible. Mrs. Wright made the lists and was at Mr. Wright's side constantly in those days, to keep things running smoothly. I think Mr. Wright might have terminated the Fellowship before the first year was out if it hadn't been for Mrs. Wright's steadying hand. Mrs. Wright brought serenity and stimulation to Mr. Wright's life, and was his intellectual equal. She established an atmosphere conducive to a creative life after so many years of upheaval.

Though Mr. Wright was in his sixties, he was truly young in spirit and bursting with energy. Having a young wife and being surrounded by devoted and eager apprentices no doubt contributed to his sense of well-being and creativity.

At Taliesin we were back to the basics of creative life, away from what Mr. Wright called "the cash-and-carry system," and away from compartmentalization and specialization.

Mr. and Mrs. Wright were concerned with all of life. Mr. Wright said,

"To be an architect is not what someone does, it is what someone is." So we were learning to be, and learning architecture from the ground up. Our feet were on the ground in southern Wisconsin and, a little later, the Arizona desert.

Our spiritual ground was the philosophy of organic architecture. In this we became rooted. . . . Sometimes [in the early morning] he would have a little sketch in his hand; other times he would sit down at the drafting table and start a drawing while an idea was still fresh in his mind. In either case he would ask me to carry on with the project. He would come back again in a couple of hours, or after he had read his morning's mail, to proceed with the project; and return again in the afternoon after his nap.

There were eight drafting tables in the old Taliesin studio, and Mr. Wright would move from one to another of these, working with each apprentice on whatever projects were on each table. Mr. Wright usually started the design of a building on the surveyor's plan of the property, which showed the contours of the land, trees to be saved, rock outcroppings, or other natural features such as orientation, or points of the compass. So, again, the land was indeed the beginning of architecture.

The floor plan was started first, followed by a cross section and an elevation. Mr. Wright's buildings were really designed from the inside out. He often said, "The reality of a building consists not in the walls and the roof, but in the space within."

Mr. Wright's tools, other than his imagination, were the T-square, triangles, the compass, and a unit system that constituted the fabric (so to speak) with which the design of his buildings was woven. This unit system almost automatically accommodated the building and established proportions not only in plan, but also in cross section and elevation. As an example: In the plan for the original Johnson Wax building the interior columns were spaced sixteen feet on centers. Therefore the plan was laid out on a unit system of 8'-0" x 8'-0" squares. It was determined that the outer screen wall would be built of oversize three inch high bricks. With a half-inch added for the horizontal mortar joints the vertical module (or unit) would be three and one-half inches. The glass tubing above the screen wall that surrounded the building was made in sizes that conformed to the vertical module [page 49].

IV

In 1932 and 1933, when the studio was still manned by faithful draftsmen who had been at Taliesin for a number of years, I began to put the drawing files in order. I also worked on whatever drawings these draftsmen would give me to do. The Malcolm Willey House for Minneapolis, new buildings for Hillside (the old Hillside Home School near Taliesin), Broadacre City, and the Two-Zone House were the projects on the drafting tables at that time. Subsequently, after these draftsmen had left Taliesin, I found myself more or less in charge of the studio for two reasons: one, I knew where the drawings were, thanks to my filing system; and two, I somehow managed to be there whenever Mr. Wright would come in.

The rear yard area of the Malcolm E. Willey residence (1933) in Minneapolis, Minnesota. The single-story residence was constructed of brick and wood. (Patrick J. Meehan)

An interior view of the Hillside Home School Theater (1933). All furnishings were designed by Wright. (*Capital Times*)

A wooden sign used in the 1930s to advertise the "Taliesin Playhouse." (Patrick J. Meehan)

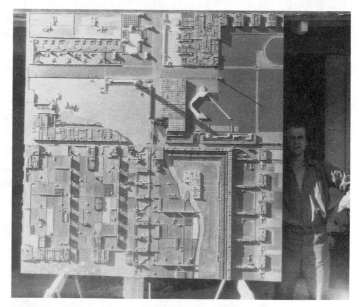

John H. Howe with the model for the Wright-designed Broadacre City Project (1934). (M. E. Diemer, State Historical Society of Wisconsin)

On entering the studio Mr. Wright often asked, "Where is everybody?" disregarding the fact that he had sent them out to build the dams, work on the construction of Hillside, or bring in the corn crop. He would then ask me why I wasn't out there helping them with these emergencies.

Mr. Wright was always in a good humor when he entered the studio; he would hum a little tune or repeat the punch line of a favorite joke. He had about seven or eight favorite jokes. Often he would mount the stairs leading to the area above the vault in which the Japanese prints were kept, sit at the old Steinway piano that was there, and roll out a few bars of his Bach-Beethoven-type improvisations. Afterwards he'd descend the stairs and work on a drawing, charged by this experience.

Mr. Wright taught me how to make the presentation drawings and how to color them with his favorite wax pencils. As I worked closely with him, I was trained to follow through with whatever he designed. Mr. Wright was receptive to any suggestions I made. He'd always explain if something wasn't a good idea, and he did the same with everyone with whom he worked.

Mr. Wright had great patience at the drafting board (if not elsewhere). He would work tirelessly, often spending hours on certain presentation drawings, coming back to them again and again for a period of several days. An example of this would be the familiar presentation view of Fallingwater that was published as background for a color photograph of Mr. Wright on the cover of *Time* magazine [January 17, 1938, issue]. The presentation drawing for the Masieri Memorial for Venice is another example. (Mr. Wright was constantly concerned that the Grand Canal wasn't looking watery enough.)

Although Mr. Wright seemed to have infinite patience in making presentation drawings, he had none at all for making working drawings. The reason was that the presentation drawings (floor plans, perspective views, elevations, and cross sections) completely expressed his design for the project, while the working drawings and specifications expressed only *how* his design was to be achieved. Mr. Wright abhorred efficiency and fought it whenever it appeared in the drafting room, not realizing that it was only by efficiency that his staff was able to keep up with him.

It became my responsibility to assign the work to the younger apprentices and to help them. Mr. Wright particularly delighted in working with the foreign students. (I think we Midwesterners were not very interesting to him.) Invariably a group would gather around when Mr. Wright was working at the drafting board. Mr. Wright enjoyed an audience. He was a teacher, although he said he wasn't. (He loved to lecture and appear on television, would cross half a continent to talk about organic architecture

on a talk show.) At times his explanation of what he was doing at the drafting board seemed to me a rationalization after the fact, for the creative process cannot be verbalized. I think that is one thing that the academic world
finds hard to understand.

Often these sessions would last too long and the staff would become
nervous, because important decisions had to be made by Mr. Wright
regarding other work. These decisions were necessary so we could proceed
with working drawings, get drawings printed and buildings under construction. Mr. Wright's signature on the red square was required on all
drawings before they were blueprinted. No drawing was made or sent from
Taliesin that didn't have Mr. Wright's express approval. (Such a practice
would likely be rare in most architectural offices.)

We were all apprentices to Mr. Wright. The charter members, who came
in 1932–33, were called Senior Apprentices. We received a stipend after a
few years and became the instructors for the younger apprentices. Mr. Wright
encouraged all of us to make drawings of projects of our own design. These
were presented to him in a specially designed box twice a year: on his birthday, June 8, and at Christmastime. (There was keen competition between
Wes Peters and me as to who would put the most drawings in the box.) At
the presentation Mr. Wright would discuss the merits and shortcomings of
each project. This was done very constructively and with kindness.

Drawings for an amazing number of great houses and buildings
designed by Mr. Wright were produced in the old Taliesin drafting room
(built in 1911 and subsequently enlarged). These would include
Fallingwater [page 131], the Johnson Wax building [page 49], Wingspread
[page 131], most of the Usonian houses [pages 67, 89, 91, 94, 141, 142,
145, 151, and 209], Florida Southern College [page 12], Auldebrass, and
the Community Church in Kansas City [page 132]. Approximately 10 years
after the beginning of the Fellowship we were able to move into our new
drafting room at Hillside. The number of apprentices had grown, and it
was now possible to provide a drafting table for each apprentice, although
some apprentices spent much less time at their tables and were less involved
in the day-to-day architectural work than others.

The weekday at Taliesin began with chorus rehearsal. During
Wisconsin summers this was followed by garden period. Generally, outdoor work (building construction, maintenance, etc.) predominated in the
Hill Garden at Taliesin. Occasionally clients or guests were present and
there was lively discussion. In cooler weather we gathered around the studio fireplace. In theory, those who had been doing outdoor work were to
work in the studio during the period between afternoon tea and dinner (at
7:00 p.m.), but that was seldom practicable. . . .

Fallingwater, the Edgar J. Kaufmann, Sr., residence (1935) in Ohiopyle, Pennsylvania, as seen from Bear Run. (Robert S. McGonigal)

Wingspread, the Herbert F. Johnson residence (1937) in Wind Point, Wisconsin. (Patrick J. Meehan)

· The Kansas City Community Christian Church (1940) in Kansas City,
Missouri. (Patrick J. Meehan)

Mr. Wright felt that music was an important part of our lives, and we
were all urged to sing in the chorus or play an instrument in the ensemble,
or both. In actuality, the urgency of the task in Mr. Wright's mind determined where one was at any hour of the day. We were always in a state of
emergency. Mr. Wright liked to be so, and we learned to understand the
value of such momentum. The life that Mr. and Mrs. Wright shared with
us was very exciting and stimulating. To have actively participated in the
fruition of so many of Mr. Wright's now famous masterpieces was a privilege for which I am most grateful.

From 1932 to the present time scores of talented apprentices have contributed to the life of Taliesin, producing drawings for and supervising construction of Mr. Wright's buildings. Despite Mr. Wright's strong distrust of
efficiency, during the final years of his life a very efficient and harmonious
architectural team developed in the drafting rooms of Taliesin and Taliesin
West.

I feel that things have worked out providentially for me. Taliesin was
my province for 32 years, making possible continuing fulfillment during
the following 25 years, first in San Francisco and later in Minneapolis,
where I have my own architectural practice.

The ground is indeed the beginning of architecture, and therein lie our
roots.

WRIGHT AND THE DRAFTING ROOM

It was hard getting Mr. Wright into the drafting room sometimes because he would be so fascinated with rebuilding the [Taliesin] dams, supervising farm work, or doing different things. Finally, after I'd go out about three times to tell him a client was waiting in the drafting room, [he'd come]. Architecture was just one part, although it was the essential part, of life at Taliesin . . .[which also included] our farm work, and the construction and reconstruction of the buildings, which went on all the time. As for drawings for these constructions and reconstructions, we drew them on big sheets of wrapping paper and, before they were even through, we would wrap them under our arms and carry them out to the site because the cement mixer was going. Keeping ahead of Mr. Wright was a real job.

He was a marvelous draftsman. He'd color up his own drawings, and he had tremendous patience. He never slapped us down. We'd gather around [him] when he was [drawing] and, being young, we would offer suggestions on them—later on. But he never slapped us down. He would always say, "Well, now that's one way to do it. I think it would be better this way." In other words, he really made an educational experience out of it. He always claimed, "I'm not a teacher and I'm not a preacher." But he came from a long line of Unitarian teachers and preachers. He really was one!

WHAT TO BRING TO TALIESIN

In coming to Taliesin what we were required to bring was no credentials, no diploma from any institution of learning, no books, just a willing spirit, a saw and a hammer, a T-square and triangles.

WRIGHT WITH HIS CLIENTS

He had tremendous rapport with all his clients. Even though they would come for just a $5,000 house, he made each client feel as if it were the most important thing to him. Mr. Wright would always closet himself with them in his office because he liked to work with them in person. He didn't let us in on the conversations with the clients. And never were [the apprentices] asked to take care of the clients. So my problem, in particular, was to find out what Mr. Wright had promised them!

On Wright's Notes and Instructions to the Drafting Room Fellows

His messages were marvelous because he would sit there at his desk and write notes [to be passed] around the corner. At first, when the studio was over at Taliesin, my drafting table was right around the corner. Later, when the large drafting room was over at Hillside, I was across the hill. . . .

Then Mr. Wright would come by to see what we'd done and what we were working on. Mr. Wright came into the drafting room about the middle of the morning every morning . . . and then he would come again in about the middle of the afternoon. So we worked between these periods catching up, bringing things up-to-date with what he had told us in the morning or what he had told us the previous afternoon.

Mr. Wright went to bed right after supper in the evenings. He thought the morning hours were the important ones, the creative ones. He would wake up at 4 or 4:30 in the morning. I'd be sleeping in the tower of Taliesin, up a steep flight of stairs. I'd hear him come with his cane on the floor and say, "Oh, Jack! Oh, Jack!" So he'd call me to the studio. He would wake up with an idea and he would sketch it out on a long roll of paper. He'd want to get it worked up in greater detail, but he was eager to get going on it. Then I would try to have that done, to some extent. . . . The more you'd put something down on paper, well, the more he knew that's what he didn't want! So then he would show what he did want. It was marvelous.

On the Taliesin Chorus

We started having chapel at the Lloyd Jones Chapel every Sunday and Mr. Wright. . .decided to have an ecumenical story. Our favorite speakers were the rabbi from Madison [Wisconsin] . . . and all of the others [from] there. We had a Fellowship hymn, "Joy and Work Is Man's Desire" . . . and we would stand up there and sing. That was the origin of the Taliesin Chorus. Afterwards we would go out into the chapel yard and have a picnic.

On Doing Away with Lunch

The worst thing that ever happened was when he decided to do away with lunch. Mrs. Wright had a wonderful way of setting things straight. She said to Mr. Wright, "Well, Frank, why don't we have just have bread and [milk]?" So, then we had bread and [milk], and later a few more things were introduced.

JOHN H. HOWE: *"We started having chapel at the Lloyd Jones Chapel every Sunday.... That was the origin of the Taliesin Chorus."* Unity Chapel (1887) at Helena (near Spring Green), Wisconsin. This building was designed by Chicago architect Joseph Lyman Silsbee, for whom Frank Lloyd Wright worked as a draftsman at the time. Wright prepared drawings for this structure under Silsbee's guidance. The chapel is at the site of the Lloyd Jones family (Wright's maternal ancestors) cemetery, where Wright lay buried from 1959 until 1985 when his remains were moved to Taliesin West along with those of his wife Olgivanna. (Patrick J. Meehan)

ON PACKING TO TRAVEL TO TALIESIN WEST

We were packing all of our belongings into the Ford truck, and Mr. Wright decided that we could more efficiently load the truck if all the suitcases and luggage were emptied. . . . We could get so much more in, and we were only taking a little trip after all. Well, a couple of people went into the house and got Mrs. Wright, and Mrs. Wright took him out and said, "Frank, it's time for our coffee and cookies." Mr. Wright was hungry. So he went into the house for his coffee and cookies while we packed up the suitcases!

2 0

WILLIAM BEYE FYFE

**The most thrilling and exciting experience in my short tenure
there was to watch Mr. Wright do a building.**

Villiam Beye Fyfe was an apprentice to Frank Lloyd Wright from June
1932 to October 1934. Fyfe had come to the Taliesin Fellowship after
receiving formal training at both Antioch College and the Yale
University School of Architecture.

ON WATCHING WRIGHT AT THE DRAFTING TABLE

The most thrilling and exciting experience in my short tenure there was
to watch Mr. Wright do a building. He just had it all in his head. He didn't
touch pencil to paper until he knew exactly what he wanted to do, and then
it just flowed out. If you were lucky enough to be in the studio at that time,
it was a tremendous experience. The rest of us would do a plan, an elevation, and a section. He would go so fast at it that he would draw little
details up here [on the paper] and a site plan down here, with the rest of it
sort of spilling out. After about an hour he'd say, "Gee, I've done this so
long I can shake them out of my sleeve!" His ability to work with the pencil was phenomenal. . . .

Some of the most beautiful architectural drawings in the world would
come out of his studio. Bob Goodall was just the best draftsman I've ever
seen in my life. He would be working away and . . . Mr. Wright would
come near him with a piece of paper or something. Mr. Wright wouldn't
touch us because Bob was a faster draftsman. Mr. Wright had us create
good drawings because he wanted us to think in three dimensions, evolving
[into] a good architect and developing the structure in our heads rather
than on paper. The only other person I know who could think that way
was Eero Saarinen.

WILLIAM WESLEY PETERS

He was more available to people than any person that I know of.
He was available to any apprentice, whether for talking or consultation
or observation of his work. He'd thrill with people standing all around
him looking over his shoulder. He enjoyed being surrounded by young
people because he drew life from them as they drew life from him.

W*illiam Wesley Peters was an apprentice to Frank Lloyd Wright from 1932 until 1959. Peters was also Wright's son-in-law; he married Wright's stepdaughter, Svetlana Hinzenberg Wright, in the 1930s. Following Wright's death, Peters became vice president of the Frank Lloyd Wright Foundation and Taliesin Associated Architects. And following Mrs. Wright's death in 1985, he became chairman of the Frank Lloyd Wright Foundation. Peters died of a stroke at Madison, Wisconsin, in 1991.*

In An Autobiography *Wright described Peters:*

Among the very first college graduates (engineering) to come to Fellowship was a tall dark-eyed young fellow who early turned up at Taliesin. . . .The lad was a fountain of energetic loyalty to the ideas for which Taliesin stood. He soon took a leading hand in whatever went on. Mind alert, his character independent and generous.

On November 1, 1984, Peters spoke at the opening of an exhibition entitled "Frank Lloyd Wright and the Prairie School Collection" at the Milwaukee Art Museum. The installation was a formal occasion. For more than an hour, Peters showed slides and talked about Wright's projects before an audience of approximately 150 people. The following question was posed after Peters's presentation: "Much has been written on Frank Lloyd Wright as a man and as a human being. As his close friend and associate, would you care to comment on that?" Peters's response, as delivered, is given here.

I think that Frank Lloyd Wright was a remarkable example of his own belief that you have to be an individual first—a fully rounded and developed individual. He was an example of that type of genius. There may be other geniuses, like Mozart, whom it's hard to explain coming full-blown into life. But Frank Lloyd Wright was [such] a person. He believed, as well, that a fully developed individual was the...direction [in] which he planned education. He himself certainly was this.

There are many legends about Frank Lloyd Wright . . . for example, that he was arrogant to his clients, that he dictated to them. I don't know of any architect in the world who had more pleased clients or faithful and successful clients and had greater, more wonderful client relationships than he did. Certainly he was strong in preserving and fighting for what he believed was principle and was right. But as far as the client was concerned, he believed definitely that the architect shouldn't [and] wasn't in a position to tell a client what he shouldn't do, that the architect should try, primarily, to tell the client how he could get what he wanted or really needed. He often took part in analyzing and judging what the particular needs of the client were or would be.

He often appeared in public life with an attitude of arrogance. He once said that if he had to early in life make a choice between honest arrogance and hypocritical humility, he would choose the honest arrogance. But I would say that people who lived and worked with him, although they sometimes were bitterly afraid of everything like that, were enriched. Frankly, everyone who worked and was close to him was enrichened. He was more available to people than any person that I know of. He was available to any apprentice, whether for talking or consultation or observation of his work. He'd thrill with people standing all around him looking over his shoulder. He enjoyed being surrounded by young people because he drew life from them as they drew life from him.

I think that many of the legends that have grown up about Frank Lloyd Wright have been centered on the development of what were termed "eccentricities". . . . And there *were* those things that seemed eccentric. But I don't know of any person who lived, almost all of his life, closer to the idea of truth, as he saw and believed it, than Frank Lloyd Wright. I don't know of any person who was with him for years who didn't love and honor and respect him, although there were . . . stormy times, too. But that's part of human life.

22

MARYA DE CZARNECKA
LILIEN

". . .I want to buy land for us." —quoting Frank Lloyd Wright

*M**arya de Czarnecka Lilien was an apprentice to Frank Lloyd Wright from January 1936 until the summer of 1937. She arrived at Taliesin with a master of architecture degree from the Polytechnic Institute of Lwow, Poland.*

ON FINDING THE LAND FOR TALIESIN WEST

When I was in . . . the west, in Arizona, for the first time, Taliesin did not exist yet. We were staying at La Hacienda, which was given to Mr. Wright by Dr. Chandler, [who] was Mr. Wright's client.

Mr. Wright went on a lecture tour and brought back a thousand dollars, which was an enormous sum. . . . He said, "This time I didn't bring you any gifts because I want to buy land for us." He went out with a real estate person . . . who took him out to the desert and showed him this marvelous valley and said, "You can have all this [land] for a thousand dollars, but there is no water." Mr. Wright said, "We will find water!" Scottsdale is there now.

Out of the desert landscape rises Taliesin West (1937) in Scottsdale, Arizona. (Patrick J. Meehan)

2 3

GORDON O. CHADWICK

. . . knowing when to be inconsistent is one of the attributes of genius.

Gordon O. Chadwick was an apprentice to Frank Lloyd Wright from 1938 to 1942. He came to the Fellowship with a degree from Princeton University.

Chadwick supervised the construction of the Frank Lloyd Wright–designed Loren Pope residence in 1940 at Falls Church, Virginia [pages 67 and 145]. In 1969 Chadwick discussed his experiences as a Taliesin Fellow with John N. Pearce, who at the time of the interview was curator of the National Trust for Historic Preservation. The interview took place in the Pope-Leighey House.

JOHN N. PEARCE: How did you get the assignment to supervise the Loren Pope House?

GORDON O. CHADWICK: I had gone to Taliesin in the summer of 1938. I think that Mr. Wright chose me in 1940 to supervise this house because I had worked on the construction of his camp in Phoenix, Arizona, for two winters. The second year I was in charge of part of the operation. Also, many of the Fellows at Taliesin were reluctant to go off on jobs; I was not.

My experience in construction was very limited; everything I had done was at Taliesin itself. I learned the hard way on this job.

The Pope House and the house in Baltimore for Joseph Euchtman were the first two houses I supervised. It was a coincidence that they were both ready to be built at the same time, and a good thing, since somebody from Taliesin had to be on hand at both sites every week.

PEARCE: Were you involved in the design of the Loren Pope House?

CHADWICK: No. I wasn't at all involved in the design. The original project had been designed before I ever saw it.

PEARCE: What was the design process at Taliesin, once the client provided a general list of wants? What attention would Mr. Wright have given it?

CHADWICK: This house was one in a series called Usonian houses that

GORDON O. CHADWICK: *"The Pope House and the house in Baltimore for Joseph Euchtman were the first two houses I supervised."* **Exterior view of the Joseph Euchtman residence (1939) in Baltimore, Maryland. (Patrick J. Meehan)**

Mr. Wright designed to be built at modest cost. Each house was planned to fit a particular site and to conform to the client's needs. What they had in common was a structural system—Mr. Wright called it the "grammar"—which gave them a family resemblance despite their variety. Certain features, such as the slab floor with radiant heating, the three-layered sandwich wood walls combined with masonry masses, and the flat roofs with overhangs, were repeated in all of them.

The plans for each house were accompanied by a Standard Detail Sheet which was applied to all houses of this type and was used over and over again. It was developed, I believe, after the initial Usonian house—the first Herbert Jacobs House (in Madison, Wisconsin)—had been built in 1937. Mr. Wright's participation—even on small projects—was more than would be customary in many architectural offices.

I remember watching him as he made revisions to the original plan for the Loren Pope House and worked out the pattern for the perforated boards, which varied from house to house. He was very fond of the

The first Herbert Jacobs residence (1936) in Westmoreland (now Madison), Wisconsin. This house was the first of Wright's Usonian houses to be built. (Patrick J. Meehan)

recessed batten designs used in the Usonian houses. Mr. Wright had developed a similar detail for interior paneling when working for Louis Sullivan, and it had received Mr. Sullivan's blessing.

PEARCE: What revisions were made to the original plan?

CHADWICK: The size of the house was cut down in the interest of economy. Loren Pope told me later that he had been getting astronomical bids from contractors. The lowest was $12,000, which might as well have been $120,000, he said, to a man making $50 a week. He was getting panicky when, one night, he received a telephone call from Mr. Wright, who told him that he realized the house was too expensive and that he was going to redesign it. The revised plan cut at least $2,000 from the cost, possibly a great deal more.

The original plan for the kitchen provided an interior room with three walls for cabinets, lighted from above by a clerestory. In the revision the kitchen has an outside wall. Just before I left Taliesin for Falls Church, Mr. Wright worked out the vertical slot window. It looked peculiar to him at first, but he made it acceptable by adding the window box at the bottom.

PEARCE: Did Mr. Wright work out the detail of the mortar joint running parallel to the sides of the kitchen window, or did you?

CHADWICK: I believe that was my interpretation of the way he drew it.

PEARCE: How much detail was given on the plans?

CHADWICK: Wright plans required interpretation. The Usonian plans were laid out in a two-by-four-foot module but without detailed dimensions. Every time you got to a doorway, a corner, or an intersection where special conditions prevailed, the dimensions had to be modified one way or another. Builders always wanted to know why they couldn't have been just like any other plans, i.e., worked out dimensionally. I think Mr. Wright wanted to emphasize the system concept; and the plans certainly looked prettier without dimensions!

Detailed dimensions were given on the Standard Detail Sheet. You had to keep checking back and forth between it and the plans, which was trying for the builder. Of course, there were some things not included on the Standard Detail Sheet which I improvised on the job.

PEARCE: Could you tell us about some of your own decisions?

CHADWICK: I devised the corner detail of the rowlock brick course on top of the foundation wall, for instance. It was no more successful than anybody else's effort in this direction.

Also, Howard [Rickert, woodwork contractor for the residence] objected to the detail for the doorjambs on the Standard Detail Sheet. He thought that the little piece of wood for the jamb was too thin and wanted to use a two-by-four section at the very least. We figured out a way of routing out the horizontal boards so that they overlapped the larger door jamb but still allowed the jamb to appear light, which is what Mr. Wright had wanted. It was one of the details he told me he liked.

Mr. Wright raised quite a fuss about my use of firebrick in the back of the fireplace. The firebrick couldn't be bonded in with the other brick because it was much wider. I told Mr. Wright it was going to get black and become inconspicuous anyway. He said to paint it black immediately!

I also designed a grate for logs instead of andirons, which Mr. Wright called much too heavy and overdesigned. "That is the trouble with all my boys," he said, "they overdesign. And," he continued, "that's my trouble, too."

PEARCE: How often did Mr. Wright visit the site?

CHADWICK: I believe he was there several times, although I wasn't present. One of his visits coincided with his presentation in Washington of the Crystal City apartments project, which was never built. William Wesley Peters . . . also came from Taliesin to visit the site and was very helpful, particularly in getting the approval of the Baltimore Building Department for the Joseph Euchtman House.

PEARCE: Were there any major structural problems in building the Loren Pope House?

CHADWICK: Mr. Wright had told me that we should put up the roof first to provide a workshop in which to construct the wall sections. They were supposed to be built on tables. Howard and I found that it was impossible to make the mitered corners of the walls fit when they were built on tables, aside from the problem of erecting and supporting the roof. Our solution was to build every other wall section on work tables and then to join them by a section built in place. This way we were able to make adjustments so that the horizontal boards and battens lined up at the corners.

Mr. Wright had two sons living near Washington at that time and they came out to the site occasionally. I suspect that Mr. Wright got news from them of what was going on. I got a summons to go up to New York and see him because, he said, I was betraying him by not putting up the roof first. I don't know how I would have managed to wiggle out of it, but when I got there he didn't seem inclined to berate me too much for not following instructions.

PEARCE: How were the furniture designs worked out? Did the client describe the pieces he wanted or did Mr. Wright decide what should be in a given space?

CHADWICK: Furniture was fairly standard for the Usonian houses. For example, this modular chair design was used in a number of houses. Mr. Wright would prepare a furniture plan which showed the dining table, modular chairs, bed frames, and anything that was built in. It was almost essential to use Wright-designed furniture, since reproduction period furniture looked out of place and most upholstered furniture was out of scale with the houses. Sometimes the furniture plan included things which the client didn't require. Mr. Wright put a grand piano in every living room. That was not necessarily what the client wanted.

PEARCE: Did he prescribe the standard Steinway in a mahogany case or did he design a piano case?

CHADWICK: Mr. Wright modified some of the pianos at Taliesin and refinished the wood, but he didn't mind the look of the traditional piano, no matter how unlike the rest of the furniture it was. He just liked pianos and thought of them as part of family life. Of course, he enjoyed playing the piano himself.

PEARCE: Did Mr. Wright try to keep in touch with his designs during their execution through visits and reports?

CHADWICK: Well, I remember going out to California with him and several other apprentices once when Mr. Wright heard that his design for a house was being tinkered with by the owner. Mr. Wright wanted no part of this. The owner was eventually forced to submit to having me and three

GORDON O. CHADWICK: *"Mr. Wright would prepare a furniture plan which showed the dining table, modular chairs, bed frames and anything that was built in. It was almost essential to use Wright-designed furniture, since reproduction period furniture looked out of place and most upholstered furniture was out of scale with the houses."* **The dining room of the Loren Pope residence (1939) in Falls Church, Virginia. This view shows the plywood table and chairs specially designed and constructed for the house. (Patrick J. Meehan)**

other apprentices rework his house.

I suppose this client was primarily interested in being able to say he had a Frank Lloyd Wright house. Mr. Wright had planned a large house for him, but until he could afford to build it, the client had completed the gatehouse and was living in that.

The exterior was supposed to be of rough-sawn overlapping boards, about 12 inches wide and one inch thick, but the owner had gotten a bargain in beveled redwood siding that was less than half the specified width and thickness. He told Mr. Wright that the building code in his community wouldn't allow the seven-foot ceilings specified for some parts of the house and that consequently he had raised the ceiling height. The combination of narrow boards and higher ceilings ruined the scale of the house, of course. A former Taliesin apprentice who was then an architect in Los Angeles was supposed to supervise it, but the client wouldn't pay for his services.

When Mr. Wright got this news, he took some of us to visit the site. There was a causeway crossing a ravine with a dry streambed way down below. The owner had outlined the sides of this causeway with stones, painted white. Mr. Wright told the fellow who was driving to stop the car. He got out, with his hat and his cane, and kicked all the stones off the driveway down into the ravine.

Meanwhile the owner kept peering over the gate, which finally opened by some magical device. We drove up and Mr. Wright got out of the car. The owner was protesting that somebody was going to run over the side of the causeway and down into the ravine. Mr. Wright said he didn't care.

On a level higher than the house, the client had built a free-form, kidney-shaped swimming pool (a shape Mr. Wright disliked), and between the pool and the house, a wooden retaining wall, which, of course, was not in the nature of materials (wood against earth equals rot). Mr. Wright went over to this wall and said, "Gordon, get the crowbar out of the car." I got it, and then he said, "Destroy that wall."

The owner kept saying, "Mr. Wright, that wall cost me $500." Mr. Wright repeated, "Gordon, destroy that wall." Then the owner's wife, trying to save the situation, announced that lunch was ready. Mr. Wright said, "I won't eat a morsel of food until that wall is destroyed." So I finished destroying the wall and then we had lunch!

Four of us boarded with this couple a month or so. There wasn't much that could be done about the siding, but we added a fascia about 18 inches deep at the overhang to lower the height of the walls visually.

Another small house on the property, a guesthouse, was sited incorrectly, and this also had to be changed. We built, I recall, a 40-foot-long masonry wall next to it to tie it into the hill. Although it was a terrible job to make these alterations, Mr. Wright would not allow these little houses to remain as built. I suspect he especially wanted to establish that there were not to be any deviations from his design for the big house when it was built.

PEARCE: Would you discuss Wright's historical innovations which are reflected in the Loren Pope House?

CHADWICK: Radiant heating was a virtually unknown thing at that time. Everybody thought we were crazy to lay wrought iron pipes under the floor. They kept asking, "What if there is a leak? You would have to dig up the whole slab." However, all the pipes were tested for almost a week at approximately 120 pounds of pressure. The normal operating pressure of the system is only 11 pounds, so we had tested far above the maximum that would ever be required. Then we had crushed stone laid around the coils to prevent damage when the concrete was being poured. From a design standpoint, radiant heating was marvelous, because getting rid of radiators—then almost universal—reduced visual disturbance.

Built-in lighting, cabinets, and bookcases have the same effect. The concrete slab continuing throughout the whole house also contributes to the sense of unity, as does the use of the same wall materials inside and out. In a small house you sense more space when not distracted by extraneous objects, especially here, where the interior is kept consistently to horizontal lines and soft natural colors.

PEARCE: How do you think Mr. Wright would have treated the landscaping of this house at its second site, here in Woodlawn?

CHADWICK: From a landscaping point of view, his primary concern in this house was the hemicycle, which should be duplicated, I think, at the second site. The land should be leveled off and given that half-circle shape as an architectural extension of the house. I also feel that the screened porch and terrace must be rebuilt. The close relationship between outdoors and indoors was one of the design principles involved. The slab of the concrete terrace was at the same level as the living room floor—unusual at that time.

Mr. Wright's favorite plant material in Wisconsin was a spreading juniper, but not the kind that is normally obtainable at a nursery. At Taliesin we would transplant them from nearby pastures—the farmers were only too glad to get rid of them. I think his preference here would also have been for native planting. His aim was usually to be natural, although, interestingly enough, in Arizona, within the confines of the camp, he took native cactus and arranged it by species in a very organized way, in contrast to the desert, where species were mixed. This only proves that knowing when to be inconsistent is one of the attributes of genius.

24

AARON G. GREEN

He had no pedagogical method. . . . It was certainly a process of teaching, learning by participation and by absorption and by emulation and, I suppose, by osmosis. By being a part of [it], you were participating in his creative activities, in a sense: the development of the buildings directly under his thumb.

*A*aron *G. Green was an apprentice to Frank Lloyd Wright from 1939 to 1943. He came to the Fellowship after studying architecture at several colleges, including Alabama State College, the Chicago Academy of Fine Arts, and Cooper Union in New York City.*

Following his apprenticeship under Wright, Green opened his own architectural office in San Francisco. Through this office Green began in 1951 to serve on occasion as Wright's West Coast representative. After Wright's death, Green continued to act as West Coast representative for Taliesin Associated Architects until 1972.

One major project in which Green played an important part during the late 1950s and early 1960s was Wright's design for the Marin County Administration Building in San Raphael, California.

ON THE TALIESIN FELLOWSHIP

I was in residence there for approximately three years. Prior to that, though, even before I met Mr. Wright, I had helped build one of his houses. I was practicing architecture a little bit during that period, and I gave Mr. Wright one of my clients. I got the client so involved and interested in Frank Lloyd Wright that I actually asked Mr. Wright to design the house. So that was a very friendly beginning—it was a professional beginning.

Most of Aaron Green's reminiscences were recorded in the late 1960s and were transcribed from Bruce Radde's KPFA-FM (Berkeley, California) radio programs "Frank Lloyd Wright: The World's Greatest Architect," "Frank Lloyd Wright: The Outspoken Philosopher," and "Frank Lloyd Wright: The Shining Brow." Printed here by permission of Pacifica Radio Archive. Three passages at the end of this chapter were transcribed from the film *Lewis Mumford: Toward a Human Architecture*, produced by Ray Hubbard Associates, Inc. Printed courtesy of Unicorn Projects, Inc.

An approach view of the terrace near the entrance court in Taliesin West (1937) at Scottsdale, Arizona. Note the integration of the building with the desert flora. (Patrick J. Meehan)

The workroom terrace, broad steps (background), and reflecting pool (foreground) at Taliesin West (1937). (Patrick J. Meehan)

When I went to Taliesin it was partly, in a sense, as a fellow professional. It was at Mr. Wright's invitation, which, as far as I was concerned, was the greatest thing that I could expect. Obviously, the thing that I was interested in most. It was, from the start, an extremely important consideration in my then life and everything that has come since.

I was extremely stimulated by everything at Taliesin and by the very close association with Mr. Wright—particularly when the group was small, when there were about 25 of us. It was in the depths of the Depression, and anybody interested in architecture was, from the point of view of economics and making a living, . . . nuts. There was no building. We were surviving at Taliesin off the land, really. Growing the crops, at times eating bread and milk for lunch because we didn't have anything else—and enjoying it! We had tremendous spirit.

Taliesin West had been under construction for just a year or so at that time. It was in the very early stages. I guess about three or four months after I was at Taliesin we moved down to Taliesin West for the winter. I remember we waited until the snow was so high we had to shovel our way out of Taliesin East, though. It was a kind of rigorous existence. We took turns staying up all night to stoke the furnace and things like that, chopping the wood.

Soon the commissions began to come in. A $5,000 or $6,000 house

The terrace at Taliesin West (1937). (Patrick J. Meehan)

Frank Lloyd Wright at his temporary office (1934–35) at Taliesin West. (State Historical Society of Wisconsin)

was a good commission that we looked forward to with a great deal of interest [page 142]. And Florida Southern College [page 12] was just beginning. My first professional task at Taliesin was the responsibility to build one of the models for the Museum [of Modern Art] show at that time. That was the main effort; getting ready for the Modern museum show of Mr. Wright's in 1940. They were preparing lots of building models, which still exist. There was a great deal of interesting activity. . . .

AARON GREEN: *"A $5,000 or $6,000 house was a good commission that we looked forward to with a great deal of interest."* The Stanley Rosenbaum residence (1939) in Florence, Alabama. Aaron Green participated in the design of this project. (Patrick J. Meehan)

Since everyone lived together and worked together, we could hardly have been any closer. It was a 24-hour day. We would see Mr. Wright at mealtimes and at worktimes. It was an extremely intimate relationship. I always assumed that it was similar to the kind of apprenticeships that must have occurred in the Middle Ages with master artisans. It did truly seem to be an apprenticeship system. . . .

Mr. Wright enjoyed talking to individuals and groups, and we would sit at his knee listening. Wherever we were—at lunch, in the drafting room, working in the fields—he came around. He was always around. . . . I've seen him get up on a tractor or a bulldozer for the hell of it; he loved to do that kind of thing. He directed everything . . . all in great detail. Whatever the activity, he had an interest in it, whether it was pulling weeds or mowing the hay or cleaning the barn or whatever it was.

He had no pedagogical method in that sense. It was certainly a process of teaching, learning by participation and by absorption and by emulation and, I suppose, by osmosis. By being a part of [it], you were participating in his creative activities, in a sense: the development of the buildings directly under his thumb. This is a highly effective learning process, I think. There were no lectures or classes in any formal way. All the youngsters were so damn dedicated that I think they were really sponges absorbing everything that was around. There was more work to be done than anyone could possibly handle. There was never any necessity for making any kind of work for educational purposes.

ON WRIGHT'S DESIGN METHOD

At the risk of great oversimplification, you could synthesize Mr. Wright's philosophies—his philosophy of organic architecture (to use his term)—as being a very direct relationship, a common-sense logical relationship, of the factors which an architect really finds, if he looks for them, around any new project. These factors have always existed and they always will. It's just that a majority of architects don't sensitively relate them all. Organic architecture means that the building itself finally is an expression and a direct result of all these various factors. There are such things as the climate in which the building is placed—first the regional climate (look at Arizona versus Wisconsin) and the local climate—where the winds, the sun, and the views are. Other factors are the topography; the native materials; the functional needs of the [building] program; the kind of human being the client is; even the budget is an important part of the final result.

Mr. Wright always started with the floor plan [when designing a building]. He felt this was the essence of the architectural scheme. I'm satisfied he had the whole thing in his mind when he did it. The whole three-dimensional aspect was all there in his mind. There's no doubt about it, because the cross sections that followed, and which he would always draw to indicate what his design was, were so directly related to a theme, a scheme he obviously—quite definitely—had in mind when he sat down. He's explained that to me as being true most of the time. He really designed on his walls, and before he got to the drawing board he pretty well had it worked out.

For instance, I will never forget [the] Marin County project [page 57]. Mr. Wright came out [on August 2, 1957] to talk to the [county] supervisors, see the site, etc.—his first trip. . . . [We] drove up to the top of one of the hills and [he] got out of the car. He hadn't experienced the site [for] more than 20 minutes when he turned to me and said, "I know what I'm going to do here!" He waved his hands, [made] a couple of gestures and said, "I'll bridge these hills with graceful arches." It wasn't until some months later that I saw him sit down at the drawing board and do just that—in a few minutes—and you can see it now [completed]. There was an aspect of inspiration in his designing—a kind of creative genius. But one that didn't require a lot of time at the site. It was pretty obvious that he very quickly knew what the main theme, the solution, would be. I certainly didn't understand it when he mentioned it. I didn't understand it until I saw him actually sketch it much later.

It might appear that he shook the design out of his sleeve, but that doesn't mean it was effortless or that he hadn't been concentrating and thinking about it for days, or perhaps weeks, before he sat down to the drawing board. So that when he sat down, the kind of complex project that might take an architect's design staff three months, or six months in some cases, to work out, Mr. Wright might easily do in an hour and a half or two hours. When he'd turn the project over to the drafting staff, all of the basic design scheme was there. He'd continue to work over someone's drafting board from then on until it was finished, but there was little change from then on. The main structural scheme, the main physical characteristics of the thing, the functional aspects, all related as they were in his work, were well set up in that initial inspirational working drawing. It was quite remarkable to watch because, again, it was without hesitation. It was sitting down to a big fresh white sheet of paper on which someone had drawn the contours for the project, surrounded with some photographs of the site (as there practically always were), to start immediately, without any hesitation, slashing away with great speed to reach a solution. To see the solution unfold even in the rough sketch form which he used was always a remarkable experience.

Frank Lloyd Wright points to a sectional drawing of the Marin County
Administration Building as an unidentified listener looks on, March 25, 1958.
(Ken Yimm, San Francisco Archives of the San Francisco Public Library)

ON THE DIFFICULTY OF COPYING
WRIGHT'S ARCHITECTURAL STYLE

Too many critics take the term "critic" seriously, and when they don't
have anything to criticize they create. The statement that Frank Lloyd
Wright . . . is difficult to copy—and using that as a criticism of him—is
quite ridiculous. It may be true as compared to Mies van der Rohe, whose
work is the simplest kind of statement. Whether that reflects on Mies van
der Rohe to his credit, or to Mr. Wright's discredit—I don't think it's perti-
nent one way or the other. As a comparison, it's simply a statement of fact,
I guess. I don't think it makes either Mies van der Rohe's work better or
Mr. Wright's work worse. Mr. Wright's followers, we might call them, persons who are affected by his architecture and who employ forms derivative
of his, tend to be singled out more often than are those who might utilize,
just as derivatively, the forms of Mies van der Rohe or some other architect, Le Corbusier . . . it's purely a matter of the fashion of the moment. . . .
But I don't take this particular kind of criticism seriously. I don't see any
point in dignifying it to that extent, because I don't think it really means
very much. It's hardly intelligent.

Frank Lloyd Wright (right), Aaron Green (center), and an unidentified man pose before a helicopter at the University of California-Berkeley in April 1957. Wright was preparing to depart for San Francisco on business relating to the Marin County Administration Building. (San Francisco Archives)

On Wright's Standards

To him architecture was so important and so great that anyone who did not maintain a high-standard relationship to it was subject to criticism. His standards were high in every endeavor. . . . He had no tolerance for mediocrity in government, in architecture, [or] in human beings. He was very forthright in saying it, of course.

He'd speak as critically, or more so [of his students]. Mr. Wright didn't like to think that anyone didn't understand his principles. But some, in lieu of understanding his principles and using them, appeared to copy his work. He had no patience for that. To him, that was mediocrity, too. He was probably more likely to criticize strongly his own apprentices and their work than anything else.

He wasn't critical of everything. He was delighted whenever he could find something which he thought was good and which he could approve of. If you consider the age in which he lived—after all, 70 years of actual professional work is a long time—you realize that when he started there was nothing which related to his idiom of quality in building construction.

He had to design all his own hardware, all his own furniture, all his own light fixtures, all the different portions of the building in his early years. Later on, when he could find something in a catalog that he thought was well designed [and] that he could specify, he got tremendous delight. And [that was also] true of other things. A piece of architecture—it might be a piece of architecture that was done by a carpenter without an architect being around. As you drove down a street he might say, "Stop the car, look at that. Isn't that a tremendously beautiful roofline? Look what it looks like up against that tree." And it might have been a tiny little cottage that didn't have an architect near it. It [was] just a thing of excellence. Sure, there weren't many examples of the product of architects that he could say that about, but if he saw one he was simply delighted. He wasn't always looking for something to criticize—quite the reverse—he was on the search for something that he didn't have to [criticize].

THE FALLACY OF THE LEGENDS

I think that part of Mr. Wright's legend is unfortunate in the sense that, as he often said himself, the newspaper didn't print the twinkle in his eye, . . . And, with very few exceptions, it was always there—that twinkle—when he made the kind of statement that would later be offered as evidence of his irascibility or arbitrariness or difficulty to get along. All of which were ridiculously untrue. The people who knew him best—his clients, his family, and so on—all knew that those things were the farthest from the truth.

[He was a] witty, personable, marvelous human being to be around and an extremely impressive one because of his tremendous strength of will, strength of character, strength of conviction, all of which were obvious. He wasn't going to hide anything that he felt, and in a very forthright way. Nor was he going to hide any criticism that he had of something that wasn't up to his idea of perfection. And those things very straightforward and, perhaps without that twinkle that we're speaking about, that wasn't fun [but] that was sincere conviction about life and everything in it, including architecture. That's where he didn't separate his philosophy of architecture from his philosophy of life. It was very strongly a matter of making decisions of all kinds based on principle. Damned few people are able to synthesize problems and come up with that kind of a solution—based on principle.

In 1979 Ray Hubbard Associates, Inc., produced a 90-minute motion picture entitled Lewis Mumford: Toward a Human Architecture *in which Aaron Green talked at some length about Wright. The following passages have been transcribed from the film.*

WRIGHT'S INFLUENCE ON DOMESTIC ARCHITECTURE

American domestic architecture, as we see it today [i.e., in the late 1970s] in its finest form—and I have to emphasize *finest form*, because the majority of domestic architecture today is not that—certainly owes everything to Frank Lloyd Wright. [It] was he alone [who] destroyed the traditional conditions that prevailed at the turn of the century and freed the architect, as well as the user, to an understanding of the advantages of space, of nature, of relating the inside of the building to the outside environment: the great emotional advantage of eliminating the claustrophobic boxes which were the rooms of the conventional houses; the advantage of using materials in their natural form, of creating a harmony of color and texture with consideration for the overall theme of an architecture—so prevalent in all his work, but particularly identifiable in the individual house. The custom house of contemporary architects is almost entirely due to Frank Lloyd Wright's influence, in my opinion, where it has become an object of fine art.

WRIGHT'S DESIGN FOR THE HANNA RESIDENCE

The Hanna House is certainly one of the most innovative and most beautiful expressions of Frank Lloyd Wright's artistry [page 209]. The ability to adapt to a hillside site in such a natural flowing, lovely, harmonious way is something that no one else has ever matched. Frank Lloyd Wright, of course, was [an] amazing genius and that was one of his main contributions.

One of the most important architectural considerations, as I think about the Hanna House design, is the ease with which it converted itself to the changing pattern of use as the Hannas' family life changed—when the children grew up. This had been [included in] the initial conception of the design. They were astute enough, and Mr. Wright was genius enough, to design the house in such a way that it was easily adjusted in the remodeling process, which I oversaw many years after the house was built. With a few minor adjustments of partitions inside the house, small bedrooms were changed in[to] spacious studies and master bedroom suites were created.

WRIGHT ON CRITICS

It's my recollection that before the war [World War II] Frank Lloyd Wright's relationship with Lewis Mumford was a very warm friendship. I recall his saying that Mumford was the only critic, the others didn't exist at all as far as being architectural critics was concerned. He hated critics.

25

JOHN GEIGER

**We had considerably more freedom of choice
in our work assignments than scholars would have you believe.**

*John Geiger was an apprentice to Frank Lloyd Wright from June 1947 to
June 1954. Geiger supervised the construction of the Wright-designed
Zimmerman House (1952–53) in Manchester, New Hampshire, and the
"60 Years of Living Architecture" exhibition in New York (1953) and Los
Angeles (1954).*

The year was 1949, and I started the working drawings of the [Henry
J.] Neils House [in Minneapolis, Minnesota] as a solo project; my first solo
set of working drawings had been for the Melvyn Maxwell Smith House
my first summer at the Fellowship in 1947 [see Chapter 14]. Jack Howe
was the chief draftsman and had assigned this house to me. As I proceeded
with the working drawings, it became evident that there were some serious
problems with the planning of the house. The lower level, which included
storage, bath, servant, and utility rooms, was confined to an area that was
woefully inadequate in size and largely below grade, requiring an excavated
area with a retaining wall to make it work at all. Meanwhile, the far end of
the living room was a full story out of the ground and marked unexcavated.

I struggled with the problem for a while but could not make it work.
Finally, [I] went to Jack and told him the house needed Mr. Wright's help.
His response was, "Don't bother Mr. Wright." I worked some more with
no success and then went to Jack again with the same request and received
the same response: "Don't bother Mr. Wright." So I said, "Okay, I won't,
but I won't complete the working drawings either."

The remainder of the summer was spent on the farm mowing hay, by
choice. We had considerably more freedom of choice in our work assignments than scholars would have you believe. Wes Peters made all work
assignments excepting household and kitchen chores. [He] was an easy
taskmaster and was respected by all apprentices for his probity.

John Geiger's reminiscences were adapted from an early draft of his "Recollection: A
Summer's Work—Not in the Taliesin Drafting Room," which appeared in the *Journal of the
Taliesin Fellows*, No. 2, Fall 1990, pp. 13–15. Copyright © Journal of the Taliesin Fellows,
1990. Reprinted with permission of the author.

Exterior view of the Henry J. Neils residence (1949) in Minneapolis, Minnesota. (Patrick J. Meehan)

It seemed that the entire summer was spent mowing that one large field across the highway from Taliesin. It extends from the [Unity] Chapel on the south on around the bend to what was then a coffee shop on the east, opposite the foot of the Wisconsin River bridge. The field was beautiful after mowing, with the concentric rows of mown hay diminishing to zero at the center. I was delighted to think that I had created all that beauty on such a vast scale with only a hay mower. The field was in full view from the Taliesin living room, and I thought afterwards that a similar view must have inspired [Wright's] abstraction that is the frontispiece for "Book Three • Work" of *An Autobiography*. (In case no one else made the connection, the frontispiece for "Book One • Family" is an abstraction of his trek with Uncle John described on page three [of that publication].) It was an altogether delightful summer. There was ample opportunity for reflection while riding the mower eight hours a day. It was not all peaches and cream, however. The first day or so out I bent the mower support arm trying to mow around edges of the field for a more manicured look. Ken Lockhart wasn't too happy about that but had the mower repaired after offering only a few pointed remarks.

Meanwhile, back in the drafting room, the working drawings for the Neils House had been completed by Steve Oyakawa without any changes. It was Mr. Wright's practice to sign drawings in the drafting room after breakfast on Sunday morning, and on this one particular Sunday I was present. Needless to say, the Neils house working drawings came up for signature. So I said to myself, "This will be interesting." Mr. Wright leafed through the

Frank Lloyd Wright visiting the home of Mr. and Mrs. Henry J. Neils in Minneapolis, Minnesota. Note the Wright-designed kettle. (*St. Paul Dispatch-Pioneer Press*, Minnesota Historical Society)

drawings, picked up a pencil, or maybe a pen, and redesigned the house on the completed set of working drawings. . . . All the lower level functions were moved [to] the upper level. The carpet swung around in line with the bedroom wing, and the roof changed from a hip roof to a gable roof. It was a total redesign and took less than half an hour. When he was finished, he stood up, tossed the pencil on the table, and said, "Well, occasionally one of these gets through without the benefit of clergy." The comment was accompanied by his wry smile.

Curtis Besinger did the working drawings for the redesign. It was our general practice to make the corrections on the original drawings and erase Mr. Wright's work as we went along. If that was done in this case, there is no record of the original working drawing set completed by Steve; probably not even a set of prints. Such was our sense of history at the time.

The Neils, because they owned the Flour City Ornamental Iron Company, produced the spherical fireplace kettle shown in the photograph. They made another in 1953 for the Usonian house at the "60 Years of Living Architecture" exhibition [of Wright's work] at the site of the Guggenheim Museum. This one was returned to Taliesin at the close of the show. The Neils also owned an abandoned marble quarry, accounting for the masonry material used for the walls of the house.

How many other works got through "without the benefit of clergy" will be the subject [of] historical inquiry one day, and hopefully there will be some documentation of particular projects by former apprentices in the intervening years. The lack of monetary concern made it possible to redo the drawings for the Neils house with no consideration other than the quality of the project. It would be interesting to speculate what this total lack of monetary concern in the drafting room had on Mr. Wright's work in the halcyon, and hence productive, years following the founding of the Fellowship.

The completed house was published in *House & Home* magazine in November 1953.

2 6

FAY JONES

"My name is Frank Lloyd Wright."—Frank Lloyd Wright to Fay Jones
"My name is Fay Jones."—Fay Jones to Frank Lloyd Wright

*F*ay Jones was a member of the Taliesin Fellowship from May to September
of 1953. He entered the Fellowship after receiving a bachelor of architecture degree from the University of Arkansas and a master of architecture
degree from Rice University.

*On April 15, 1958, during a lecture to architecture students at the
University of Arkansas-Fayetteville where Jones was a professor, Wright made the
following comment about Jones's work:*

So, where is architecture today? Where do you see it? Fay Jones has
built a little house over here with some of it in it. Go and look at it. And
there are other little houses, there is a feeling coming. Join it, get wise to
what the substance is in it, because it is not merely a matter of taste . . . it
all begins back there with a study of nature—the study of nature.

*Although his tenure with the Fellowship was short, Jones's practice of creating
organic architecture, under the principles established by Wright, has been
remarkable. Jones was the 1990 recipient of the American Institute of Architects
Gold Medal—the Institute's highest honor and only the 48th such award to be
presented by the institute. The AIA Gold Medal is one of the most important and
prestigious awards that an architect can receive. Wright was the recipient of this
same honor in 1949. Jones is the first of Wright's apprentices to be so distinguished.*

*After receiving the AIA Gold Medal, Jones stated: "I never intended to be a
small Frank Lloyd Wright, which I used to worry about until I was reminded
that there is no such thing as a small Frank Lloyd Wright."*

*The following passage is based on an interview in which Jones recalled his
first meeting with Wright.*

Fay Jones's reminiscences were recorded by Allen Freeman in *Accent on Architecture: Honors
1990*. Copyright © 1990 The American Institute of Architects. Reproduced with permission
under license number 90089.

[In 1938] a movie short about Wright's new Johnson Wax headquarters building in Racine, Wisconsin, convinced Jones, then 16 years old, that he wanted to be an architect. Today the Wright legacy imbues Jones's architecture. "Wright and the principles of organic architecture have had the greatest influence on my architecture," he says.

Jones's first face-to-face encounter with Wright was in 1949 in Houston during the AIA convention at which Wright accepted the Institute's 16th Gold Medal and lectured its leaders for being so presumptuous as to call him a great architect. As a fourth-year student in the first architecture class at the University of Arkansas, Jones had driven to Houston with fellow students hoping to attend the ceremony. Jones was in a corridor of the new Shamrock Hotel just when Wright was looking for a way to escape a cocktail party in his honor. "The doors of the room burst open, and here's my first glimpse of Frank Lloyd Wright," Jones recalled years later in *Arkansas Times* magazine. "I just plastered myself up against the wall to leave him plenty of room to walk by. He must have seen my fright, because he came up to me and stuck out his hand and said, 'My name is Frank Lloyd Wright.'

" 'My name is Fay Jones.'

"By this time the president of the AIA and two or three other people were trying to get Mr. Wright back into the party. He said, 'No. I've had enough of that. This young man and I are going to look at this hotel that we've been reading so much about.' So he took me by the arm like I was Charlie McCarthy, and I was a prop for about half an hour."

VERNON D. SWABACK

**The greatest lesson to be learned from Frank Lloyd Wright
is not to be found in the look of his buildings, no matter how exciting
they may be. The lesson is that it is immensely rewarding to think
independently, wherever that might take a person . . . and that to do
otherwise is to waste the opportunity.**

*V*ernon D. Swaback, who was a teenager when he became an apprentice to
Frank Lloyd Wright, was a member of the Taliesin Fellowship from
1957 to 1978.

*Now, more than 25 years after Wright's death, Swaback's work is flourish-
ing. Swaback is president of a 12-person architectural and planning firm in
Scottsdale, Arizona. He is a member of the Taliesin Council, a group that acts in
an advisory capacity to the Frank Lloyd Wright Foundation. He is also on the
advisory boards for both the College of Architecture and the Department of
Planning at Arizona State University. His work has been widely published, both
locally and nationally.*

The following interview was conducted by Hoyt Johnson, publisher of
Scottsdale Scene Magazine, *in 1986.*

HOYT JOHNSON: Vern, when was the first time that you met Frank
Lloyd Wright? What were the circumstances that led to that memorable
occasion, an event that so significantly influenced your life?

VERNON SWABACK: I had wanted to meet Mr. Wright, and I had wanted to become a member of the Taliesin Fellowship, for as long as I could
remember. I grew up near Oak Park, Illinois, where so many of Mr.
Wright's first homes were built. I saw those homes, and I knew of Mr.
Wright's work through architectural publications.

For me, Taliesin had almost an unapproachable mystique. I knew that
it existed but didn't know how to get to it, and somehow I had the feeling
that people rarely entered or left Taliesin.

JOHNSON: Vern, I'm sorry for interrupting, but let's establish when this

Hoyt Johnson's "Conversation with Vernon Swaback" was originally published in *Scottsdale
Scene Magazine*, Vol. 4, No. 4, April 1986, pp. 102–08. Copyright © 1986 *Scottsdale Scene
Magazine*. Reprinted with permission.

VERNON D. SWABACK: *"I had attended a celebration of Frank Lloyd Wright Day, proclaimed by the mayor of Chicago, and had had the opportunity to meet a few people from Taliesin. Soon after that, I wrote a letter to Mr. Wright and boldly asked if I could come to Taliesin to be interviewed for the Fellowship."* Chicago's Mayor Richard J. Daley (left), Madison's (Wisconsin) Mayor Ivan Nestingen (right), and Frank Lloyd Wright at a Frank Lloyd Wright Day testimonial dinner in Chicago on October 17, 1956. (*Capital Times*)

was. I think you previously told me that it was in 1956, and that you were a first-year architecture student at the University of Illinois. Is that correct?

SWABACK: Yes, that is correct.

JOHNSON: Well, at that time, what did you know about Taliesin? Had you seen pictures of Mr. Wright's home in Spring Green, Wisconsin?

SWABACK: I had attended a celebration of Frank Lloyd Wright Day, proclaimed by the mayor of Chicago, and had had the opportunity to meet a few people from Taliesin. Soon after that, I wrote a letter to Mr. Wright and boldly asked if I could come to Taliesin to be interviewed for the Fellowship. I remember that I mailed the letter about noon, and two hours later I was so anxious that I called. Very fortunately, I was invited to come to Taliesin the next weekend.

JOHNSON: How do you explain the fact that you were able to just make a phone call and arrange a visit with the world's most renowned architect?

SWABACK: Actually, when I called I talked to Gene Masselink, who was Mr. Wright's secretary, and he made the appointment for me.

JOHNSON: But, nonetheless, Vern, to be able to schedule an interview with Frank Lloyd Wright . . . most people perceived him as being almost untouchable . . . was a great stroke of good fortune.

SWABACK: I was amazed—a bit bewildered, perhaps—and terribly excited. I believe it was fate . . . an inevitable course of events: writing the letter first, and then deciding to call; having Gene Masselink answer; finding Mr. Wright at Taliesin so he could approve the appointment.

JOHNSON: Please tell me about your visit with Frank Lloyd Wright.

SWABACK: My mother and father were with me. We were ushered into Mr. Wright's studio, and he was extremely simple about everything. He asked me why I wanted to come to Taliesin. I told him, "Because at the university they are beginning to teach preconceived solutions." Thereupon he turned to my mother and my father and asked, "Where does he get it? From you, or you?" And that was all there was to the interview. I told him I wanted to finish the semester at school and that I would journey to Arizona in January.

That brief encounter set the course for my life. Please know, however, that my experience was not totally unique, because Mr. Wright was constantly alert to young, dedicated architectural students who wished to work and study at Taliesin. In fact, some people have referred to the creation of "little Frank Lloyd Wrights," but that is the farthest thing from what Mr. Wright wanted to do.

I'm reminded of the first time I brought a design to show to Mr. Wright. He looked at it and said, "This all looks familiar to me. Next time, why don't you show me what *you* can do!"

JOHNSON: Vern, when you finished the semester at the University of Illinois and boarded the train to travel to Taliesin West in Scottsdale, you were very young, perhaps 17. You had never been to Arizona before; you had only experienced one very short visit with Mr. Wright; you had never really been away from home before. My God, you must have been overdosed with emotion as that train creaked its way over the tracks heading west.

SWABACK: It was eerie. I was thrilled and scared. I felt almost as though I was going to another planet, to a destination somewhere unknown. I arrived at Taliesin at night, and as I walked across the gravel courtyard I was mesmerized by the very romantic lights in the distance, and by the dreamlike awareness that I was at Frank Lloyd Wright's home in the desert. I had the feeling that I was being totally immersed in a sense of greatness.

JOHNSON: Even though you were so young and so new, did you feel you were making a total commitment to Mr. Wright, to Taliesin . . . and did you plan to remain with the Taliesin Fellowship for the rest of your life?

SWABACK: It was clear to me that I was making a total commitment to my life's work, but, strangely enough, I had been counseled by one of my professors at the University of Illinois not to get "too swallowed up" in the Taliesin situation. So I had sort of predetermined that I would remain for only one year. I never really changed my mind, but 21 years later I was still there! The experience was constantly challenging and there was never a reason to leave.

JOHNSON: Were there any immediate disappointments upon your arrival at Taliesin? Did you ever want to get back on the train and return home?

SWABACK: The only disappointment I experienced was finding out that some of the new students were not as excited about, not as committed to, the program as I was. It surprised me greatly because, to me, being at Taliesin was a lifelong dream of immeasurable magnitude. I mean, what was powerful was just meeting Mr. Wright—nothing else mattered—so I didn't understand their attitude. Of course, they didn't last, they didn't stay, they didn't become part of the Fellowship.

JOHNSON: Let's talk about Mr. Wright. Was there ever any disappointment regarding his professional and personal character?

SWABACK: Never! Absolutely not! There's an old saying, "No man is a hero to his valet," that did not apply to Mr. Wright. The closer a person got to Frank Lloyd Wright, the more heroic he became. There was no "behind the scenes" about him that was a disappointment. Instead, he got better and better.

JOHNSON: Was Frank Lloyd Wright really 100 percent Frank Lloyd Wright? Or was he a perpetrator of mystery, a man who enhanced his reputation as an architectural genius by wearing a cloak of personal mystique?

SWABACK: I think he played "the role" to some extent. Early in his life he used to take his own picture; he created—or, perhaps better, cultivated—an image that he considered appropriate for his esteemed place in our society.

I remember a conversation that took place when Mr. Wright and I were with movie producer Mike Todd and his wife at the time, Elizabeth Taylor. Todd, who had just completed filming *Around the World in 80 Days*, was surely one of the great Hollywood show people, and at one point during the conversation he turned to Mr. Wright and said, "Hell, Frank, you're the greatest showman of us all." Mr. Wright just laughed.

I think that if he "acted" just a little, however, it was a legitimate part of the aesthetic sensitivity that he displayed for almost everything. He felt that we should not only design beautiful buildings, we should create beautiful dress, we should plan beautiful parties and dinners. He paid a lot of attention to the way he dressed—his tailor made his clothes—and the way he combed his hair. It was all consistent with the position of a great man at the helm of a legacy.

In a 1932 essay on power, Charles de Gaulle wrote: "There can be no prestige without mystery, for familiarity breeds contempt. In the designs, the demeanor, and the mental operations of a leader there must be always a 'something' which others cannot altogether fathom, which puzzles them, stirs them, and rivets their attention. Aloofness, character, and the personification of greatness, these qualities it is that surround with prestige those who are prepared to carry the burden which is too heavy for lesser mortals."

Frank Lloyd Wright knew of that "something". . .

JOHNSON: What do you consider to be the greatest lesson to be learned from the work of Frank Lloyd Wright?

SWABACK: The man produced a great body of work, and there is a tendency to view that work as his greatest contribution. For followers of Mr. Wright it is very easy to fall too much in love with his work, however, and there is a danger in doing that because what he represented more than anything else was a discarding of the old classical order and the creation of what he called "thought-built" architecture.

If the work he produced is loved too much, the result is a new classical order. More in keeping with what Mr. Wright was really all about in his admonishment to think for yourself, don't rest on your laurels, and don't look backwards. It is in the nature of architecture as he professed it that it must be continuously fresh, constantly new, or it isn't living up to its potential.

JOHNSON: I think you just told me why you left Taliesin.

SWABACK: Could be, could be.

I don't think I love Mr. Wright's work any less than a person who is limited by that love. I simply cannot view the work that he did as a justification for the way that I do my work. That was his work, it is what he did, and I can't do what he did as well as he did, and if I tried, I wouldn't find out what kind of "music" I have within me.

JOHNSON: And you wouldn't be doing what he taught you to do.

SWABACK: Right. Now, on the other hand, to egotistically ignore the work of Mr. Wright is to turn your back on what has been this civilization's greatest single insight regarding what architecture can do for mankind. His teaching, his work, was a great contribution to making life more interesting, more beautiful, more stimulating, and more appropriate.

If we can accept Mr. Wright's work as principle, look at circumstances entirely different from what he faced, and listen to clients who speak differently. . .our clients don't come in and say, "I love Frank Lloyd Wright, please do something for me." They come in and they want to make money, or they want to solve problems, or they want to achieve rezoning, or they want to do all kinds of other things that preclude having the initial presentation be a cultural statement because it is one of need, of self-interest, or whatever. . . . If we listen very carefully to what they say, we become so close that we share their problem, or their dream. In doing that, we get very close to what I think Frank Lloyd Wright was all about: that every new person, every new site, represents an opportunity which is new in nature, an opportunity that nobody has ever faced before. And if you give that person or that site what you did last, you are squandering that opportunity.

JOHNSON: You certainly have alluded to your answer, but I repeat: What is the single greatest lesson to be learned from Mr. Wright?

SWABACK: I think it is important to answer that question by defining what it *isn't*. The greatest lesson to be learned from Frank Lloyd Wright is not to be found in the look of his buildings, no matter how exciting they may be. The lesson is that it is immensely rewarding to think independently, wherever that might take a person . . . and that to do otherwise is to waste the opportunity.

There is a second part of the lesson: that there has to be a consistent relationship between all the elements related to whatever a person is doing. Frank Lloyd Wright related furniture to the houses he designed, and the houses to their sites.

In our current work, we've carried that concept further, relating the elements of entire communities. It's a powerful idea that has no bounds, and if we can just take any given assignment and forget everything we've seen that has been done before, we are then getting close to the great way that Mr. Wright saw things. There was nothing familiar to him; he regarded familiarity to be an enemy to artists. The more we can take on that freshness of interpretation, the closer we get to the greatest lesson that I think Mr. Wright offered to us.

PART V

FRIENDS AND
ACQUAINTANCES

2 8

ALAN REIACH

**It was quite impossible not to be moved by his charm and sincerity.
The last memory I have of him is of leaving Taliesin for the plane
at eight o'clock on a brilliant sunny morning when the desert was fresh
and the cacti cast long shadows. He waved me off at the door of his office.
"Good-bye," he said, "and be a good boy!" I felt somehow that had I been
a man of 70 he would have still said that, and that one would
not have taken offense.**

Alan Reiach, senior partner of the Edinburgh architectural firm of Alan
Reiach, Eric Hall & Partners, met Frank Lloyd Wright on three occasions and visited Taliesin twice.

I first met him in New York in 1935. He had been lecturing to a
Women's Club and was surrounded by an ardent throng of admirers.

Nothing daunted, I pressed forward and, after saying how much I had
enjoyed his discourse, asked for some guidance in the New World!

He looked at me, sized me up, and then came the inevitable pronouncement: "You want to see our great country?"

"Yes," I replied.

"Then buy a secondhand Ford and keep away from the schools!" Then,
as an afterthought: "We will be glad to see you anytime at Taliesin." Be it
said I didn't follow his advice implicitly. However, I duly presented myself
some months later [in 1936] at Taliesin.

It was dark, and the Master had gone to bed. I discovered afterwards
that he almost invariably retired early. I was met at Spring Green station by
a young man who said he was his secretary. This was difficult to believe, as
he appeared to be far from the commonly accepted ideas of a secretary—
open-necked shirt and flannel trousers. Still, he was affable enough and
drove me up to the house and showed me to my room. I was to be an honored guest and was in the Master's own quarters. Owing to some fault in
the electrical generating system, the place was plunged in darkness and we

Alan Reiach's "Meetings with Frank Lloyd Wright" originally appeared in *Concrete Quarterly*
(England), No. 100, January/March 1974. Reprinted with permission of the British Cement
Association.

Frank Lloyd Wright's bedroom at Taliesin in Wisconsin in the late 1950s. (Richard Vesey, State Historical Society of Wisconsin)

were reduced to using candles—it all added up to the strangeness of my introduction to one of the fountainheads of architectural wisdom.

I can remember there was a private shower off my room, but it didn't work—this was reassuring, and gradually one became aware that many things of that kind abounded. This to me, fresh from the old world, was comforting!

In the morning, after early rising with the students and then breakfast, I was informed that the Master would expect me to breakfast privately with him and the family. So a second meal was to be faced!

Afterwards we strolled through the gardens—me plying him with questions and F.L.W. answering, with majestic calm, the brash outpourings of a student! I can remember asking him his opinion of modern architects' work in Europe. Unhesitatingly he replied, "What modern architecture needs today, young man, is more love." This impressed me enormously at the time, as did his remark when, after saying that I hoped to see the Ford Works [automobile factory] at Detroit, he said, "Yes, see that . . . you will see what is wrong with us." And so we talked, or rather he talked and I lis-

tened, just dropping a word from time to time to let him expatiate on top-
ics that ranged from literature to religions, from D. H. Lawrence to
Buddhism. Suddenly in the midst of all this he said, "Well, I must be doing
work—enjoy yourself," and with a wave he disappeared into his office. I
was left to wander about the school, his house, and the gardens at will.
Feeling rather tired and not a little overawed, I was glad of the day or two
in such an atmosphere, an oasis in the middle of a continental trip.
Notwithstanding the aura of hero worship that was everywhere evident, the
sheer beauty of the place and the extraordinary sense of being at the source
of such inspiration was itself immensely stimulating—if rather heady for an
impressionable student.

The next time we met was in London when he was giving his Sulgrave
Manor lectures at the RIBA [Royal Institute of British Architects] in 1939.
After one of these, I remember coming up to him and saying, "You won't
remember me, but you were very kind to me at Taliesin in 1936 and let me
stay with you when I was feeling rather tired and far from home." "Well,"
he replied, "you are looking better now." Another architect, Erno
Goldfinger I think it was, told him by way of introduction that he had
spent two years in the States, to which Wright answered laconically, "Oh,
what did you leave us for?"

We did not meet up again until 1957, and then only after two or three
fruitless attempts to get in touch by letter. A reply eventually came from his
secretary to say that the Master would not be in Wisconsin at the time I
had proposed to come, but would be glad to see me next time I was that
way again. The opportunity did, however, occur later on, and a stay with
him at his desert home in Arizona became possible.

I flew in from New Mexico, where I had been staying with friends, and
took a chance on finding him at home despite no answer to my further letters. I had got quite used to this one-sided correspondence and took the situation as being normal. Taliesin West is some 20 miles from Phoenix, and,
as the Wrights had no telephone in their winter quarters, I had to take a
taxi from the airport and drive up to the mountains armed with some money and a good deal of hope. After what seemed an interminably long distance from town, we picked up the trail on a dirt road through the cactus
desert—a kind of treasure hunt, it seemed, whose clues were the Taliesin
symbol signpost of Wright's own design. After we had carried around several sharp bends and left all trace of human life behind, we saw, on the
horizon, an encampment [pages 139, 149, and 150]. I can only call it that;
it gave the impression of a kind of caravanserai in the desert. In a few
moments the driver set me down in the car park at the entrance to the
estate. This was Taliesin West.

Wright's Arizona school had, of course, become a mecca for the faithful long before, and it had all the appearance of such. It seemed more like a resort than the usually accepted notion of a school. One could not but be impressed by the extraordinary building forms that the students had evolved under his direction.

Again, just as at my first visit 20 years before, it was evening, Wright had retired for the night, and his secretary (the same man as the first time, now grown old in service) said that he would be pleased to see me in the morning and wished me a pleasant stay.

I was shown to my room on a balcony overlooking the desert and told that supper would be ready shortly. Afterwards, strolling around the encampment, one had time to admire at leisure the art works built into the walls of the buildings and the great variety of desert plants in the cactus garden. The Wrights' own quarters were set a little apart. There were several houses dotted about the landscape, as well as tents for the apprentices.

Hours are long at the school, and we were wakened at six o'clock for a 6:30 breakfast. A Chinese gong was struck to summon "the faithful," and after a simple meal I was left to await the Master's pleasure. Just as in 1936, I had a second breakfast with the Wrights. The same almost ritualistic atmosphere was observed. This time, however, the old man seemed more mellow, especially in his relations with his colleagues. He talked freely and pleasantly about this and that and seemed especially moved by his recent visit to Wales (the land of his ancestors), where he had received an honorary degree at Aberystwyth the year before. The countryside had impressed him more than the Welsh, one gathered!

He seemed to sense my unexpressed wonder at seeing him so active and in such fine fettle, and vouchsafed the view that perhaps one of the reasons for his fame (apart from the notoriety that had followed him through life, and which he hated) was the fact "that he had been here so long"— which of course was, I suppose, just the plain truth. After a short discussion, he had work to do and left me, as before, to my own devices to walk at leisure through the house, the gardens, and the studios.

In the afternoon he held court for some young architects who had made the pilgrimage from the West Coast, and sat and talked at length of his early days in Chicago. It was quite impossible not to be moved by his charm and sincerity. The last memory I have of him is of leaving Taliesin for the plane at eight o'clock on a brilliant sunny morning when the desert was fresh and the cacti cast long shadows. He waved me off at the door of his office. "Good-bye," he said, "and be a good boy!" I felt somehow that had I been a man of 70 he would have still said that, and that one would not have taken offense.

2 9

R O B E R T   L .   Z I E G E L M A N

**I contacted Mr. Wright, and he agreed to speak to the student body
under one condition: the lecture was to be for students only;
professors, spouses, and friends could not attend.**

W*right often lectured to students of architecture at universities across
the country. These lectures were usually well attended by students and
faculty alike. For the students, they tended to be special occasions
indeed.*

*In October 1957 Wright visited the College of Architecture and Urban
Planning at the University of Michigan. This visit was at the invitation of
Robert L. Ziegelman [B. Arch., 1958], who shares the following anecdote.*

At the time, I was a fifth-year senior and president of the Class of `58.
My duties included responsibility for all lecturers coming to the
Architecture School. I contacted Mr. Wright, and he agreed to speak to the
student body under one condition: the lecture was to be for students only;
professors, spouses, and friends could not attend. I, of course, agreed to
this stipulation and posted the requirement along with the announcement
of the upcoming lecture.

A couple of classmates and I picked Mr. Wright up at a downtown
Detroit hotel and had lunch with him at the house he had designed for
William and Mary Palmer in Ann Arbor [page 95]. At the appropriate
time, we proceeded to Room 215 in Lorch Hall. Every architecture student
in the university was in attendance, as well as the entire faculty, and everyone's spouse and friend. There was one notable exception: my wife.

She never forgave me.

Robert L. Ziegelman's "Letter on Frank Lloyd Wright's Visit in October 1957" was originally
published in *Portico*, Vol. 5, No. 3, Spring 1989. Reprinted by permission of the College of
Architecture and Urban Planning of the University of Michigan; Robert L. Ziegelman, FAIA;
and Philip B. Margelin.

Frank Lloyd Wright talking with architecture students at the University of
Michigan in October 1957. (Philip B. Wargelin, College of Architecture and
Urban Planning, University of Michigan)

Frank Lloyd Wright talking with Robert L. Ziegelman
(left) and architecture students at the University of
Michigan in October 1957. (Robert L. Ziegelman, FAIA)

3 0

ALINE B. SAARINEN

Then back to his bedroom-workroom, where he pulled toward him a skyscraperlike box with thin layers of cantilevered wood. In the core of each of the many "storeys" was a medal: he showed them off, commenting on the heaviness of the pure gold in the British RIA [Royal Institute of British Architects], the gaiety of the Mexican one, the de' Medici medal from Florence, an honor "Dante coveted."

Aline B. Saarinen, wife of the architect Eero Saarinen, was an architecture critic and a friend of the Wrights. In August 1954 the New York Times *published her account of a visit to Taliesin.*

A dapper figure in white, from his flowing hair and immaculate suit to his socks and neat buckskin shoes, Frank Lloyd Wright walked debonairly into his living room. It was a sprightly entrance: his 85 years and one month sat lightly.

The five expectant visitors—including two wide-eyed, T-shirted students from the Chicago Institute of Design and two respectfully silent Italian and American architects—made an intimate greenroom audience. This was prelude to the weekend's activities, when the entire Fellowship of about 60 apprentices would welcome "the Master" back, after a few weeks' absence, to Taliesin—"Shining Brow"—the house and buildings that sit on the hillside overlooking the lush green Wisconsin valley.

Simultaneously he distributed the Los Angeles catalogs of his exhibition and the news that the building he had designed to shelter that show, along with the adjacent house he had built for Aline Barnsdall in 1913, would be permanently preserved as Los Angeles's first Municipal Center.

But soon he warmed to the theme which was to sound like a threnody throughout the weekend: the loss of dignity in the architectural profession. His tone was haughty when he dealt with the denigrating rat race, but filled with humility when he spoke of architecture itself.

"Architecture is a profession new in theory, not in practice," he said

Aline B. Saarinen's "Taliesin Weekend: Frank Lloyd Wright, 85, Vitally Works On" appeared in the *New York Times* on August 8, 1954. Copyright © 1954 The New York Times Company. Reprinted by permission.

The pavilion (1954) designed by Wright in Los Angeles for the "60 Years of Living Architecture" exhibition of his work. (Patrick J. Meehan)

The view from an elevated terrace overlooking an interior garden court (foreground) at Hollyhock, the Aline Barnsdall residence (1917) in Los Angeles. (Patrick J. Meehan)

sternly. "The AIA let this happen. It should be a noble association of builders, men of ideas with respect for architecture in their own hearts as the greatest necessity, the highest need of a culture."

Contemptuously he described many architects today scrambling after jobs "like donkeys with a bundle of grass dangled before them"; witheringly of how jobs are gotten through the influence and pressure of advertising agencies; scornfully of certain large firms as "plan factories."

But then his mood mellowed, and he swept his guests into his bedroom-workroom [page 173]. He showed the treasures he had brought back from New York, enhancing them with an agilely phrased commentary.

There were splendid editions of prints by Hokusai and Hiroshige (smilingly, "Here, not in the International Style, 'less is more' is a virtue."); an austere Chinese seated figure ("Rodin's 'Thinker' is a bit sentimental. This is really a thinker."); and a book on whose cardboard pages sections of a Chinese scroll had been pasted ("Look, look here at this palace. The terraces, the second floor when you went for this view with what is, I guess, the first picture window," unconcernedly ripping the pages apart. "Look how they did it—terrain, water, buildings, people, all one," then pulling at another page. "It's good to look at these lessons. They are so far from us you can't copy them.").

Chinese bell mounted to a white oak tree at Taliesin (1925) in Wisconsin. (Patrick J. Meehan)

At this point, Mrs. Wright, serene and stately, ushered the guests outside. Frank Lloyd Wright led the way through the profusely flowered inner court up the hillside, brandishing his cane as if it were "my extended forefinger," pausing to pose for a photograph and remark, "Oh dear, I've almost forgotten how to look arrogant!" stopping to ring boyishly the great Chinese temple bell on an enormous white oak.

Thus summoned to his presence and to Saturday-night sweet punch, the apprentices appeared in groups of twos and threes. Some shyly, some reverentially, they paid their respects and then fell back. As dusk closed in, the architect led the procession down the hill into the main living room,

The living room of Taliesin III (1925) in the late 1950s. (Richard Vesey, State Historical Society of Wisconsin)

expounding en route on such extraneous matters as the indestructibility of plastic drinking glasses, the cost of building the Guggenheim Museum, and the monogamy of swans.

The flowing space of the living room seemed magically to contain the eighty-odd people in an orderly fashion as they ate at small tables. At dinner, prepared and served by several of the apprentices (who rotate the household and maintenance chores as a mandatory "privilege"), Frank Lloyd Wright talked to his guests of architecture.

"Form follows function—that has been misunderstood," he said. "Form and function should be one, joined in a spiritual union." He mentioned a well-known architect. "He exposes all the function on the top and puts the form below. It's as if you were to wear your entrails on top of your head."

Then back to the theme of people shopping for architects. "As if you would telephone several doctors and ask each how he would treat you if he got the job," he said disdainfully. "That's what my mother does," one of the architect guests remarked. Mr. Wright's reply was rapid: "Then your whole family is depraved."

There was breakfast in the main dining hall and then the Sunday morning "discussion"—at which Mr. Wright spoke exclusively. His talk was spontaneous but nonetheless peppered with epigrams.

"Our new theater at Taliesin is an experiment, not experimental.

Experiment—a man who knows certain factors to be true from experience and tries from there. Experimental—a man who is always interested in anything new no matter what it is. . . . An original idea in America is only good for the number of substitutes that can be born from it. . . . The heart is the chief feature of a functioning mind."

He led the way to the new theater, explaining its ideas: the audience sitting on two sides of a 90-degree angle so everyone gets a three-quarter view of the performance: a wood floor with space beneath to act as a virtual drumhead, intended to give resonance without reverberation.

Then back to his bedroom-workroom, where he pulled toward him a skyscraperlike box with thin layers of cantilevered wood. In the core of each of the many "storeys" was a medal: he showed them off commenting, on the heaviness of the pure gold in the British RIA [Royal Institute of British Architects], the gaiety of the Mexican one, the de' Medici medal from Florence, an honor "Dante coveted."

We noticed a large Japanese scroll painting over a door. "People often ask why I, a modern architect, have so many old things around. Why not? I, too, belong to tradition—back to the oldest American architecture, that of the Mayans, and to the Japanese and others. All of them are brought into now."

It was perhaps more than anything else the truth behind that statement that gives a Taliesin visit its special quality of enrichment. The buildings themselves—their design beginning in 1902 but announcing many principles and many of the details of modern architecture—and the man himself combine timelessness with contemporaneity. He belongs to the present, alive, vital, imaginative, and progressive, but in his work and in the standards and ideals he holds for his profession he is a link with the past. One feels all over again, both in the man and in his creations, a sense of never-ending richness, potential, heart, and meaning.

Interior view of the Taliesin Theater (1952) at the Taliesin Fellowship Complex in Wisconsin. (Patrick J. Meehan)

3 1

J O A N   W .   S A L T Z S T E I N

**I had first met Frank Lloyd Wright in 1930 at the University of
Chicago, where I was a student and he a visiting lecturer. When I
introduced myself as the granddaughter of Dankmar Adler, the architect
with whom he had been associated in his youth, his face lit up, and in that
warmly resonant voice he cried, "The Big Chief, your grandfather, how
wonderful to find you! How is your mother? I must see her."**

D*ankmar Adler and Louis Sullivan, partners in the Chicago architectural firm of Adler and Sullivan, were Frank Lloyd Wright's employers
in the early days of his career. Wright always had a particular fondness
for Dankmar Adler.*

*Joan W. Saltzstein, Adler's granddaughter, was a frequent visitor to
Wright's home near Spring Green, Wisconsin—particularly during the early
days of the Taliesin Fellowship.*

It was in the thirties, the Depression years, that I first visited Taliesin
East, Frank Lloyd Wright's lovely, peaceful Shangri-la at Spring Green,
near Madison. Those were difficult times for Frank Lloyd Wright. He no
longer had to face the confrontations with the authorities that had plagued
the early years of his marriage, and his family life with his wife, Olgivanna,
her little daughter by a previous marriage, Svetlana, and their baby,
Iovanna, was tranquil and happy. But commissions were almost nonexis-
tent, the creditors demanding, and public acclaim, at least in the United
States, was slow in coming.

I had first met Frank Lloyd Wright in 1930 at the University of
Chicago, where I was a student and he a visiting lecturer. When I introduced myself as the granddaughter of Dankmar Adler, the architect with
whom he had been associated in his youth, his face lit up, and in that
warmly resonant voice he cried, "The Big Chief, your grandfather, how
wonderful to find you! How is your mother? I must see her."

It had been many years since he and my mother had met, but they had
many delightful reminiscences to share of the Adler and Sullivan office in

Joan W. Saltzstein's "Taliesin Through the Years" originally appeared in *Wisconsin Architect*,
Vol. XL, October 1969. Reprinted with permission.

the old Borden Block, where, as a little girl, my mother used to stand at his elbow and adoringly watch him sketch, and he would give her little presents of paper clips and rubber bands to carry home. My mother followed his career with interest, but they did not meet again until I brought him to call on her that spring [1930]. Mr. Wright was in the process of writing his autobiography and was anxious to learn more about the personal life of his Big Chief. Soon we became frequent guests at Taliesin.

By 1932 the Taliesin Fellowship was founded and students were enrolling in what Frank Lloyd Wright called a "direct work experience." That first year there were 23 apprentices working in the fields, gardens, and vineyards and helping to restore the long neglected buildings of the neighboring Hillside Home School that Wright had built in 1902 for his two aunts. Students came from all over the country and the world, willing to work with only limited time in the drafting room, for the privilege of sharing in this adventure with the man they considered to be the prophet of the new architecture.

Eugene Masselink came among the first and stayed nearly 30 years, until his death, his own creative skills willingly sublimated to those of the Master. He was secretary, factotum, friend—a gentle, gifted, creative person. Many years later he was responsible for the icons in the Wright-designed [Annunciation] Greek Orthodox Church in Wauwatosa [Wisconsin]. Edgar Tafel, later to become one of the most successful of Wright's students, was there in those early years, and, for a short time, Edgar Kaufmann, whose father commissioned Fallingwater, the spectacular house constructed over a waterfall near Pittsburgh [page 131].

In 1932 William Wesley Peters arrived, a giant of a man who had to bend his huge frame to get through Taliesin's low doorways. Some years later he married Mrs. Wright's daughter, Svetlana, who, with one of their sons, met a tragic death in an automobile accident in 1946. Wes Peters went on to become a distinguished designer and the chief architect of the Frank Lloyd Wright Foundation.

There were girls in the Fellowship, too—a few as wives of the architects; others, like Cornelia Brierly, sharing the work both on the grounds and in the drafting room on equal footing with the men apprentices.

Frances Coan joined the Fellowship in 1946, fresh from her job as acting director of the Milwaukee Art Institute. Her two children grew up at Taliesin.

Those early years of the Fellowship were far from affluent ones. The students' tuition, which began at $650 and was later raised to $1,100, including board and lodging, barely covered expenses. Quite a few students who could not pay the full amount were enrolled anyway, because of their special ability.

Lights were dimmed at 8:00 p.m. to save electricity. There was no out-going telephone service and almost all food was homegrown and produced. There was no outside help of any kind, and the apprentices' day usually began at 5:00 a.m. But entertainment was plentiful. Students were expected to have some talents other than their ability as architects, and on Sunday nights the Fellowship String Quartet played in the living room, grouping themselves around the music stand that Mr. Wright had designed: four slanting wooden tracks surrounding a central lighted platform on which a bowl of flowers might rest.

On Saturday nights neighbors and guests were invited to a movie in the theater at Hillside [pages 127, 128, and 182]. There was first a formal dinner for the Fellowship and guests, who were seated at small tables with gaily colored linens. The movies were usually foreign films, although the family had their favorite comedies and Westerns that were often repeated. Visitors were charged a dollar, and they came from nearby towns and from as far away as Madison.

The story of the Fellowship had quickly become news, and, weekends, the curious would wind their way up the hill to see what was going on. It was decided to charge 25 cents a head to show them through the grounds, and the apprentices were allowed to keep what they collected. On Saturdays and Sundays they would station themselves on the hill overlooking the road so that they could spot and claim the cars as they drove in.

There were always many children at Taliesin. The apprentices brought their families with them or married while they were there. The carriage house with its collection of old buggies and wagons that had been a part of the original farm was always a source of fun, and the windmill called Romeo and Juliet, which Mr. Wright had built for his aunts in 1896 as his first architectural project, was a marvelous place for games of hide-and-seek.

The annual Halloween masked ball became a tradition weeks-long in the planning, and the celebration of Mr. Wright's birthday on June 8 was a time for elaborate decorations, surprise gifts, and dance, music, and drama performances by the apprentices.

Sunday picnics were a favorite recreation. Trucks would carry the supplies to selected spots, a fire would be laid, and pots of stew or corn and enormous bowls of homegrown tomatoes and lettuce would be readied. Gutzon Borglum Point was one of the popular spots, so named by the sculptor himself on one of his visits to Taliesin. Many celebrated guests came to Taliesin in those years, but there were also many lesser known people in whom Mr. Wright took an equal delight: a pixie of a woman who had written a book called *Round the World on a Penny* and who arrived with

JOAN W. SALTZSTEIN: *". . .the windmill called Romeo and Juliet, which Mr. Wright had built for his aunts in 1896 as his first architectural project was a marvelous place for games of hide and seek."* **The Romeo and Juliet Windmill for Nell and Jane Lloyd Jones (1896) near Spring Green, Wisconsin. (Patrick J. Meehan)**

props, including a trunk on wheels; local masons, farmers, and carpenters; former pupils of the Hillside School; and others who asked to come.

He loved to play with the children and there were always a few at his feet.

Picnics were a gala event, and everyone was urged to dress accordingly. Mrs. Wright and Svetlana sometimes wore beautifully embroidered red suede jackets, and Iovanna a gaily decorated one from Mexico. Mr. Wright especially liked to see his wife in a large red hat that was particularly becoming to her, and the family resembled a royal procession as they came up the road to the picnic grounds, Mr. Wright in his flamboyant tweed cape, his beret and bright scarf, carrying a cane. After lunch everyone would rest under the trees or gather flowers for the house, Mr. Wright happily picking great armfuls.

The house, with its beautiful living room dominated by a great stone fireplace, was the evening gathering place where Mr. Wright would often discuss his philosophy or we would listen to recordings on the Capehart phonograph.

Sometimes the family and quests gathered in the smaller sitting room and Iovanna would peek down from her little room on the balcony above. She was her father's darling, and he admitted with pride that he spoiled her. His other children, frequent visitors to Taliesin, were all grown, with children of their own, and she was the adored child of his later years.

Svetlana shared equally in his love. Gentle, dark-haired, and beautiful, she always seemed to be a uniting force at Taliesin. As a member of the family, an apprentice in the school, and a talented musician, she bound together all the elements that made up the Taliesin complex. When she was a little girl, she delighted in designing and making her own clothes. When her warm and glowing smile was gone, much of the light of Taliesin was forever dimmed.

The first commission to break the Depression lull for the Fellowship was Fallingwater. It was followed by the administration building for the Johnson Wax Company in Racine [page 49].

Soon the huge drafting room, which the apprentices had rebuilt with their own hands at Hillside, was alive with activity. There were other commissions for the Johnson family, including Wingspread [page 131]. The huge Broadacre City plan, Mr. Wright's vision of an ideal city, was laid out on plywood and dramatically displayed in the small gallery next to the drafting room, where it still remains today [page 128].

Mr. Wright would talk about his work, explaining to his guests with great patience the plans, blueprints, and models. He made them feel that he was interested in *them*, in what *they* were doing and planning. When, in later years, I brought my family to see him, he would sit down with my children and talk to them as if they were as important to him as he to them. Fame had now come his way in full measure, and he seemed surprised to find himself swimming with the tide instead of fighting against it.

3 2

EGON WEINER

**. . . deep down he was a modest man. Just look at his home at Taliesin.
Instead of cutting down a tree, he built around it. He had a sensitive
feeling to the creations of God. How could such a person be conceited?**

I*n the 1950s Egon Weiner sculpted a bust of Frank Lloyd Wright. The following passage is based on Weiner's own account of that experience.*

The intruder sat at the piano playing the Turkish March from Mozart's
Sonata in A Major with Variations. Behind him suddenly he heard an
impatient tapping. It was Frank Lloyd Wright striking his cane on the
floor.

The intruder was Egon Weiner, a vibrant Vienna-born sculptor who
had finessed his way into Wright's Taliesin East home in Spring Green,
Wisconsin. With him he had brought a wood case with an unfinished
bronze head of Wright. He was determined to finish the head. "I needed
Frank Lloyd Wright himself to pose for me," Weiner recalls. "I would have
gone disguised as the milkman!"

Weiner, who teaches now at the Art Institute of Chicago, was given an
"in" by a friend who arranged for him to be invited to Wright's home—but
only by posing as an architecture student.

The sculptor eagerly went up to Wisconsin, but had to walk the 20
miles from Madison carrying the heavy case, because a storm had washed
out the roads. Wright was out when he arrived.

"Once there," Weiner says, "I found the den, lifted the bust, and placed
it on top of an imposing grand piano in the corner." Then he sat down to
play the Mozart until he heard Wright's tapping.

Weiner began to blurt out his reason for being there. Wright was just
about to dismiss him, but looked at the sculpture. "All at once his face soft-
ened," Weiner says. " 'That is a strong head,' he said. " 'Very strong.' "

Instead of throwing Weiner out, Wright invited him to stay around as
long as necessary to complete the head.

"Weiner and Wright" was originally published in *Inland Architect*, Vol. XIV, May 1970.
Reprinted with permission.

**Part of the Taliesin Fellowship Complex near Spring Green, Wisconsin, is
built so as to accommodate existing trees. (Patrick J. Meehan)**

"By the way, sculptor," Wright said to Weiner while pointing to his
own jaw, "was it exasperating working with this steel trap?"

Weiner stayed at Wright's home to complete work on the head. Every
morning for a week he and Wright met in the den. The very first morning
Weiner found Wright sitting at the piano, playing powerfully. It was just
what he wanted.

"Don't move!" Weiner said.

"Hindemith?" asked Wright

"Wright!" came the reply.

**Weiner's bust of Frank
Lloyd Wright, now at the
entrance to Austin Gardens,
Oak Park, Illinois.**

Weiner completed the head in time for
the great architect's 80th birthday, and in
doing so reinforced his feelings about
Wright's personality. "I have the impression
that he had the inner dignity of an artist since
his youth," Weiner says. "He didn't flatter
people, and because of this some were against
him.

"But deep down he was a modest man.
Just look at his home at Taliesin. Instead of
cutting down a tree, he built around it. He
had a sensitive feeling to the creations of God.
How could such a person be conceited?"

3 3

WILLIAM T. EVJUE

**I asked Mr. Wright about his concept of God. I asked this question
in the midst of the flaming bougainvillea on the premises and the
beautiful desert flowers which were beginning to appear. Mr. Wright said
quickly, "Nature is my manifestation of God. I go to nature every day
for inspiration in the day's work. I follow in building the principles
which nature has used in its domain."**

William T. Evjue was the editor of the Capital Times, *a newspaper published in Madison, Wisconsin. Evjue was also a close friend of Frank
Lloyd Wright.*

*In the 1930s Evjue invited Wright and his Taliesin Fellows to contribute to
the* Capital Times *a series of newspaper columns called "At Taliesin"; these
columns allowed Wright a regional forum for his ideas and opinions. Later, in the
1950s, Evjue afforded Olgivanna Lloyd Wright the same opportunity; the result
was her "Our House" column. Evjue was also a staunch supporter of Wright's
architectural projects in the Madison area, including the Monona Terrace Civic
Center project of the late 1930s and the mid-1950s.*

Twice—in March 1958 and again in March 1959—I spent nearly five
weeks at Taliesin West as the guest of Mr. and Mrs. Wright. I rate these
visits to Taliesin as among the greatest experiences of my life.

We sat for an hour and a half at the breakfast table at times. At least
three cups of coffee were poured while we discussed such subjects as the
origin of the universe, the lack of culture in the United States, the persis-
tence of war as the only method by which mankind could settle its disputes,
the failure of education, the continued surrender of government to an
alliance of big business and the military. There was also much talk in which
the word *organic* was used.

One morning at breakfast I asked Mr. Wright about the word *organic*.
I said, "Mr. Wright, do you remember when we were on the Nakoma golf

William T. Evjue's "Two Men in Wisconsin Who Had Greatest Influence on Editor" was
originally published in the *Capital Times* (Madison, Wisconsin) on June 9, 1959. Reprinted
with permission.

Frank Lloyd Wright and William T. Evjue at Taliesin in Wisconsin in 1956.
(C. A. Thompson, *Capital Times*)

course years ago, after you had been invited to draw plans for a new Nakoma clubhouse? Do you remember that I asked you then to give me your definition of the word *organic*?"

Mr. Wright had looked down the fairway on which we were standing, leaned over to pick up a handful of Nakoma soil, which he patted flat in the palm of his hand, and said, "That's what I mean when I use the word *organic*."

It was about the time when he was contending that the United States should have a prairie architecture indigenous to its own soil and character, and that the use of the ancient forms of architecture in Italy, France, and England should not have priority in a great land like the United States.

I asked Mr. Wright about his concept of God. I asked this question in the midst of the flaming bougainvillea on the premises and the beautiful desert flowers which were beginning to appear. Mr. Wright said quickly, "Nature is my manifestation of God. I go to nature every day for inspiration in the day's work. I follow in building the principles which nature has used in its domain."

Cassanova [Wright's dog] was there, too, and he stretched out in slumber as world problems were being solved at the breakfast table.

Following Mr. Wright's death, the newspaper with which I am associated said:

> To Mr. Wright, nothing was more precious than freedom; nothing more hateful than the government or the social customs that bound the freedom of expressions and movements that he considered necessary to the development of human dignity. He fought his battles in the world of ideas; he never ducked a battle and never gave quarter. He despised the stupidity of war. It is in the world of ideas that his enduring monument will be found. His thought is part of the stream of human life and nothing but complete annihilation can remove it.
>
> There is nothing that can destroy an idea that has the power of truth and beauty. Frank Lloyd Wright gave the world some of those ideas, and he lived his life in the faith that only in leaving enduring ideas can man give the world a lasting heritage.

3 4

B E N   R A E B U R N

By 1950 I just about had the autobiography memorized.

D*uring a 1949 conversation with radio personality Mary Margaret
McBride, Wright reflected briefly on his writing of* An
Autobiography:

I wrote that book that my little family might continue to eat. It was a
purely defensive affair. I had never written a book and didn't want to write
a book, but I thought that perhaps it was the only way I could get some
money. . . . So I wrote the first *An Autobiography* under very trying circumstances . . . Well, I've read it recently again—portions of it—and I like a
number of things in it."

*An Autobiography was first published in 1932. It was subsequently revised,
and a new edition was published in 1943. For 16 years after that, Frank Lloyd
Wright revised the book still further, and it was published once more in 1977, this
time by Horizon Press.* An Autobiography *now stands as Wright's final effort to
recount the experiences of his life and to make clear his revolutionary architectural
philosophies.*

On the occasion of the third publication of An Autobiography, *the magazine* Publishers Weekly *visited Ben Raeburn, president and editor of Horizon
Press, in his office on lower Fifth Avenue in Manhattan. Raeburn, who was
Wright's publisher and close friend in the last years of his life, lit a cigarette as he
reminisced about his association with Wright.*

"When I was in my early 20s," Ben Raeburn recalls, "I read one or two
sentences that were quotes of Frank Lloyd Wright's. They were in the *New
York Telegram*, I think. Wright said that the city will die unless it's decen-
tralized." The quotes appeared sometime around 1932, about the time the
first version of the autobiography was to be published by Longman's,
Green. Wright's words made a profound mark on the young Raeburn, who

Ben Raeburn's reminiscences first appeared in *Publishers Weekly*, July 25, 1977, published by
R. R. Bowker Company, a Xerox company. Copyright © 1977 Xerox Corporation. Reprinted
by permission.

bought the autobiography as soon as it was published. As was his wont, Wright never ceased working, and he continued to rewrite and refine the published autobiography. In 1943, Duell, Sloan & Pearce published the second version.

"By 1950 I just about had the autobiography memorized," Raeburn comments now. Horizon Press was founded in 1951 and Raeburn's dream was to publish Wright's works. In 1952 he wrote the architect a letter, and apparently he composed it artfully, for Wright responded via telegram two days later. The following Sunday, Raeburn was summoned to the Plaza Hotel to meet Wright. The architect asked Raeburn why he should align himself with a fledgling publisher. Raeburn brashly said, "Because I know your work better than you do." Wright was soon convinced, and Horizon Press became his exclusive publisher.

In 1953 *The Future of Architecture* was published, the first of the books by Wright to be published by Horizon. *An Autobiography* is the 17th title of his to appear from Raeburn's company.

When Wright was alive, however, the autobiography eluded Raeburn. He knew that during the years after the second version had been released, Wright had not let up on revising the text. "It was not that mistakes needed correcting," says Raeburn, "but what concerned him was a constant clarification of his prose and his ideas of architecture." Working on a printed edition of the autobiography, Wright made linear alterations, crossing out words and sentences, adding new thoughts, reorganizing the material. He wrote in the margins and between the lines. (A facsimile of Wright's unorthodox manner of revision is reprinted as the front endpapers to the book.)

"He did it all himself," Raeburn remarks. "He'd give it to me to read, and we would talk about what he might add." Early in 1959 (the year of his death) Wright handed the reworked autobiography to Raeburn, saying, "Here, Ben, it's yours." Raeburn put the manuscript in a vault. He felt hamstrung, he says, because the rights to the book were not his.

At that time, rights to *An Autobiography* were still held by Duell, Sloan & Pearce. Later, Duell, Sloan & Pearce was no more, and the books under its imprint became a trade division of Meredith Press. In due course, the people at Meredith came to know the architect's widow, Olgivanna [Lloyd] Wright, and at last the property was relinquished to her and the Frank Lloyd Wright Foundation. And then Raeburn received permission to go ahead.

Not only does Horizon's edition of the work contain the entire book as originally published and subsequently emended by Wright, it also concludes with a section called "Broadacre City." It had been Wright's intention to append this to his autobiography. "Broadacre City" was first meant to be a pamphlet designed by Wright for his own use. It relates to his ideas of the future city, government, politics, and is much more a philosophical piece than the rest of the book. Photographs from the first 1932 edition are in the book (the 1943 version was unillustrated), as are additional photographs of Wright's work, even some taken after his death.

Raeburn notes that there will be still other books: "There is no diminution of interest in Wright's work and thought," Raeburn says, snubbing out a cigarette.

3 5

REV. JOSEPH A. VAUGHAN, S.J.

**When I returned the next morning, Mr. Wright was still hovering
over the bed as if the dying man were his own son.**

The architect Francis C. Sullivan was a friend of Wright's who worked
intermittently in Wright's studio at Taliesin. In the book The Prairie
School: Frank Lloyd Wright and His Midwest Contemporaries
H. Allen Brooks writes:

In 1916, at the age of 34, Sullivan found himself suddenly without
work. . . . His health also failed. . . . In 1916 he had revisited Taliesin,
where he worked on the drawings for the Imperial Hotel, but by 1917 he
was back in Ottawa. . . . Again [in the late 1920s] Sullivan's health broke;
he was operated on for throat cancer. Later Wright, himself beset with
problems, mercifully took Sullivan to his winter camp, Ocatillo, in Arizona,
and for over a year he remained with Wright, until his death in 1929.

*Following Wright's death in 1959, the Reverend Joseph A. Vaughan, S.J.,
recalled the occasion of Sullivan's death three decades earlier.*

About 30 years ago I was stationed at St. Francis Xavier Church in
Phoenix, Arizona. A sick call came in from one of the many tubercular sani-
toria scattered around the parish. As I entered the cabin, a distinguished-
looking gentleman in cardigan jacket and knickers welcomed me. A young
man named Sullivan was lying in the bed.

"Are you a relative of the sick man?" I asked.

"No, Father, my name is Wright; I am working on a hotel in
Chandler; this morning I was watching this man tottering with the weight
of a wheelbarrow; suddenly he fell to the ground and spouted blood. So I
picked him up and brought him here."

Only late that night did it dawn on me that the good Samaritan was
the internationally famous architect Frank Lloyd Wright. When I returned

---

"A Priest Tells of Wright" was published in the *Capital Times* (Madison, Wisconsin) on May
4, 1959. Reprinted with permission.

the next morning, Mr. Wright was still hovering over the bed as if the dying man were his own son.

When Mr. Sullivan died about noon, Mr. Wright—there to the end—asked, "What do I do now, Father?"

"Has he any relatives?" I asked. Mr. Wright answered that he had a wife in Chicago. I suggested that any mortician would ship the body.

"I'll see it through, Father," said Mr. Wright.

Did not Christ say something about a cup of water, etc., etc.?

3 6

L O U I S E   M E N D E L S O H N

**My husband was greatly impressed by Frank Lloyd Wright—
with his personality—greatly impressed.**

T*he German architect Eric Mendelsohn (1887–1953) initially visited
Wright at Taliesin near Spring Green, Wisconsin, in November 1924.
Wolf von Eckardt, in his book* Eric Mendelsohn, *reported on the visit:*

Mendelsohn and Wright, it seems, agreed on the relationship between
music and architecture but disagreed on American materialism.
Mendelsohn defended his beloved Bach against Wright's partiality for
Beethoven, and Wright defended his country against Mendelsohn's criticism. Since Mendelsohn spoke little English at the time, [Richard] Neutra,
who was working with Wright, did the interpreting. He recalls that he considerably toned down both Mendelsohn's somewhat disparaging remarks
and Wright's rather haughty retorts to the young German blade. "I am
proud that my translating job cemented a lifelong sympathy between the
two."

The second morning of Mendelsohn's visit, a pleasant Sunday, was
devoted to a walk along the Wisconsin River. According to the Swiss architect Werner M. Moser, who was also present, the smooth river bank tempted Wright to draw in sand, and he playfully suggested a contest.
Mendelsohn, Moser remembers, drew one of his round, flowing fantasies,
while Wright sketched an angular building, typical of his style at that time.
Mercifully, there seems to have been no judgment to wreck Neutra's
diplomacy.

*Wright and Mendelsohn became friends. Many years later Eric
Mendelsohn's widow talked about her husband's opinion of Wright.*

My husband, was greatly impressed by Frank Lloyd Wright [in
1924]—with his personality—greatly impressed. I had the impression that

Louise Mendelsohn's reminiscences were recorded in the late 1960s and were transcribed from
Bruce Radde's KPFA-FM (Berkeley, California) radio program "Frank Lloyd Wright: The
World's Greatest Architect." Printed here by permission of Pacifica Radio Archive

Frank Lloyd Wright with Eric Mendelsohn at Taliesin in November 1924. (Frank Lloyd Wright Home and Studio Foundation, Maginel Wright Barney Collection)

they had much in common, very much in common their attitude toward architecture. He thought so highly of Frank Lloyd Wright—he thought he was the only great genius in all of America—an artistic genius. He always believed that there were great geniuses in [technology] and industry and all this, but not in an artistic way; and so he thought one should honor Frank Lloyd Wright. He suggested that [Wright take his work] to the Academy of Art; he had a heavy hand in this exhibition and [he] opened it. [The reaction among architects] was great interest [in Wright's work], great admiration. He was very much admired; he was actually much more known in Europe and in Germany and in Holland than [in] America.

LEWIS MUMFORD

**One could not be in the presence of Wright for even half an hour
without feeling the inner confidence bred by his genius.**

*L*ewis Mumford (1895–1990) was one of 20th-century America's pre-
mier social philosophers, historians, and urban-planning and architecture critics. He was a prolific writer—a frequent contributor to The
New Yorker *and the author of more than 30 books. Influenced early in his career
by the work of the English planner Patrick Geddes, Mumford became an advocate
of creating regional cities with surrounding greenbelts as a solution to the conges-
tion associated with today's cities. This was an idea not dissimilar to Wright's own
philosophies. Bruce Brooks Pfeiffer, in his book* Frank Lloyd Wright: Letters to
Architects, *states: "Lewis Mumford was the first American critic to see into the
character of Organic Architecture, to perceive its significance, and to write well
about it."*

*The long, sometimes turbulent friendship between Wright and Mumford
extended from about 1928 until Wright's death. Indeed, many of the characteristics inherent in both men were the source of the occasional turbulence in their
relationship. The friendship was important enough to Mumford that he reflected
upon it at some length in the later years of his life.*

I must say something about my encounters with Frank Lloyd Wright,
that architect of genius who loomed so high above the American horizon
between 1890 and 1950. In the twenties, when I became personally
acquainted with him—indeed, before I had had more than a fleeting glance
at his buildings—his planet was in all but total eclipse. He was one of the
handful of people I have known who, through the direct impact of their
personalities, I would place at the same level as Patrick Geddes. Yet that
very force, I must ruefully admit, remained at the end—as with Geddes—an

obstacle to the deeper and closer attachment that both men at one time or another openly sought.

Our first contact came about through my book *Sticks and Stones*, for Wright had written me, unexpectedly, an appreciative letter about it. At the time I wrote that book I was so little acquainted with Wright's buildings that I dared mention them only in passing. Even when in 1925 I had contributed a pathetically meager and tentative article on Wright's significance for Henric Wijdeveld's presentation of his work in Wijdeveld's Dutch architectural review, *Wendingen*, I still lacked even a literary acquaintance with Wright's work. But Wright himself opened the door to me; and he followed up his letter, in 1927, by inviting me to lunch with him alone in his favorite New York hotel, the Plaza.

One could not be in the presence of Wright for even half an hour without feeling the inner confidence bred by his genius. Certainly it was no flattering appreciation of his work by me that had led him to seek me out. Nor had I approached him in turn with the handicap of being a worshipful disciple: we met under the sign of friendship, which erases distinctions and inequalities. There was, I found, a curious softness about Wright's face that somehow brought the word *cornfed* immediately to one's mind: a sort of family resemblance to Sherwood Anderson that increased my pleasure later when, at the Guggenheim Museum's big show of Wright's work, I discovered that while Anderson was still in a publicity agency in Chicago he had written the copy for an advertisement of a prefabricated house Wright had designed.

Wright and I were never more friendly and at ease than we were at that first exploratory luncheon; he was disarmingly candid: almost painfully so, as sometimes happens more easily with a stranger than with an old friend or future associate. He confessed at the beginning that he was financially broke; indeed he had come to New York to find someone who would purchase his collection of Japanese prints, so as to stave off his ever-threatening creditors. But before long he was also unrolling the story of his second marriage, with the older woman who had rescued him from his desolation, indeed, restored him to life after that grim holocaust at Taliesin in which Mrs. Cheney, who had left her husband to live with Wright, was murdered with an ax wielded by a demented butler as she and her two children fled from the house he had set on fire.

Wright survived the gruesome murder of his beloved mistress as he survived the shattering publicity that resulted from his later persecution by his second wife, who became an avenging angel when he left her for Olgivanna, his younger, final mate. None of the tragedies of his life, none of the harassing episodes that had followed, had corroded his spirit or sapped his energies: his face was unseamed, his air assured, indeed jaunty. Was he, then, lacking in sensitiveness or sensibility? Yes or no! More probably, I am driven to believe, his ego was so heavily armored that even the bursting shell of such disastrous events did not penetrate his vital organs. He lived from first to last like a God: one who acts but is not acted upon.

Perhaps this explains why, for all the friendliness that developed between us, we never became intimate: strangely, neither of us ever saw the other in his own home, nor did we ever spend so much as a whole evening together in conversation. So I never had direct contact with the central creations of his family and working life: Taliesin East and Taliesin West. This was not for lack of good will on Wright's part—or on mine. In the early thirties he actually invited me to take up residence in Taliesin to help him run the school he had started there. This came after he had prudently withdrawn his earlier invitation to his admiring Dutch friend, Wijdeveld. With good reason, Wright suspected that "Dutchy's" ego and even his original talents in architecture, stage design, and typography were too insistently visible to blend with his own.

Our relations were not merely friendly; in the early thirties, before I had begun to weigh Wright's work and his underlying philosophy more circumspectly, they were affectionate—as Wright's letters to me testify. But Wright could not understand my willingness to abandon my vocation as a writer to have the honor of serving his genius; and he was puzzled, almost nettled, over my unreadiness to break into my work at any given moment to be his guest.

For all that, during the next dozen years I did my best to put forward Wright's name and extol his achievement, at a time when he was still being passed over for commissions only he could have audaciously filled—including the two world's fairs, Chicago in 1933 and New York in 1939. The failure then to turn even a single exhibition over to Wright, who was in every sense a great exhibitionist, was revelation of the limitations of fashionable taste in the thirties—both that of the exponents of the so-called International Style and that of Wright's more favored rivals, whose work now bears the derisory name of Art Deco.

Though I never made an exhaustive firsthand study of Frank Lloyd Wright's entire work, I kept my eyes open for his buildings wherever I traveled, whether in Buffalo, Minneapolis, Los Angeles, or Palo Alto. And by good luck I had the opportunity to examine closely two of his most original structures—the Midway Gardens in Chicago [page 203] and the Larkin Building in Buffalo [page 46]—before both were torn down. The exuberance, the imaginative energy visible in these designs—even after the struc-

Midway Gardens (1913, demolished 1929) in Chicago, Illinois. (*The Life Work of the American Architect Frank Lloyd Wright*, H. Th. Wijdeveld, ed.)

tures had been deserted—overweighed the chronic technical lapses and human oversights that had become as much a mark of Wright's character as is a mole on the cheek of a beautiful woman.

With Wright's extravagant gestures, his princely airs, his confident dismissal of other historic architectural epochs, along with his open contempt for most of his peers—likewise his disgracefully unparental jealousy of younger followers as possible rivals—went an innate desire to dominate and subdue those around him. So after our early meetings, my relationship to him became one of wary mutual respect: the rebellious disciple who had refused to see the panorama of Edinburgh from Geddes's Outlook Tower through his master's eyes was equally rebellious, though smilingly so, when Wright reproached me at lunch for not following his example. He was pained, for example, one hot day, when I insisted on having my favorite Irish whiskey on ice rather than in plain water—or, at another time, for my not walking with my toes pointed outward—an old military style which Wright still favored against the more natural "Indian walk" of my generation!

Yet Wright and I were both steeped in that part of the American tradition which had found literary expression in the culminating phase I had called the Golden Day: the period that found its voice in Emerson, Whitman, Thoreau, and Melville, and that then, in the generation after the Civil War, found concrete expression in buildings, parks, and the suburban communities of Frederick Law Olmsted. For both Wright and me the source and exemplar of that indigenous culture was Emerson; and though our roots were in our native soil, we, no less than Emerson, drew spiritual nourishment from remote cultures and lands: Emerson himself from Persia and Brahmin India, Wright from the newly discovered architecture of the Aztecs and Mayans, I from China and pre-Platonic Greece.

But if this common ancestry drew us together, between our conscious and political philosophies there were wide gaps. Like old Geddes, Wright demanded a complete, uncritical acceptance of his outlook and his way of life. To question his preeminence in any sphere was to become a defector. At an early stage I sensed that if our friendly relations became too close, I would surrender my right as a critic to pass an unfavorable judgment on any of his sacred beliefs or achievements. In certain vital places these differences in temperament and outlook went deep. So in time my relation to him was not a little like that of Chekhov to Tolstoy. In order to retain our admiration for the master, both Chekhov and I were forced out of self-respect to maintain a certain spatial and psychological distance.

In the late thirties our different political views widened the gap between Wright and me; and over the issues raised by the Second World War, we, alas! inevitably parted company. Such fissures in friendship were not unusual then; for I lost more than one friend or associate, at least temporarily, through my militant opposition to Hitlerism and Stalinism, as well as to all other demoralizing later forms of dictatorship, including that of the Pentagon, the Atomic Energy Commission, the FBI, and the U.S. Central Intelligence Agency. And though I was able to remain friends with Robert Frost, who was as bitter an isolationist as Wright, this was possibly because we both discreetly smothered our differences in silence.

To Wright's public denunciation of the handful of Americans like myself who at that time advocated active military resistance to Fascism and Nazism, I replied with a passionate counterindictment. In that crisis our friendship had come to an end; so much so that I did not open till years later the New Year's messages he continued to send me. But I smiled grimly when I received a greeting from him—sent at a time when there was a stringent paper shortage—in an envelope 18 inches long, containing a folded greeting on heavy paper twice the length of the envelope! During the early forties that insolent symbol seemed final.

Happily, we came together again soon after Wright's great exhibition of his life work in Florence in 1950, the first of such choral triumphs punctuated by gold medals. He sent me a catalog inscribed, "In spite of all, your old F.Ll.W." When I saw this, I turned to Sophia and said, "I've just written a book in which I've said that without a great upsurgence of love we shall not be able to save the world from even greater orgies of extermination and destruction. If I haven't enough love left in me to answer Wright in the same fashion as this greeting, I'd better throw that book out the window." So I wrote him, repeating my words to Sophia; and he answered in his characteristically generous fashion by sending me an inscribed print of a winter scene by Hokusai. And neither of us referred to that breach thereafter.

How consoling it would be to report that from this time on we drew closer, and that, as a by-product of our restored friendship, it would be I and not a young colleague, Henry-Russell Hitchcock, who would attempt the first definitive criticism of Wright's architecture, for by then Wright's imagination, released and exalted by the opportunities offered him after the Second World War, was enriching the vocabulary of modern forms. If at this time architecture had been my dominant concern, I might, perhaps, have been tempted to make such a study. But what had already happened to the world around us since 1935 made it clear by 1945 that, though Nazism had been undermined in the end by the delusions of its psychotic leaders, Hitler had nevertheless won the war. Well before the end, Nazism's methods had infiltrated the minds and plans of his enemies and had begun to dominate the science, the technology, and the politics of the so-called Nuclear Age. I did not think that architecture, as the favored masters of modern form still conceived it, would serve as an instrument in our salvation. But without such a change in the American political and moral climate, a closer relation with Wright would be impossible. By 1950 we were each too firmly rooted in our individual allotments and commitments.

My difficulty in doing complete justice to Wright's achievements in architecture was based on the fact that, the better I knew his work, the more I found in its whole span to admire—no one else could rival him in sheer fertility of imagination and constructive innovation—and the more I found to question in his unwillingness to admit, as copartners in shaping the design, his individual clients, the contributions of his disciples or rivals, or the communal traditions that support and enhance every work designed to meet the varied needs of life. Too often with Wright showmanship took precedence over workmanship, and dramatic originality often flouted tested experience. If, on my estimate of Wright's early buildings, the Cheney House shows Wright at his human best, was this perhaps, I have asked myself, due to the fact that in this building the client he passionately loved had had an active influence over her lover's design?

My reservations about Wright's most characteristic insignia came to a head in my response to the retrospective exhibition held on the site of the still unbuilt Guggenheim Museum, in a temporary building Wright himself designed. In viewing his whole life's work, I now had the good fortune to have Wright himself as my commentator and guide. But in seeing his life, so to say, spread before me, with his voice as a persistent undertone, I realized as never before how the insolence of his genius sometimes repelled me: notably in his transforming the tempting site of Pittsburgh's Triangle, a hillside plot formed by the dramatic juncture of the Allegheny and Monongahela rivers, into a typically Wrightian "fun" area. That exhibition-istic idea was hardly more worthy of so grand a site than the unplayful mass of mediocre buildings later erected there.

Despite all such doubts and reservations, what remained, what indeed dominated this exhibition was, for me, still magnificent: so rich, so resourceful, that it seemed the work not of a single individual over a limited period of time but almost of a whole culture, over a century-long span. Not merely that, but Wright had met and conquered his rivals at their own game. In Fallingwater, designed for Edgar Kaufmann [page 131], he had created a dynamic multidimensional composition that made Le Corbusier's buildings seem flat cardboard compositions; while in the Johnson Wax Laboratory at Racine, Wisconsin [page 49], he had experimented with untried glass forms that made Mies van der Rohe's blank glass facades blanker than ever. So I spelled out my critical evaluation of Wright's *oeuvre* in two *New Yorker* Sky Lines: the first favorable, the second tempering my praise with questions, though seeking to do justice, in spite of Wright's belligerent Americanism, to his truly universal bequest from other cultures and other ages.

Wright read my first article in a plane; and he became so angry about it that he then and there wrote me a letter that trembled with rage as if from some mechanical vibration. His references to me were all in the third person—"He says that"—as if it were a Letter to the Editor. To settle matters, he dismissed me—whom he had once put on a par with his favorite writer, Emerson—as a "mere scribbler," an "ignoramus"; and he was sure, he said, that his clients would rise up in their wrath to denounce me. This looked like the second end of our friendship.

When I answered him promptly, I told him that I respected his greatness too much to belittle it by sweetening my critical appreciation with undiluted praise; and that I had written about him in the same unsparing manner in which I had written in *Green Memories* about my young son's life, out of admiration and love. When I reached the end of the letter, I was about to sign it in my usual fashion, but a sudden impish impulse prompted me to sign it instead in the style of Frank Lloyd Wright himself: "With all respect and admiration, as from one Master to another, Ever yours . . ."

Wright tacitly accepted that explanation and that declaration of equality. At all events, he made no comment on my second article, despite its unsparing severity. Possibly in the meantime too many of his admirers had praised my first

Frank Lloyd Wright presenting his design for the Mile-High Illinois Skyscraper Project in Chicago on October 16, 1956. (Chicago Historical Society)

article as a fine tribute to his life and work—which it actually was.

At the end, alas! I missed my final chance for a warm reconciliation with Wright when he invited me to take Robert Moses's place at a dinner in Chicago where Wright himself was to be the chief speaker. As usual, I was reluctant to break into my work; but I had already drafted an acceptance when a closer reading of the invitation made me realize that this dinner was part of an effort to launch Wright's design for a "Skyscraper a Mile High." In that project all of Wright's egocentric weaknesses were crystallized in an ultimate fantasy, conceived as if by a lineal descendant of Kublai Khan. What a monument of futility—even more absurd, humanly speaking, if that were possible, than the later World Trade Center in New York. Naturally, I could not lend myself to a proposal that violated every canon of Wright's own conception of an organic architecture, as well as my own. If this was what old age had done to Wright, I had no desire to exalt his mummified remains.

Not a long while after this I was scheduled to give a public lecture at the University of Pennsylvania, where I was then Ford Research Professor; but up to the last week I had hesitated to choose the theme of the lecture. Almost at the last hour, the theme announced itself. The news of Wright's death came to me that morning. On approaching the old building of the School of Design I saw that the flagpole above the entrance showed the American flag at half-mast; around the mast itself the students had suspended black streamers of mourning. The students' swift response touched me, and I realized that there was only one possible subject for the lecture that night—Frank Lloyd Wright's life and work.

Though I have given many extemporary lectures, good and bad, I can remember only two in which all the deeper resources of my experience as well as self-knowledge were brought to bear. One of them was to a small class in biography at Dartmouth, under Professor Arthur Wilson: my subject was Vincent van Gogh. And the other, even fuller, profounder, and infinitely more audacious, was this lecture on Frank Lloyd Wright. In it I did something like justice to both his actual and his potential greatness; and at the same time I related his work to the vicissitudes of his personal life; and not least to the insidious temptations to which his success alike as a creative architect, as an outstanding public figure, as a seminal personality, had laid him open.

Speaking to the young audience, especially about their future careers in architecture, I pointed out that Wright's expansive ego, his own uncritical self-love, his naive self-righteousness had made him too lenient toward his own weaknesses and errors, and too ready to transfer self-reproach to a hampering family, to jealous rivals, to unscrupulous imitators, to inefficient or recalcitrant workmen, to unimaginative clients. While he preached "democracy," his practice was that of a Renaissance despot; for he built *himself* into every building, and even in the intimacies of the marital bedroom of the Hanna House, Wright's presence was inescapable. What is more, he regarded the minimal modifications necessary to meet practical exigencies he had not foreseen as an insult to his genius.

Though I never favored Walter Gropius's ambitious concept of "total architecture" in this increasingly totalitarian world, I must admit that my Wright lecture came near to being, in quite another sense, "total criticism," since I did not spare myself any more than I spared Wright. As with my van Gogh talk, there is no record of what I actually said: not so much as a penciled scribble. And even if the words had been recorded on tape, the lecture itself, with its passion, its exuberance, its harassing search for truth, likewise in my self-exposure and self-criticism, which underlay the very

The playroom terrace on the west side of Honeycomb, the Paul R. Hanna residence (1936) in Stanford, California. The name Honeycomb was derived from the hexagonal modular-unit system used in constructing the house. This is one of Wright's largest Usonian houses and the first with a pitched roof. (Patrick J. Meehan)

words I addressed to Wright, would all be missing. This was not a psycho-analytic diagnosis: it was a dramatic act, set within the vast theater of Wright's own genius. If that was not to be my last word on Frank Lloyd Wright, it deserved to be. And the highest honor my own life could possibly receive would be to serve as the subject for such a drastic, ego-transcending performance by a mind capable of meeting my work on equal terms—"As from one Master to another!"

ON THE DIFFICULTY OF TALKING ABOUT WRIGHT

It is difficult for me to talk with complete objectivity about Wright and to say all the negative things that I have observed and could dwell upon because we were friends. From the moment that he read *The Golden Day*, which came out in 1926, and wrote me a letter. . . . he saluted me as the real successor of Emerson. He could give no higher praise.

ON WRIGHT'S CREATIVE MIND

Wright was undoubtedly the most creative mind we have had in architecture. He could have created a dozen possible styles, all more or less in harmony with the life that we'd like to live in this culture, but that only a few, of course, can ever achieve. There is no doubt about the quality of his imagination.

ON WRIGHT'S DESIGN FOR THE HANNA RESIDENCE

I lived there [in the Hanna residence] for a week. Well, one learns a great deal about a house by living [in it] for a week. I learned a great deal about the Hannas, a great deal about Frank Lloyd Wright, and something about myself as well by living there. Outwardly, it's a very successful building [page 209]. [It is] beautifully sited on a hill and with a good landscape around it, with an excellent view from the main living room and from the bigger social room that adjoins the main room. [It] shows Wright, in some ways, at his very best. . . .

On the other hand, he was not merely a man of genius but he had the effect of a genius, an overwhelming ego and an arrogance in thinking that his way of life was the only way of life, that what he wanted was right for everyone else.

There was one part of him that had a great feeling for abstract form. In the Hanna House he seized upon the hexagon as a module for every room. Every room was to have six sides to it, not four. As a matter of fact, that's a much less adaptable room than a four-sided room given the equivalent amount of space. He was so rigorous in his logic that once he'd used a hexagon he kept on using it for every part of the house . . . [except] in an inner room, like the kitchen, which he made as much as possible like that of a drugstore lunch counter. In the bedroom, of course, you notice first of all the weakness of the hexagonal plan. The original beds he supplied had to be made to order, and they had to be made on hexagonal principles to fit with a hexagonal wall. Therefore, it had a very interesting effect on marital relations between husband and wife. Because the husband and the wife didn't sleep on the same level, and that was the least of it. As the housekeeper, Mrs. Hanna was faced with the problem of getting special sheets made to order that could be used on a hexagonal bed. Finally, after living in the house for awhile, they threw out the hexagonal beds and introduced two comfortable beds, side by side, where a decently married couple could enjoy all the pleasures of domesticity without one of them being out of reach of the other. This kind of arbitrariness on Wright's part was one of his great failings.

PART VI
FAMILY

Mr. and Mrs. Frank Lloyd Wright during the mid- to late-1950s at Taliesin West. (Frank Lloyd Wright Home and Studio Foundation, Maginel Wright Barney Collection)

3 8

OLGIVANNA LLOYD WRIGHT

His whole life was *truth*, he was truth.

Olga Iovanovna Lazovich Hinzenberg married Frank Lloyd Wright
on August 25, 1928. She was his third and last wife. Olgivanna Lloyd
Wright was born in Cetinje, Montenegro (now a part of Yugoslavia),
in 1898. She was the daughter of a chief justice of the Montenegran Supreme
Court. Her grandfather, Duke Marco Milianov, was a celebrated Balkan general and national hero. Olgivanna and Frank Lloyd Wright had one child together, Iovanna Lloyd Wright. Together they also established the Taliesin Fellowship
in 1932. Following Wright's death, Mrs. Wright became the president and
chairman of the Frank Lloyd Wright Foundation.

In 1980, five years before her own death, Olgivanna Lloyd Wright was
interviewed by James Auer. It is interesting to note that at the end of the interview, Mrs. Wright alludes to the autobiography she is writing. As of the publication of Frank Lloyd Wright Remembered, Mrs. Wright's autobiography
remains unpublished.

JAMES AUER: Mrs. Wright, your husband was a man of genius and of
many contrasts. Is there any way he can be summed up in a word?

OLGIVANNA LLOYD WRIGHT: His whole life was *truth*, he was truth.

AUER: He never dissimulated?

WRIGHT: He did not conceal, he spoke as he believed. At the same
time he had the ability to bring everybody to his level. He could talk to a
15-year-old or to a 70-year-old person with the same equality. I personally
believe that to be a rare ability. People always try to gauge; he never
gauged. Anything he said was absolute truth.

What he accomplished is what is most important. As to his contrasting
experiences, that is another matter altogether. He was a complex individual,
and you cannot very well categorize him on any particular grade or level of
life.

AUER: Why can't you?

James Auer's "Mrs. Wright Talks About the Man" was published in the *Milwaukee Journal* on
August 24, 1980. Reprinted with permission.

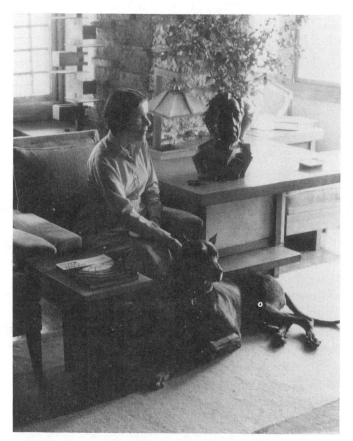

Olgivanna Lloyd Wright on September 12, 1981, in the living room of Taliesin in Wisconsin. (Patrick J. Meehan)

WRIGHT: Because he is beyond those categories. For instance, his communion with nature was of such tremendous understanding—it seemed as though they were one, as though nature favored him and always gave him dramatic scenes. He told me that on the night he was born a terrible storm raged in Richland Center, Wisconsin. I said, "That's why your life, and mine with you, is stormy but interesting."

AUER: He unified many gifts within himself, didn't he?

WRIGHT: He was incredible. To describe him in any kind of conventional language seems an impossibility. Whatever he did, he did well—he was an avid reader, a wonderful speaker, a marvelous skater. He rode horseback as if the horse and he were one.

AUER: His propensity for straight talking sometimes got him into difficulty, didn't it?

WRIGHT: Yes, indeed it did. Great difficulty. He had many enemies because people were jealous or they did not understand him. If they really understood him, they would have supported him in his work. Only later in his life was he recognized by the intellectuals of the world as the great leader in living architecture—not dead architecture, but a living organism as Taliesin is—a living, breathing organism.

AUER: How did he see his relationship to the environment?

WRIGHT: He believed the influence of environment to be extremely important. No matter how low a man might feel, as everyone does at times, going back to his home he will be regenerated if that home has a harmonious atmosphere.

AUER: Do you feel that architecture as a whole has improved as a result of Mr. Wright's life?

WRIGHT: Yes, very much so. Architecture the world over has profited by his work, notwithstanding the truth that no other architect can possibly be on his level. He despised imitation—that was a falsehood to him. He said, "I hate to go around and see my own regurgitations. Why can't they do something with a little inspiration? I want people to be inspired, not to be imitators."

AUER: Were other architects inclined to imitate the superficials of his life without accepting his principles?

WRIGHT: Life is difficult; an architect has a wife and children to support. Sometimes he feels he must compromise simply to get the job. If he has been related in some way intellectually or emotionally to Frank Lloyd Wright, he will feel bad about the work he has done. Whenever I came across this instance, the architect always told me, "I had to do it."

My husband felt very different about the same situation. When a young architect explained to him that he went against principle in a building he designed because he "had to earn his living," Mr. Wright would ask, "Why? If you cannot build buildings that are honest, then go and get a job digging ditches to support yourself."

As to people who were of an older generation, there were very few that understood him. He mainly gave his inspiration to the young, hoping to establish a wonderful basis for them, which I try to carry on here at Taliesin, developing real architects.

AUER: Are you pleased with what your students have produced over the years?

WRIGHT: With some, yes. With others, no. It is the same as in everything else. Some have gone out and done very well. They have become successful without having to sell down the river this principle of integrity in building.

There are architects who build on fine principles. We have trained many. They frequently return to visit us as to Mecca, in order to refresh themselves, to remember once more their youth at Taliesin and their experiences here.

AUER: What was Mr. Wright's reaction to new building materials? Did he welcome them?

WRIGHT: As civilization moves on, there come new materials such as steel, concrete, reinforced concrete, metals. Glass had existed as a material for centuries, but with the modern method of rolling it into large sheets, my husband saw it as a totally new material and used it accordingly. He used every material in the nature of its innate characteristics—stone, wood, brick, steel, textiles.

He combined materials such as canvas and glass in a most beautiful way in our Taliesin West [pages 139, 149, and 150] on the Arizona desert. This might be rather difficult for some people to understand, but he made a beautiful combination of the two. He later replaced canvas with acrylic materials as they were developed. Whatever worthwhile new building products were being manufactured, he put into use in his buildings. If he were designing today, he would be using plastics, vinyls, and other materials in a harmonious way. He said that architecture is not just sticks and stones. It is much more than that, and he was able to put the breath of life in everything he built.

AUER: Then he drew much from his study of nature?

WRIGHT: Yes, he most certainly did. There was a bond between the two of them.

He believed in moving with the time, but at the same time he was timeless. As you know, his buildings today are still 50, 100 years in advance of anything else that is being built.

AUER: They're buildings like no one else's.

WRIGHT: Yes, he showed that he knew how to make everything sing. His work always had a melody or was like a symphony. Take this house, Taliesin, for example—or any house that he has designed—it sings. His architecture is many-dimensional architecture, including the people, the terrain, the site, the sky, the climate—everything that goes into it.

AUER: Do people experience a spiritual dimension, living with the architecture Mr. Wright created?

WRIGHT: That would naturally depend upon the people themselves. But I personally believe that the world is filled with people who have some creative substance in them. They might be business executives or they might be humble laborers and workmen—it doesn't matter in what strata of society they are placed. A very humble farmer, living the hard way, came into Taliesin and said, "Mr. Wright, you live like a king." My husband was always pleased when things came to him from so-called "ordinary" people. Of course, no one ever admits to being ordinary, and there really is no such thing as an "ordinary man." I believe that to be true.

AUER: He seems to exist in his buildings?

WRIGHT: Yes, his presence is permeating everything. How can it be otherwise? He built every building with love. Once a client said to me, "Mr. Wright's buildings are—mystical. I believe Mr. Wright is a mystic, but he does not know it!"

AUER: You are a mystic, are you not, Mrs. Wright?

WRIGHT: How do you define "mystic?" That you live in another dimension? Yes, I believe that people either realize or fail to realize that a force exists which is superior to ours. If we believe in and adhere to that force instead of our purely animal natures, the whole body can be illumined by it. You ask difficult questions.

AUER: You've been interested in metaphysics for a long time, haven't you?

WRIGHT: I would not call it metaphysics. For me it started in my child-hood in Europe. My whole life was very difficult from the typical life of the times. My father, who was blind, developed in me a great sense of deeper values. I always wondered how he could be so self-contained in the face of such a dreadful tragedy that all of a sudden struck him and deprived him of his eyesight. I was with him a great deal of the time and read to him whatever he wanted—newspapers, literature, poetry. Through that training, through read-ing books, through hearing him speak to me about the ballads and fairy tales of Montenegro, my native country, I grew somehow to believe that although information may be useful, it is interior content that is significant.

AUER: It was your father, then, who planted in you the seeds of intel-lectual curiosity?

WRIGHT: Yes, all that mixture made me interested in ideas. I read Nietzsche, I read Schopenhauer, I read Kant, I read Santayana—I read all the philosophers and studied all the philosophies. I wanted to discover how to achieve and develop these deeper qualities as a living part of my life.

AUER: How did you happen to visit Taliesin? Had you known of it before?

WRIGHT: Yes, I had met Mr. Wright in Chicago, and later he asked me to visit Taliesin here in Wisconsin. My life, in a worldly sense, started then. He told me, "Olgivanna, from this time on you won't be seen for the dust." He was right! It was a very stormy, difficult, and yet wonderful life. And I would not trade it for anything, ever. But now you are asking me questions which I am answering in my autobiography. Do you think it is fair that I tell you that which I am writing?

LLOYD WRIGHT

He was an archindividualist. The individual came first, last, and all the time. And I understand why now, as time passes and my experience enlarges in life; it is all-important.

Lloyd Wright, Frank Lloyd Wright's eldest son, was born in Oak Park in 1890 and grew up in the environment of his father's Oak Park studio. As a boy Lloyd Wright occasionally worked for his father, and in 1910 he accompanied him and Taylor Woolley on a trip to Europe to help in the preparation of Ausgeführte Bauten und Entwürfe von Frank Lloyd Wright, *also known as the Wasmuth portfolio.*

Lloyd Wright became a distinguished architect in his own right. Among his projects were the Swedenborg Memorial Wayfarer's (1946–71) Chapel in Rancho Palos Verdes, California, and two designs for the Hollywood Bowl (1924–25 and 1928) in Hollywood, California. During the 1940s and 1950s he collaborated with his father on several architectural projects in California.

In October 1977 Lloyd Wright spoke at a conference entitled "An American Architecture: Its Roots, Growth, and Horizons" in Milwaukee, Wisconsin. At the time Lloyd Wright was already in his late eighties, and his voice and tone were strongly reminiscent of his father's. Eric Lloyd Wright, who is also an architect, assisted his father on this occasion. It was one of Lloyd Wright's last public appearances; he died of a stroke, following a bout with pneumonia, on May 31, 1978, in Santa Monica, California.

LLOYD WRIGHT: Now this is going to be too much off the cuff. I like the freedom of it and I need it. We all should have it. Winston Churchill was once asked, "Have you any geniuses in your country?" And he said, "Yes, one, Frank Lloyd Wright." So there now I've said it. You've asked me to talk about a genius—my father. And I shall do so—Wright on Wright.

He was an archindividualist. The individual came first, last, and all the time. And I understand why now, as time passes and my experience

---

Lloyd Wright's reminiscences in the second part of this chapter were recorded in the late 1960s and were transcribed from Bruce Radde's KPFA-FM (Berkeley, California) radio programs "Frank Lloyd Wright: The Outspoken Philosopher" and "Frank Lloyd Wright: The Shining Brow." Printed with permission of Pacifica Radio Archive.

enlarges in life; it is all-important. I used to think [the individual] was supposed to be self-centered—nothing of the sort. You couldn't begin to commence in architecture until you recognize the individual, and his quality is the essential matter.

As time has gone on, [my father's] presence has become stronger. . . . His contribution has not yet been fully understood or comprehended, certainly not by his peers, the architects. I'm sorry to say they're awful backsliders in their recognition of this man's genius, capacity, and contribution. I won't explain why, all you need to do is research it yourselves and then try to help others see it for the good of the community, which is a unique one— that is, the new world of the U.S.A. to which he contributed so much.

About 20 years ago he gave a talk to the USC in which he said, "I don't usually name my talks, they're usually ad-lib, but tonight I'm going

Lloyd Wright as a child. (Frank Lloyd Wright Home and Studio Foundation)

to name it: 'What is the matter with America?' " America, whom he loved very much and for whom he had great respect and much concern. What is the matter with America? Twenty years later, what he said came to fruition in the Watergate, etc. America was losing its original courage and honesty, and it still is. It's a great shame. I think we're facing up to the question now more clearly than we have heretofore for decades. But we're still not answering the question, and we still have to find our original courage and honesty.

The schools, unfortunately, do not seem to be able to help us. The academic runaround, bureaucracy, gets in the way. In this connection, and in connection with our performance in our professional fields, there are many, too many, coattail riders. I believe you understand what I'm referring to, and I don't want to waste time going into details which you're already aware of.

I would like to tell you a little story. It isn't a story, it's a real experience

Lloyd Wright in the Swedenborg Memorial Wayfarer's Chapel (1946–71) in Rancho Palos Verdes, California, in the mid-1970s. The chapel was designed by Lloyd Wright. (Wiener; The Wayfarer's Chapel)

of mine and my father's on the West Coast. He had finished the Imperial Hotel [page 241]. He had employed [Rudolph M.] Schindler and [Richard] Neutra to assist him; not so much Neutra as Schindler. And after he had returned [from Japan] and gone into the business on the Coast, these two, whom he had taken under his wing—because of troubles in Europe—and given jobs for several years, taking in their families, decided that they were geniuses, or at least that they were great architects—they had each built one building. They opened an office on Wilshire Boulevard, and they posted in the front of it three photographs: one of each of them on either side of Frank Lloyd Wright. And they proclaimed themselves the coming modern architects to the good U.S.A. Father heard about it, and he took with him Lewis Mumford. (You all know Lewis Mumford, or [have] heard of him. He's still alive—he'll verify this tale.) Father was fit to be tied. He didn't like that kind of thing. But Mumford came to his assistance and said, "Cheer up, Frank, Christ was crucified between two thieves!"

AUDIENCE: [*Loud laughter and applause*]

WRIGHT: So that was part, and is part and parcel of our problem today. And the sooner we face up to it, the better and the sooner we can take care of it.

The Swedenborg for whom I built a retreat [Wayfarer's Chapel in Rancho Palos Verdes] for the tourist—the passing man—had already formed and recounted and described the philosophy which I had understood. I hadn't understood that my father had been working with it and that it was his credo, too. I hit it on the head anyway, because I had been prepared for it by the man who understood it—Frank Lloyd Wright. Transcendentalism at its best, and it's still at work. We're going to have the day when we see as clearly as these two men saw, and as they worked with it, and as we in time, and in due course, [will] do the same.

My son says it's about time for us to take questions from the audience. So we'll try—we have a little time. Where do I get one? You'll have to talk up because my hearing isn't good.

QUESTIONER: Can you tell us something about the [Frank Lloyd Wright] Studio and House in Oak Park and what it was like to grow up in that house?

WRIGHT: It was a very exciting experience. I must say so, all the time, and in all ways, and we had a large family—there were six children. There were also clients. And there were contributions which my father was making to the culture of our nation. It was very involved. It couldn't have been more interesting or more vivid.

My father furnished us up with a beautiful room that brought to life the cultures of other nations—Japan, Germany, every part of the world. My mother took care of kindergarten groups from the neighborhood for years in that beautiful room—the playroom we called it.

QUESTIONER: Did your father plan your career like his mother planned his?

WRIGHT: If he did, he didn't let me know about it!

AUDIENCE: [*Loud laughter*]

WRIGHT: Any more [questions]?

QUESTIONER: Yes, Mr. Wright. When your mother was teaching you and other children in the playroom, did she use the Froebel toys? [It should

The Frank Lloyd Wright residence (1889) in Oak Park, Illinois, is a structure clad with wood shingles. (Patrick J. Meehan)

The Frank Lloyd Wright studio (1895) in Oak Park, Illinois. Like the adjoining Frank Lloyd Wright residence (1889), this structure is covered with wood shingles. (Patrick J. Meehan)

be pointed out that the questioner was the former Frank Lloyd Wright apprentice Edgar Kaufmann, Jr.]

WRIGHT: She certainly did, and if we didn't use the Froebel toys we made them "à la Froebel." The geometry of the Froebel system was essen-

The playroom of the Frank Lloyd Wright residence (1889) in Oak Park, Illinois. (Jon Miller, Hedrich-Blessing; Frank Lloyd Wright Home and Studio Foundation)

tial to this transcendentalism, and the playroom floors, and the figures, the patterns on the floors and movement of the dancers, all of it [was] a coordinated, rhythmic concentration and discipline which we need now just as much as then, and which, maybe someday, we'll get generally in the education system. But we haven't got it yet.

QUESTIONER: Mr. Wright, what is your comment on the apprenticeship training of your father? How were young architects trained in the studio in Oak Park? How were they trained when they came to work for him?

WRIGHT: They weren't trained in the studio in Oak Park in the aesthetics; they learned from actual work on the project with him, as a pencil in his hand. That's what they came to him to do—be a pencil in his hand— and that's what he insisted on them being. He had no intention of formally educating them in any cultural development except as they found it out in the process with which he was involved and in which he involved them.

QUESTIONER: How is it that you have applied yourself to architectural work? Are you still active?

WRIGHT: Every moment of the day and night.

QUESTIONER: What is your most recent project?

WRIGHT: Well, there is one that fascinates me. It is a desert project to utilize what is known as wasteland, where the sun is its essence—sun power, solar energy. These magnificent deserts of ours on the West Coast are the center of my present interest, and they're most fascinating. They are getting their energy from the sun and converting it. They're the areas to drain, and I hope we can make them a suitable environment for humanity.

QUESTIONER: I wonder if you can comment on Taliesin West and on what the people are doing out there. What I mean by that is replacing your father's two-by-two blocks with styrofoam blocks painted like wood, and the tract homes they have designed out there.

WRIGHT: I think they are trying their best to follow his directions and his lead.

QUESTIONER: What about the tract homes they designed?

WRIGHT: Well, I haven't been critical of their work or their effort— that's theirs. You ask them!

AUDIENCE: [*Loud laughter*]

QUESTIONER: I read your book several years ago. Do you know if that's still available?

ERIC LLOYD WRIGHT [answering for Lloyd Wright]: What book are you referring to?

QUESTIONER: *My Father Who Is On Earth.*

ERIC LLOYD WRIGHT: That was by my father's brother, John Lloyd Wright. John passed away about two years ago. The book is not available unless you can find it in a used bookstore. I don't think it's been reprinted.

QUESTIONER: Mr. Wright, what to you is your own greatest accomplishment?

WRIGHT: To stay with this problem.

AUDIENCE: [*Loud applause*]

QUESTIONER: I understand, Mr. Wright, that you introduced your father to Alfonso Iannelli.

WRIGHT: I did. I found a kindred soul in Alfonso in Los Angeles, and we spent nights and days together in his workshop on Spring Street. I saw a mark of genius there which I recognized and which was familiar to me. My father was building the Edelweiss Center [i.e., Midway Gardens in Chicago; see page 203] at that time, and I recommended that he get Iannelli to help him with the figures. Iannelli was having trouble getting the kind of stylization he needed. Dicky Bock [the sculptor Richard Bock] at that time had been doing things, but it was a little too much for Dicky— it was too abstract. And so Iannelli came on and never returned—he remained in Chicago. Iannelli and I were very close indeed.

QUESTIONER: Mr. Wright, when you were growing up, did your father talk about his experiences on the Eastern seaboard when he was a child?

WRIGHT: No. No, he didn't. He never referred to that. I think because of his mother, who didn't like to discuss it. It was painful for her, so he never talked about it to us. Now I still must visit Richland Center and acquaint myself with more of the details of that background, because it is important to me and to all of us.

QUESTIONER: Mr. Wright, do you remember your grandmother?

WRIGHT: Oh, quite well—she was a very strong woman!

AUDIENCE: [*Loud laughter*]

QUESTIONER: Did she have the same perfected diction that both you and your father have?

WRIGHT: Oh, I think that the diction was extremely clear—I never had any difficulty understanding it!

AUDIENCE: [*Loud laughter*]

WRIGHT: And I loved her. But she was very definitive.

QUESTIONER: Mr. Wright, was there ever any tension between your mother and your grandmother?

WRIGHT: Well, there would naturally be . . . My grandmother had very definite opinions as to what she wanted to do; and my young mother, naturally, had her own concepts, which were not the same.

QUESTIONER: Do you have any favorites among the works of your father? Did he ever express to you whether he did any work that he considered his best?

WRIGHT: Yes, every time he built a building it was particularly great!

AUDIENCE: [*Loud laughter*]

QUESTIONER: Do you have any favorites?

WRIGHT: No, I can't play them in my work or his. They're all different. They're all dealing with different situations, environmental and otherwise. And so they're not really comparable. Any other questions?

QUESTIONER: Mr. Wright, did you ever meet Louis Sullivan?

WRIGHT: Yes, several times.

QUESTIONER: Can you tell us something about that?

WRIGHT: It was a great experience. My father saw to it that I saw him soon before he died. We had a luncheon at the Tip-Top Inn in Chicago. [It was] very moving. He was a very gentle person, suave, graceful, small, but wise. What else?

QUESTIONER: Did you discuss your feelings of the Johnson Wax Building [page 49]? Do you have any memories of it—of Frank Lloyd Wright talking about it?

WRIGHT: Well, I discussed all of Frank Lloyd Wright's buildings with him at one time or another—upside-down and downside-up, and round and round.

QUESTIONER: What sort of experiences did you have as a draftsman in your father's office? Were the other draftsmen resentful? Were there any problems? [The questioner, in this instance, was Patrick J. Meehan.]

WRIGHT: Well, the other draftsmen were all interesting individuals. There was [William E.] Drummond and Marion Mahoney [Griffin], and the secretary, Isabel Roberts Jones, and so on and on and on. They took good care of me, as a junior member, and they helped me up on the stools to make tracings of their glasswork for them. I commenced to do that when I was about seven or eight years old, and never quit thereafter.

ERIC LLOYD WRIGHT: You know, it might be interesting to talk about the *Ausgeführte Bauten und Entwürfe von Frank Lloyd Wright* and when you were in Italy.

WRIGHT: My father turned to me again and again. I was going to the University [of Wisconsin in Madison]. He took me out of the University to come and help him with the *Ausgeführte Bauten*. I stayed there [in Italy] almost a year, and it was a wonderful experience. He hired a villa, [the] Villa Fatuna [*sic*], just below the Plaza of Michelangelo, in Firenze. What an experience! I and the draftsman, [Taylor] Woolley, a Mormon from Salt Lake City, were my father's aides in that adventure. In the villa—we got there in the winter and it was cold—the floors were made of stone and there was no heating except braziers, and we warmed our hands and drew with cope felt [*sic*] pens. We made tracings of all the work he had done up to that time . . . It was a marvelous experience. We'd go down to town, in between sessions, and we'd discover the works of—what was his name at that time, the great sculptor of that time?—and we'd think we had discovered the works of Michelangelo!

AUDIENCE: [*Laughter*]

WRIGHT: Well, of course, we did have this figure of David just above us.

So it was very complex and very interesting, and very vivid, and we were working all the time to good purpose, and the Germans took these drawings that we made with the cope felt [*sic*] pens over all sorts of pencil drawings, ink drawings, and watercolors, what have you, and Father put them in order, checked them, and did some of the drawing himself. They then coordinated with our stones—their photographic stones—into a marvelous work that isn't equaled anywhere to my knowledge, since or before.

The Germans were marvelous technicians. They had invited him over there to do this work and he surely did it [pages 45 and 46]. This was the kind of man he was. He was indeed a genius.

LLOYD WRIGHT: "He hired a villa, [the] Villa Fatuna [sic], just below the Plaza of Michelangelo, in Firenze. What an experience! . . .We got there in the winter and it was cold—the floors were made of stone. . ." The studio building in Florence, Italy, where Frank Lloyd Wright, Lloyd Wright, and Taylor Woolley produced the drawings for *Ausgeführte Bauten und Entwürfe von Frank Lloyd Wright.* (Clifford Evans Collection, University of Utah Libraries)

AUDIENCE: [*Loud applause for several minutes as Lloyd Wright leaves the podium*]

The following passages were transcribed from programs that aired on KPFA-FM radio (Berkeley, California) in the late 1960s.

ON THE OAK PARK YEARS

I remember my earliest experiences on Chicago Avenue in Oak Park. The feeling of mystery and awe and the possibilities—it felt like "Beauty and the Beast." I felt the beast was out there and might come in at any moment. Because my father had built this home with funds extended by the *lieber Meister*—his employer—Louis Sullivan. [My father] had his mother in the home right adjacent to him . . . which happened to be a landscape architect's home. And he had planted exotica in it—wonderful things. I can only liken it to the story of "Beauty and the Beast." The beast was there, the beauty was there, and it was eminent. It half frightened me, and yet it intrigued me, and yet it was marvelous.

[Living in my father's house] was sort of a dream. His life was very quiet, relatively, in the home. The home, which at that time was . . . lovely, with aluminum ceilings and so forth; and his affection for beautiful things such as Oriental rugs. As a boy I helped him open up these Oriental rugs, studied them, saw them . . . and heard his reactions and [I] learned therefrom. But no, he went into the big city in the earlier days on the elevated trains, which were electrified at that time. That was the early beginnings of the modern technology. He would go and come back and the life went on very well, quietly that way. Occasionally we had visitors but not very often—he was too busy. He had too much to do to indulge in entertaining. If he did any, it might have been downtown. But, then, not much of that either because he had to earn a living and he had these children coming on. I was the first of six. My mother was very busy taking care [of us] and she didn't have time for social contacts. She was young and inexperienced and she wouldn't have known much what to do with [free time] even if she had it. So she was there and she was involved, deeply involved, with the children, and he let her be so because he was deeply involved with what he was doing. And he was doing a very creative thing indeed. I grew up and took it for granted [because] I wasn't aware—it was just soaked in like a sponge.

Well, I got up on the [drafting] stool before I could hardly climb up on it. So I was in the studio [and] it was just part of the life . . . in line with this business of the individual artist's expression in his creative world. He abhorred the machine and the industrial thing that was showing its head in the restriction of creative action. Even though he worked in [Adler and] Sullivan's office, it was a factory and he didn't want a factory. He didn't want to extend that industrialization. So when he came out there to Oak Park he set up an establishment which was highly individualistic. He would have his studio where he could go to it at will and not have to travel the route down to the big city and back again, as he had for years, which consumed time and destroyed the continuity and progressive action. And he went about the business of creating a grammar—architectural grammar—for the new day, the new world, and he did it! I can remember night after night, when I was maybe six or seven [years old], or earlier than that because I went to Hillside [Home School at Spring Green] at that time. . . . He'd come up [to his room] dead tired, dead tired because he was struggling on the [drafting] board himself—nobody else—at night because there wouldn't be any interference. And it was right next to the home, and he could come up and go into bed . . . at two or three o'clock in the morning night after night, day after day, week after week, month after month, year after year. And he'd come up dead tired and I'd be lying in bed. His father taught him how to play [the piano] beautifully. Well, he could play [the piano] as well as he could draw. He did Schubert, it was a great favorite and, of course, [the] pieces of Beethoven. He would relax at the piano and I'd hear this; it was as though I could cry—it was beautiful. . . .

ON HIS FATHER'S ARCHITECTURAL GRAMMAR

This is not too good an example, but it will, in some way, indicate what he was doing. Now here you have the Japanese print—there was a high culture, great sophistication, beauty's essential best in human expression, highly organized, architectonically based, and disciplined, highly disciplined. Here we have the western Europeans . . . in [their] most sophisticated productive era. . . . Now here comes an abstract of Frank Lloyd Wright's small or simple, which is a square with a never-ending line which he adopted . . . Then there are these symbols [of the circle and triangle] into this composition, which is linear, and yet it is also in depth in its overlaying well with the other. So, in the development out of these primary considerations into the present and using the techniques of the trade—the triangle and the T-square—and the architectural approach, which meant correlation, integration, and ideas symbolized—the poetry of condensation and all the rest of it. And out comes this figure . . . here [he points to a design by his father]. Now this is neither European nor is it Japanese. It is U.S.A. 20th-century democracy. No other source! You will find this nowhere else!

[Frank Lloyd Wright's use of the square as his autograph block] as a simple block, as a simple concept of architectonic incorporation. . . . went further than that as you see [in his buildings] based upon the primary forms. He went back to primaries, not to the cluttered and oversophisticated and weak products of the . . . European Renaissance, which to him was decadent; which to [Louis] Sullivan was decadent. They were creating something much stronger-based, more creative, not so imitative, not so bound to a weak and dying tradition, moving ahead on its own volition, with its own original contributions and with the guts to do it. And they gave themselves to it! And they died doing it!

ON TEACHING

He came, on one side, from a family of ministers (those who were dealing with the abstract and religious phenomena, human relationships) and, on the other side, from leading educators (they were professors)—families of teachers and preachers. If he had a contempt for it, the contempt was for those who abused the process of teaching and preaching. He was against teaching and preaching as a profession but not teaching and preaching as to the work that was to be done, because he was himself a teacher and a preacher. And every man has to be that, but he didn't put that first; he didn't make it professionalism and he didn't want to see it made a professionalism. He didn't want to see it become a fixed dead thing. It should be a living one. What bothered him about the academic world which he knew so well was the "dead fish" part of it; the thing that went dead because of the professional sterilization. One of the troubles with the academic world is that it gets ossified in this fashion and is not creative. It is responsible for the destruction of creation and the confusion of youth in its search for help in its creative efforts and growth. This is what he resented, and what he tried to do to the boys who came to him [at the Taliesin Fellowship] was to free them from these plecades [*sic*] of the academic fixation. . . .

He would welcome revolution. He was a revolutionary himself. . . . He was interested in beauty. He was interested in the things that the establishment was not. He was an out-of-liner. The trouble with him was that he would never stay in line. He was not only a "drop out" but a "kick out." He proceeded to construct his world as he knew it should be and well could be constructed. And it took a great deal of courage, determination, and genius, which he had . . . .

This thing of being fashionable, he fought fashion all his life because of its dead hand. Because it standardized and stopped growth. . . .

ON HIS FATHER'S ONE MOST IMPORTANT CONTRIBUTION TO ARCHITECTURE

If I were to sum it up for you it would really be a poem. It would be an extreme abstract—it would have to be, because it would be a summation of many forces . . . and many interrelated parts. Now, of course, that's the business of the architect. So I ought to be able to give it to you in a package right now, maybe, if I wanted to. The question is whether I want to sew it up into a package; the question is whether I could! And I certainly don't want to. This business in . . . packaging everything is doing us in. Let's keep [the work of Frank Lloyd Wright] open and let's not frame it as being the end-all and complete—because it never is. It's always proceeding and, I hope, always enriching.

40

CATHERINE DOROTHY WRIGHT BAXTER

His drama was very evident, I felt, in projecting his thoughts, and [he was] fully aware of it—quite conscious of it. Quite conscious of it, I'm sure. He was very fond of theater. He probably would have been a great actor. . . . I don't know how many lecturers that you know in this past generation . . . who stomped onto the platform the way he did and gave a performance. But, along with the performance, he usually had something to say. Though I'm afraid at times I would shiver a little bit and feel a little bit embarrassed for him and for some of the things he would say that hurt others—actually they did at times. I felt that they could have [been] better left unsaid. But they suited the public.

*C*atherine Dorothy Wright Baxter, Wright's eldest daughter, was born in 1894 and, like her brother Lloyd Wright, grew up in the environment of her father's Oak Park studio. Unlike her brothers Lloyd and John, she did not become an architect. Catherine, who had three children, among them the film actress Anne Baxter (see Chapter 42), died in 1979.

ON WRIGHT'S BIRTH DATE

We still don't know why, but he took my aunt's—his sister's—birth year and just appropriated [it] as his own. He was actually born in 1867, and his sister's date was 1869. I researched a great deal on it, and the thing that finally settled it for me was that Aunt Jenny mentioned the fact that he had [also] changed his mother's birth date, which shocked me [to] no end. He said that it was a confession of the soul, and I didn't like to press him further. I still don't know why father did it. . . . The two years made very little difference.

Catherine Dorothy Wright Baxter's reminiscences were recorded in the late 1960s and were transcribed from Bruce Radde's KPFA-FM (Berkeley, California) radio program "Frank Lloyd Wright: The Shining Brow." Printed with permission of Pacifica Radio Archive.

Frank Lloyd Wright's eldest daughter, Catherine
Dorothy Wright, c. 1896. (Frank Lloyd Wright Home
and Studio Foundation)

LIFE IN THE WRIGHT HOME AROUND 1900

Of course, my only comparison was to see other peoples' homes, which were very conventional. I used to feel disturbed that ours was so different. . . . We had specially designed lamps and, of course, the . . . chair design was entirely different than the things we saw in other places, and we didn't have any cozy corner in our house. . . . The living room . . . in our first house was a little place . . . with seats facing each other. It was nice in our dating days—it was a nook then, but not a cozy corner. The cozy corner of my friend's [house] was hung with swords of Egyptian patterns and things of that kind . . . they were really something . . . the plush curtains and all that sort of thing [page 222].

We had scatter rugs over concrete . . . this was when the studio was built. It had concrete floors. The house was built in 1889, or 1890 perhaps, because mother and father were married in 1889, and they immediately had this house which, as I say, had to be remodeled. . . .

I think that one of the things that always amused me was father having his room—a very beautiful room—with all built-in furniture. . . . It was quite unusual then for the dressers and all the different commodes to be built-in. His room was directly next to the bathroom and, of course, we children had to go to school. We were up at 6:30 in the morning after his working all night. It was a little bit harrowing for him to have to listen to a lot of chatter, with one bathroom for six children—five at least in those days! So it was a very annoying experience, but he lived through it and so did we.

The passageway between our house, the original house, and the studio—father turned that into a kitchen. So mother and I, being the kitchen police of the family, used the kitchen. Father did not want to destroy the lovely willow tree, so he used that as a place for the ice box to be set. The ice box was set in between the two arms of the willow tree, and it was all very well until it rained; which it often did in the city. So mother and I very often did our kitchen police around puddles of water, which was not the concern of my father at all. . . . Even though the trunk of the tree had these sheet-metal things around it, when the tree began to weave back and forth it didn't do much to benefit the water coming down . . . [*laughter*]. The tree has very definite memories [for me] of being . . . a menace, but we circumvented it somehow.

I do recall one of our loveliest rooms was our playroom [page 223]. As near as I can recall, it must have been [added to the house] close to 1900, maybe before then. But father's growing family felt that this was a room that could be a family room, and we didn't have very many family rooms. . . . It was one of the most beautiful rooms I have ever seen, proportionwise and any way. Of course, it was used by the six children as a gathering place. One of my vivid memories is the Christmas parties where the tree was in the center of the room. And, of course, the ceiling was vaulted with one of the most beautiful pieces of scrollwork I have ever seen; [it] was a very great disappointment when I returned to the house to find that it had disappeared. At the end of that room was a beautiful drawing—or a painting, rather—of "The Fisherman and the Genii." It was above the fireplace, which was usually going in the wintertime. At the opposite end [of the room] was a balcony and a small attic. The balcony was used as a gallery for plays that we performed. It provided many hiding places for hide-and-seek and what have you. In that room, too, in those days, father had a [statue of] the "Winged Victory" set up on a pedestal, and that was quite something. I recall it very vividly. Later, father never liked the looks of the grand piano, so he had it shoved underneath the back stairs [of the playroom] and you only saw the keyboard . . . . True to father's tradition, the fact that any-body over five-foot-three (but I mean the grown-ups) would bump their head on the back stairway didn't make any difference [to him] because we could use the front stairway if we wanted to.

Father did play piano, but he loved the aeolian—that was one of his investments—which rolled up to the piano. Father used to work nights, and the piano would be going at all hours of the night—the roller—and he could express himself very beautifully, using these rollers to express himself loud . . . [*laughter*]. He had many sessions which could have bothered us to no end for noise, but it was a great outlet for him when he wasn't able to perform Mozart or Beethoven or what have you on the piano.

On Wright's Dramatic Talents

His drama was very evident, I felt, in projecting his thoughts, and [he was] fully aware of it—quite conscious of it. Quite conscious of it, I'm sure. He was very fond of theater. He probably would have been a great actor. . . . He had very sane thoughts and projected them beautifully at times when he was not on stage. . . .I don't know how many lecturers that you know in this past generation, in the early 1900s, who stomped onto the platform the way he did and gave a performance. But, along with the performance, he usually had something to say. Though I'm afraid at times I would shiver a little bit and feel a little bit embarrassed for him and for some of the things he would say that hurt others—actually they did at times. I felt that they could have [been] better left unsaid. But they suited the public. Perhaps I was more sensitive because I was part of the family picture, and sensitive to criticism also because I had so much of it all my life. . . . I will never forget [that] . . . in San Francisco he waited about three-quarters of an hour to appear on the platform. Then he came swooping on because he had his cape on . . . the great dramatic entrance. I don't think it was unstudied.

41

ROBERT LLEWELLYN WRIGHT

**It is nice having a house my father designed for us.
Most fathers leave their children money. I'd rather have this house.**

*I*n the years from 1955 through 1957, Frank Lloyd Wright designed and completed construction of a house in Bethesda, Maryland, for his youngest son, Robert Llewellyn Wright. Robert Llewellyn once quipped:

Robert Llewellyn Wright, c. 1909. (Frank Lloyd Wright Home and Studio Foundation)

I was an unusual client because I was never asked to pay for any of the extensive architectural services I received. My siblings always complained that my father was overgenerous with me. He did not make me earn money for a college education, for example—an indulgence my brothers, said was denied to them. I think he would have been delighted to design a house for any of his children. He did for my brother Dave. My architect brothers, Lloyd and John, designed their own houses, and my sisters, Frances and Catherine, never asked for a Frank Lloyd Wright house.

Sarah Booth Conroy's "The Right Home for Wright's Son" was published in the *Washington Post* on July 13, 1974. Copyright © The Washington Post. Reprinted with permission.

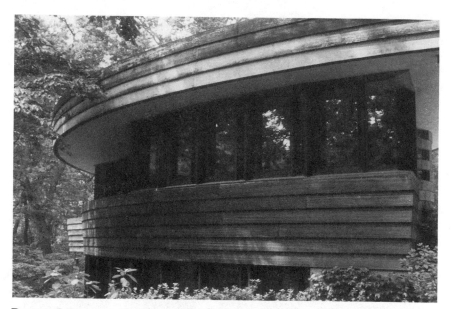

ROBERT LLEWELLYN WRIGHT: *"I don't think he really built for posterity. I think he thought everything would be rebuilt, better, by him."* **An exterior view of the Robert Llewellyn Wright residence (1953) in Bethesda, Maryland. (Patrick J. Meehan)**

In 1974 he was interviewed by the Washington Post. *That interview follows:*

Robert Llewellyn Wright, a Washington lawyer, remembers a particular night his father, Frank Lloyd Wright, spent with the son's family.

"Early in the morning my wife and I heard someone sawing. We quickly came down the stairs to see my father sawing off the back legs of a chair he'd designed and given us 20 years ago. 'I thought about this chair for 20 years,' he said. 'And this morning I realized why it isn't comfortable. The back legs need to be shortened.' And he was right."

From the suburban Maryland road, the only evidence of a house designed by the best-known American architect of the last 100 years is a mailbox set into an "FLLW" red square ("FLLW" was Wright's signature on his structures). The house itself is set below the hill's summit, snuggled into the slope.

Visitors drive into an "arrival court" covered with gravel. From there, the guest sees the curve of the slag block wall, with a towerlike protuberance for the kitchen.

Greeting visitors, a constant occurrence for the owner of any Wright house, is Robert, the youngest of the architect's children by his first wife. The son now is in his early seventies.

ROBERT LLEWELLYN WRIGHT: *". . .my father would turn up at the house without notice and rearrange the furniture. I think he always did indeed feel that any house he had designed still belonged to him."* The David Wright residence (1950) in Phoenix, Arizona. Frank Lloyd Wright originally called this design for his son "How to Live in the Southwest." (Patrick J. Meehan)

He pointed to the curve of the kitchen. "That was the biggest change my wife and I made in my father's plan. He had intended the kitchen to be two stories, but we felt we needed a second bathroom because the three children were home then. There should have been a tall, thin window going up two stories to light the kitchen." You could see that, after the years, the change still worried the son.

"The Taliesin apprentice (Robert Beharka, now of Los Banos, California) who supervised our house was shocked that my father would let us make such a major change in the plan."

"But I'm glad we did," Mrs. [Robert Llewellyn] Wright interrupted.

"We found him very accommodating," his son said, "though everybody's heard stories about how he treated his clients. But, then, if you just wanted somebody to draw up your plans, you shouldn't pay the money to hire Frank Lloyd Wright. My sister Catherine, for instance, built four houses, none of them designed by my father, but then I think she always liked her own way better.

"My brother David, who lived near my father in Arizona, not far from Taliesin, used to have a bit of trouble with him. Dave's wife was a meticulous housekeeper. But my father would turn up at the house without notice and rearrange the furniture. I think he always did indeed feel that any house he had designed still belonged to him. He liked change. He was always tearing down and rebuilding Taliesin. I don't think he really built for posterity. I think he thought everything would be rebuilt, better, by him."

Today, Robert Wright worries about the fungus and the carpenter bees attacking the Philippine mahogany bent to girdle his house.

"I would hate to have to find somebody today who would understand how to wet and bend the boards like these," he said.

The house is shaped almost like an almond, opposing the hill's slope. The same curve, the house's basic module, is scored into the red concrete which forms the floors of the first story. Stools and a table in the living room all echo the house's shape.

"It's funny how people are still afraid of anything unusual," Robert says. "I couldn't get an upholsterer to put new fabric on that stool. So I did it myself. That was why my father always had to send an apprentice to act as contractor—the workmen didn't know how to build his way. They always said those glass corners couldn't be done." (Most Wright corners are made of two pieces of glass butted against each other.)

The apprentice cut the block himself in the fireplace to let heat from the chimney into the room.

"It's strange now to remember that when we built this house in 1956, we couldn't get a bank loan on the design. We had put off having my father do us a house for years, because back then he insisted that we have at least an acre of land, and we couldn't afford it.

"Finally, we took his advice and bought a two-acre lot the builders didn't want. It was his sort of site, on a slope with lots of natural planting.

"We borrowed from a friend to get the house constructed. Then we had a time finding an appraiser who would say it was worth half what it cost. It cost $40,000, and we wanted a $20,000 mortgage. Well, it's all paid for now, anyway. The appraisers didn't like the site or the slag block, but they just weren't used to anything different."

The only things the Wrights regret now are the places where the design had to be scaled down to fit the budget.

"The dining area, for instance. When he came to stay with us, after the house was built, he thought it looked too cramped, so he put in wall-to-wall mirror to reflect the outside.

"I think that the play of light and shadow was his greatest thing. He really understood it. It's a practical thing, too. The house is oriented south by southwest. In the winter the living room and the three bedrooms upstairs are flooded with light. In the summer, because of the overhang, the sun doesn't come in at all. It certainly saves on both heating and air conditioning.

"We put in an attic fan, though my father said we wouldn't need it, and we didn't for cooling. We put the air conditioning in because of the humidity."

Besides the light patterns, caused by the deep windows with their protruding mullions (framing pieces), the house has another Wright characteristic—the sand-colored, textured plaster ceilings Robert remembers from his childhood in the house in Oak Park, Illinois [page 222].

The fireplace, just the height of Mrs. Wright, is another Wright characteristic—the fireplace as the focal point. The Wrights admit this one sometimes bumps heads.

The house has double decks. One extends the living room on the first floor, with a lily pool sunk into the center of the curve. On the second floor, the balcony curves off the master bedroom and the Wrights' daughter's room. (The three children are now grown and away from home.)

The deck springs a bit as you walk on it. "A friend of mine used to tease me and say, 'If you jump up and down on it, you'll tip the house over.' "

Robert, as did his father, enjoys repartee, but, though he jokes about the house, he's very serious about the pleasure in it.

"It is nice having a house my father designed for us. Most fathers leave their children money. I'd rather have this house."

4 2

A N N E   B A X T E R

**He enjoyed my career and I revered his genius. We laughed a lot together.
He taught me to mistrust facades and always to observe life beneath
the surfaces; to find excitement in a seed pod or beauty in a carpenter's
hammer. He gave me other, inner eyes. I gave him pleasure as a lively
audience and as his favorite Taffy's daughter.**

*The Oscar-winning movie actress Anne Baxter (1923–85) was Frank
Lloyd Wright's granddaughter. She was the daughter of Wright's eldest
daughter, Catherine.*

*Anne Baxter won an Academy Award as best supporting actress for her per-
formance in the 1946 adaptation of Somerset Maugham's* The Razor's Edge.
*She was also nominated for an Oscar four years later for her portrayal of the
scheming young actress in the film* All About Eve. *Her many other films include*
Angel on My Shoulder *(1946),* The Ten Commandments *(1956), and*
Chase a Crooked Shadow *(1957).*

*Following her grandfather's death, Anne Baxter traveled to Australia and
set aside her acting career for a significant period of time*

My suitcase was half-packed for the trip home tomorrow. I'd discovered that for an extra fifty dollars I could fly back to California through the
Orient, a part of the world I'd never seen. Friends had armed me with letters of introduction, and I was hungry for the whole adventure. The high
points would be Angkor Wat and a stay in Tokyo's Imperial Hotel, which
my grandfather had designed in [1915]. Frank Lloyd Wright was my
mother's father. She was the favorite as a child and he used to call her
"Taffy." She was beautiful and saucy and thoroughly individualistic, all of
which he loved. But when the family broke apart she'd understandably sid-
ed with her mother and there had been many painful scenes. He and I had
no such ravines between us and had discovered deep affection easily. He
enjoyed my career and I revered his genius. We laughed a lot together. He
taught me to mistrust facades and always to observe life beneath the surfaces; to find excitement in a seed pod or beauty in a carpenter's hammer.

He gave me other, inner eyes. I gave him pleasure as a lively audience and as his favorite Taffy's daughter. . . .

Japan was hovering on the brink of very early spring. I was ushered into the lobby of the hotel it had been my lifetime wish to see, only to find I'd been housed in the "new" non–Frank Lloyd Wright wing, a tasteless glass box. I threw a polite fit, and with abject apologies the management changed me

Anne Baxter with uncles David Wright (center) and Lloyd Wright at a Wright family reunion at the Frank Lloyd Wright Home and Studio Foundation in Oak Park, Illinois. (Frank Lloyd Wright Home and Studio Foundation, Wright Family Collection)

to one of Grandfather's elegant small suites. Of course it was small-scaled. Grandfather had designed the whole place for the Japanese people, not rangy overgrown Americans, for God's sake. He always said anyone over 5'10″ was a weed. Grandfather was 5'10″.

The army of occupation had painted cheap gold paint in between every poured-concrete design. Awful. What a legacy. Never mind, that romantic building still triumphed over earthquakes and armies.

And now home. Home and Katrina, my seven-and-half-year-old. I wanted to have some days alone with her before we went to Grandfather's for Easter in Arizona.

Taliesin means "shining brow" in Welsh; Grandfather had named both his homes Taliesin (Tal-ee-*es*-in). Easter celebrations at Taliesin West were unlike any in the world. Arizona is dramatically beautiful in spring, and Grandfather loved drama. He had designed a theater for me when I was three years old—sowing a potent seed. . . .

We drove out across the Paradise Valley on the dirt road to Taliesin. That Easter morning was soaked in blinding desert sun. The sweep of buildings cut clean lines into an intense blue sky, as married to that rock-strewn desert floor as anything he'd ever built [pages 139, 149, and 150].

View of the pool (foreground) and main entrance of the lobby wing at the Imperial Hotel (1915), reconstructed at the Museum Meiji Mura near Nagoya, Japan (1976). The original building was constructed in Tokyo and, because of its unique structural design, survived the earthquake of 1923. (Juro Kikuchi)

"Look at the balloons!" cried Katrina, her green eyes flashing. They were marvelous, straining straight up on their strings, shouting with gay color in windless air. Everything and everyone formed kaleidoscopes of multi-color. Desert flowers festooned the long tables. Young men and women apprentices from the Fellowship moved to greet the arriving guests; we embraced other Wright family members; of the six in Grandfather's original family, three were there: David, Lloyd, and Mother, each with children and grandchildren to join the celebration—not only of Easter, but of their father.

There he came, arm in arm with my step-grandmother, who wore a bright straw hat with flowers in her hair. Though almost 92, he walked with small panther-smooth steps, the most graceful man I ever knew. He was dressed in white linen, a dashing soft-brimmed straw hat shaded his merry eyes, and he exuded geniality and delight.

We greeted one another with joy. The quality of our time together had been matchless, and we both savored that rare fact.

The apprentices sang songs, from ancient Gregorian chants to spirituals, and we all deeply felt the perfection of those sun-drenched moments in another world. Or was it the quintessence of the best of this one: an atmosphere conceived by a magnificently creative spirit, whose explosive, husky laughter infected us all with ebullience?

The day ended with more music; a concert by a fine young pianist named Carol Robinson. Music was something else my grandfather and I shared; it was a necessity to both of us. How he loved to play grandiose Beethoven-like chords on finely tuned pianos! . . .

A few days later Grandfather fell dangerously ill. An operation was performed and he rallied with incredible stamina. Two nights later I wakened from a peculiarly distressing nightmare: in a vast twilight valley a great dark bird with mile-wide wings bore down upon me, roaring with speed. Cold with fright, I snapped on the light. It was three o'clock. I tried to calm myself reading, and as I turned out the light an hour later the phone rang; it was my mother.

"Anne—Papa died an hour ago." I comforted her as best I could, put down the phone, and wept.

A thousand comments were made about Grandfather's extraordinary genius, his stormy life, his work—all to do with his public self. San Francisco's educational television station planned a memorial show, as his last building was being completed just north of the city. They called and asked if I would talk informally about his more private self, his early family days. Mother and I discussed it, and it seemed to help her to talk about the helter-skelter Wright family and the fun they shared, as well as the hardships. With her blessing I said I'd contribute what I could to a truthful image.

The show was beautifully done and very moving. Grandfather's roots were so vibrantly American that just speaking about him made you believe all over again in native American space and beauty and tenacity and daring.

When it was over, I walked away shaken by emotion and oddly aimless. . . .

[Later] I felt drawn there [to Taliesin West] by a yearning to once again be where his genius reverberated. The students would have gone north to Taliesin East in Wisconsin. Only a few hardy caretakers would be there. June could be fierce, and Grandfather never air-conditioned the free-flowing desert air at Taliesin. The three of us [Baxter, Katrina, and Baxter's husband Randolph ("Ran") Galt] took off for Arizona. . . .

Taliesin [West] was unutterably depressing to me. He was gone. The spirit was gone. The genius loci had gone. Only the stones were warm from baking desert. Later I wandered off alone. Ran found me standing in the gloom of the empty theater where we all had supper and chamber music at Easter. He gathered me in his arms without a word.

"We shouldn't have come," he said after a moment.

"I'm OK," I muttered into his shirt. "I had to take one more look. Thank God you're with me."

I took a farewell look, and never went back to Taliesin again.

We'd rented a car and, sensing my solemn mood, Ran changed the subject as we drove back to the sprawl of Phoenix.

ANNE BAXTER: *"I took a farewell look and never went back to Taliesin again."* **The entrance gate at Taliesin West (1937). (Patrick J. Meehan)**

EPILOGUE

Arch Oboler, a client, once asked Wright about the future of his work after his death. Oboler reported the following response:

> . . . all the animation and the fun he had in his face—he always had a sparkle in his eye when we talked . . . the fun went out of his face. He thought a while and said, "I really don't know, I really don't know." Because he knew what I meant was not a continuation of his style of work but a continuation of his genius.

Flying back from Wright's funeral in Wisconsin, John Noble Richards, then president of the American Institute of Architects, wrote the following:

> His continuing influence assured.
> This century's architectural achievements would be unthinkable without him.
> He has been a teacher to all of us.

NOTES

PART I: IN HIS OWN WORDS

Chapter 1

Wright's appearance at the American Municipal Association conference was described in the November 27, 1956, edition of the *Capital Times* (Madison, Wisconsin).

One of the most noteworthy of Wright's debates with William Zeckendorf took place on April 22, 1956, in the studios of WRCA-TV in Washington, D.C., and was broadcast on the NBC television program "The American Forum of the Air." The complete text of that debate appears in Patrick J. Meehan's *The Master Architect: Conversations with Frank Lloyd Wright* pp. 134–52.

Chapter 3

Wright's testimony before Representatives Mahon, Scrivner, Deane, and Whitten is extracted from the public record of the Military Construction Appropriations for 1956. Hearings before a subcommittee on the Department of the Air Force, 84th Congress, 1st Session, 1955, pp. 554–61. Wright's testimony before Senators Chavez, Stennis, and Saltonstall is extracted from the public record of the U.S. Senate Committee on Appropriations. The Supplemental Appropriations Bill, 1956. Full committee hearings on H.R. 7278, 84th Congress, 1st Session, 1955, pp. 337–40.

Although Wright prepared a design for the U.S. embassy in Japan, there is evidence that he was never retained for this design. See Michael Kopp's "Mr. Wright in Japan: Beyond the Imperial," *Architecture*, Vol. 78, No. 1, January 1989, p. 72.

For a discussion of Wright's attempt to secure the commission for the National Cultural Center (the John F. Kennedy Center for the Performing Arts) in Washington, D.C., see Patrick J. Meehan's *Truth Against the World: Frank Lloyd Wright Speaks for an Organic Architecture*, pp. 412–41.

PART II: ARCHITECTS

Chapter 4

Bruce Goff's introduction to the work of Frank Lloyd Wright has been described briefly in Patrick J. Meehan's *The Master Architect: Conversations with Frank Lloyd Wright*, pp. 169–72. The most extensive published account of the friendship between Wright and Goff can be found in David Gilson Delong's *The Architecture of Bruce Goff: Buildings and Projects, 1916–1974* and *Bruce Goff: Toward Absolute Architecture*.

The dialogue between Wright and Philip Johnson is explored in greater detail in Bruce Brooks Pfeiffer's *Letters to Architects: Frank Lloyd Wright.*

Chapter 5

Wright's discussion with University of California architecture students about R. Buckminster Fuller can be found in Patrick J. Meehan's *The Master Architect: Conversations with Frank Lloyd Wright*, p. 213.

Chapter 6

For a discussion of the Princeton Conference and the text of Wright's speech at the conference, see Patrick J. Meehan's *Truth Against the World: Frank Lloyd Wright Speaks for an Organic Architecture*, pp. 275–82.

Chapter 7

An interview in the early 1980s can be found in Charles Jencks's *Kings of Infinite Space: Frank Lloyd Wright and Michael Graves*, back cover.

Chapter 8

Details of Frank Lloyd Wright's initial meeting with Ludwig Mies van der Rohe can be found in Edgar Tafel's *Apprentice to Genius: Years with Frank Lloyd Wright*, pp. 69–80. During this initial visit Wright presented Mies his concept for Broadacre City. See Patrick J. Meehan,s *Truth Against the World: Frank Lloyd Wright Speaks for an Organic Architecture*, pp. 349–61. For a record of Wright's correspondence with Mies van der Rohe, see Anthony Alofsin's *Frank Lloyd Wright: An Index to the Taliesin Correspondence.*

Wright's conversations with Carl Sandburg can be found in Patrick J. Meehan's *The Master Architect: Conver-sations with Frank Lloyd Wright*, pp.243–70.

PART III: CLIENTS

Chapter 12

Loren B. Pope's Twenty-Five Years Later: Still a Love Affair" was adapted from Helen Duprey Bullock and Terry B. Morton's *The Pope-Leighey House.* Courtesy of The Preservation Press, National Trust for Historic Preservation.

Chapter 15

Wright's discussion of his design for the proposed Nicholas P. Daphne Funeral Chapels can be found in *Architectural Forum*, Vol. 88, No. 1, January 1948, p. 116. Also see Patrick J. Meehan's *Truth Against the World: Frank Lloyd Wright Speaks for an Organic Architecture*, pp. 191 and 203.

Anthony Alofsin's *Frank Lloyd Wright: An Index to the Taliesin Correspondence* indicates that Wright and Daphne corresponded from August 1944 through August 1948.

Chapter 18

For a more complete discussion of Wright's efforts on hospital design, see Patrick J. Meehan's *Truth Against the World: Frank Lloyd Wright Speaks for an Organic Architecture*, pp. 185–209.

PART IV: APPRENTICES

The reminiscences of other former apprentices of Frank Lloyd Wright's—Kamal Amin, Aubrey

Banks, Richard Carney, David Dodge, Minerva Montooth, Frances Nimton, Ling Po, John Rattenbury, Kay Schneider, and Michael Sutton—can be found in Bruce Brooks Pfeiffer's *Frank Lloyd Wright: The Crowning Decade, 1949-1959*, pp. 169–94.

Chapter 20

William Beye Fyfe's reminiscences are excerpted from a panel discussion, "I Remember Frank Lloyd Wright," held on May 11, 1982, at Unity Church in Oak Park, Illinois.

Chapter 22

Marya de Czarnecka Lilien's reminiscences are excerpted from a panel discussion, "I Remember Frank Lloyd Wright," held on May 11, 1982, at Unity Church at Oak Park, Illinois.

Chapter 23

The reminiscences of Gordon O. Chadwick were extracted and reedited by Patrick J. Meehan from *The Pope-Leighey House*. Courtesy The Preservation Press, National Trust for Historic Preservation. The dialogue, as published in that book, was edited by Marguerite B. Gleysteen. Gleysteen's text was reworked for this collection by the editor.

Chapter 24

Aaron Green recounted his experiences assisting in the design of the Marin County Civic Center in his book *An Architecture for Democracy: The Marin County Civic Center*. A detailed account of Wright's 1957 visit to Marin County, California, can be found in Patrick J. Meehan's *Truth Against the World: Frank Lloyd Wright Speaks for an Organic Architecture*, pp. 381–411.

See Chapter 37 for further discussion of the Hanna residence. Still more information on the Hanna residence can be found in Paul R. and Jean S. Hanna's *Frank Lloyd Wright's Hanna House: The Client's Report*. Correspondence with Aaron Green can be found in Paul R. and Jean S. Hanna's *The Hanna House Documents*.

Chapter 25

The original preliminary drawings of the Neils House appear as illustrations 506 and 509 in Bruce Brooks Pfeiffer's *Volume 7, Frank Lloyd Wright Monograph 1942-1950*, pp. 260–61. Other drawings and photographs in that publication are of the revised house.

Chapter 26

Wright's remarks at the University of Arkansas are taken from Patrick J. Meehan's *The Master Architect: Conversations with Frank Lloyd Wright*, p. 234.

Jones's remarks after receiving the AIA Gold Medal are excerpted from "In Wright's footsteps: Ark. architect Jones accepts Gold Medal," *CNPN Convention News: Recap Edition*, p. 15.

PART V: FRIENDS AND ACQUAINTANCES

Chapter 29

Detailed accounts of three visits that Wright made to universities—Oklahoma (May 2, 1952), California-Berkeley (April 24 and 27, 1957), and Arkansas-Fayetteville (April 15, 1958)—can be found in Patrick J. Meehan's *The Master Architect: Conversations with Frank Lloyd Wright*, pp. 169–240.

In October 1957 Wright also addressed the Michigan Society of Architects at the Ford Auditorium in Detroit. See Patrick J. Meehan's *Truth Against the World: Frank Lloyd Wright Speaks for an Organic Architecture*, pp. 143–55.

Chapter 34

The excerpt from Wright's conversation with Mary Margaret McBride is taken from Patrick J. Meehan's *Truth Against the World: Frank Lloyd Wright Speaks for an Organic Architecture*, p. 3.

Chapter 37

The relationship between Frank Lloyd Wright and Lewis Mumford is further illuminated by 12 of Wright's letters to Mumford reprinted in Bruce Brooks Pfeiffer's *Frank Lloyd Wright: Letters to Architects* (pp. 140–52); these letters span the period from 1928 through 1958. In addition, Anthony Alofsin's *Frank Lloyd Wright: An Index to the Taliesin Correspondence* reveals that there were 69 pieces of correspondence from Wright to Mumford between 1928 and 1958 and 74 pieces from Mumford to Wright between 1926 and 1958. These letters, as well as Mumford's recollections and remembrances of Wright, offer insight into the evolution of their friendship.

Further information on the Hanna residence can be found in Paul R. and Jean S. Hanna's *Frank Lloyd Wright's Hanna House: The Client's Report*. Also, correspondence by Lewis Mumford can be found in Paul R. and Jean S. Hanna's *The Hanna House Documents*.

PART VI: FAMILY

Chapter 38

Further reminiscences by Olgivanna Lloyd Wright, as well as reminiscences by the Wrights' daughter, Iovanna Lloyd Wright, can be found in Bruce Brooks Pfeiffer's *Frank Lloyd Wright: The Crowning Decade, 1949-1959*, pp. 99–168.

Chapter 41

Robert Llewellyn Wright's quip is excerpted from his article "A Son as Client," *The Frank Lloyd Wright Newsletter*, Vol. 3, No. 2, Second Quarter 1980, p. 7.

EPILOGUE

See also Chapter 13 for Arch Oboler's reminiscences.

John Noble Richards's comments are extracted from his article "Frank Lloyd Wright's Funeral, April 12, 1959: Impressions Written on an Airplane," *AIA Journal*, Vol. XXXI, May 1959, p. 44.

BIBLIOGRAPHY

Alofsin, Anthony, ed. *Frank Lloyd Wright: An Index to the Taliesin Correspondence*. New York: Garland, 1988.

American Institute of Architects. *Accent on Architecture: Honors 1990*. Washington, D.C.: American Institute of Architects Press, 1990.

Auer, James. "Mrs. Wright Talks About the Man," *Milwaukee (Wis.) Journal*, August 24, 1980, part 5, p. 4.

Baxter, Anne. *Intermission: A True Story*. New York: G. P. Putnam's Sons, 1976.

Blake, Peter. "A Conversation with Mies." In *Four Great Makers of Modern Architecture: Gropius, Le Corbusier, Mies van der Rohe, Wright*. New York: Trustees of Columbia University, 1963.

Brooks, H. Allen. *The Prairie School: Frank Lloyd Wright and His Midwest Contemporaries*. New York: W. W. Norton, 1972.

Bullock, Helen Duprey, and Terry B. Morton, eds. *The Pope-Leighey House*. Washington, D.C.: Preservation Press, 1969.

Busignami, Alberto. *Gropius*. London: Hamlyn, 1973.

Conroy, Sarah Booth. "The Right Home for Wright's Son," *Washington Post*, July 13, 1974.

Cook, Jeffrey. *The Architecture of Bruce Goff*. New York: Harper & Row, 1978.

DeLong, David Gilson. *The Architecture of Bruce Goff: Buildings and Projects, 1916–1974*, New York: Garland, 1977.

_____. *Bruce Goff: Toward Absolute Architecture*. New York and Cambridge, Mass.: Architectural History Foundation and MIT Press, 1988.

Donoian, John, and Dennis Doordan. "A Magnificent Adventure: An Interview with Mrs. Sarah (Melvyn) Maxwell Smith about the Smith House by Frank Lloyd Wright," *The Journal of Architectural Education* 39, no. 4 (Summer 1986), pp. 7–10.

Dunlap, Beth. "An Original American Genius," *Miami Herald*, April 1, 1984, pp. 1E and 4E.

Evjue, William T. "Two Men in Wisconsin Who Had Greatest Influence on Editor," *Capital Times* (Madison, Wis.), June 9, 1959.

Fitch, James Marston. *Walter Gropius*. New York: George Braziller, 1960.

"Frank Lloyd Wright," *House & Home*, May 1956, pp. 164–68.

Gebhard, David. *Lloyd Wright, Architect: 20th Century Architecture in an Organic Exhibition*. Santa Barbara, Calif.: University of California, 1971.

Geiger, John. "Recollection: A Summer's Work—Not in The Taliesin Drafting Room," *Journal of the Taliesin Fellows*, no. 2 (Fall 1990), pp. 13–15.

Goff, Bruce. "Die Drei Feinde Moderner Kunst," *Baukunst und Werkform*, July 1953, pp. 374–76.

Gordon, Elizabeth, ed. "A Great Frank Lloyd Wright House," *House Beautiful*, January 1963, entire issue.

Green, Aaron G. *An Architecture for Democracy: The Marin County Civic Center*. San Francisco: Grendon Publishing, 1990.

Griggs, Joseph. "Alfonso Iannelli, The Prairie Spirit in Sculpture," *The Prairie School Review 2*, no. 4 (Fourth Quarter 1965), pp. 5–23 and covers.

Gropius, Walter. *Apollo in the Democracy: The Cultural Obligation of the Architect*. New York: McGraw-Hill Book Co., 1968.

_____. *The New Architecture and the Bauhaus*, Cambridge, Mass.: MIT Press, 1968.

_____. *Scope of Total Architecture*. New York: Collier Books, 1962.

Hanna, Paul R., and Jean S. Hanna. *Frank Lloyd Wright's Hanna House: The Clients' Report*. New York and Cambridge, Mass.: Architectural History Foundation and MIT Press, 1981.

Hitchcock, Henry-Russell. *In the Nature of Materials: 1887–1941, the Buildings of Frank Lloyd Wright*. New York: Duell, Sloan and Pearce, 1942.

Howe, John H. *John H. Howe: Architect/Visiting Professor, Nihon University*. Tokyo: Nihon University, 1975.

"In Wright's footsteps: Ark. architect Jones accepts Gold Medal." In *CNPN Convention News: Recap Edition*. Chicago: McGraw-Hill, 1990.

Jencks, Charles. *Kings of Infinite Space: Frank Lloyd Wright and Michael Graves*. New York: St. Martin's Press, 1983.

Johnson, Hoyt. "Conversation with Vernon Swaback," *Scottsdale (Ariz.) Scene Magazine*, April 1986, pp. 102–08.

Johnson, Philip. "The Frontiersman," *Architectural Review* CVI (England), August 1949, pp. 105–06.

_____. *Mies van der Rohe*. New York: Museum of Modern Art, 1947.

_____. *Mies van der Rohe*. Rev. ed. New York: Museum of Modern Art, 1953.

Manson, Grant Carpenter. *Frank Lloyd Wright to 1910: The First Golden Age*. New York: Reinhold Publishing Corp., 1958.

Meehan, Patrick J. *Bruce Goff, Architect: Writings 1918–1978* (Architecture Series: Bibliography A-73) Monticello, Ill.: Vance Bibliographies, August 1979.

_____. *Lloyd Wright: A Prairie School Architect* (Architecture Series: Bibliography A-3). Monticello, Ill.: Vance Bibliographies, July 1978.

Meehan, Patrick J., ed. *The Master Architect: Conversations with Frank Lloyd Wright*. New York: John Wiley & Sons, 1984.

_____. *Truth Against the World: Frank Lloyd Wright Speaks for an Organic Architecture*, New York: John Wiley & Sons, 1987.

Mumford, Lewis. *Sketches from Life*. New York: Dial Press, 1982.

"A New House by Frank Lloyd Wright Opens Up a New Way of Life on the Old Site," *House & Home*, November 1953, pp. 122–27.

Noble, Charles. *Philip Johnson*. New York: Simon and Schuster, 1972.

Oboler, Arch. "He's Always Magnificently Wright," *Reader's Digest*, February 1958, pp. 49–54.

Owings, Nathaniel Alexander. *The Spaces in*

Between: An Architect's Journey. Boston: Houghton Mifflin Co., 1973.

Pfeiffer, Bruce Brooks. *Frank Lloyd Wright Treasures of Taliesin: Seventy-Six Unbuilt Designs.* Fresno, Calif., and Carbondale, Ill.: Press at California State University and Southern Illinois University Press.

Pfeiffer, Bruce Brooks, ed. *Frank Lloyd Wright: The Crowning Decade, 1949–1959.* Fresno, Calif.: Press at California State University, 1989.

_____. *Frank Lloyd Wright: Letters to Apprentices.* Fresno, Calif.: Press at California State University, 1982.

_____. *Frank Lloyd Wright: Letters to Architects.* Fresno, Calif.: Press at California State University, 1984.

_____. *Frank Lloyd Wright: Letters to Clients.* Fresno, Calif.: Press at California State University, 1986.

_____. *Volume 4: Frank Lloyd Wright Monograph 1914–1923.* Tokyo: A.D.A. EDITA, 1985.

_____. *Volume 5: Frank Lloyd Wright Monograph 1924–1936.* Tokyo: A.D.A. EDITA, 1985.

_____. *Volume 6: Frank Lloyd Wright Monograph 1937-1941.* Tokyo: A.D.A. EDITA, 1986.

_____. *Volume 7: Frank Lloyd Wright Monograph 1942-1950.* Tokyo: A.D.A. EDITA, 1988.

_____. *Volume 8: Frank Lloyd Wright Monograph 1951-1959.* Tokyo: A.D.A. EDITA, 1988.

_____. *Volume 10: Frank Lloyd Wright Preliminary Studies 1917–1932.* Tokyo: A.D.A. EDITA, 1986.

_____. *Volume 11: Frank Lloyd Wright Preliminary Studies 1933–1959.* Tokyo: A.D.A. EDITA, 1987.

Pierre, Dorathi Bock. *Memoirs of an American Artist: Sculptor Richard W. Bock.* Los Angeles: C. C. Publishing Co., 1989.

Pope, Loren. "The Love Affair of a Man and His House," *House Beautiful*, August 1948, pp. 32-34, 80, and 90.

Reiach, Allan. "Meetings with Frank Lloyd Wright," *Concrete Quarterly* (England), no. 100, January/March 1974, pp. 38–40.

Saarinen, Aline B. "Taliesin Week-End: Frank Lloyd Wright, 85, Vitally Works On," *New York Times*, August 8, 1954, p. 8X.

Saltzstein, Joan W. "Taliesin Through the Years," *Wisconsin Architect* XL, (October 1969), pp. 14–18.

Sergeant, John. *Frank Lloyd Wright's Usonian Houses: The Case for Organic Architecture.* New York: Whitney Library of Design, 1976.

Sergeant, John, and Stephen Mooring, eds. "Bruce Goff: AD Profiles 16," *Architectural Design* 48 (London), no. 10 (1978), entire issue.

Snyder, Robert, ed. *Buckminster Fuller: An Autobiographical Monologue/Scenario.* New York: St. Martin's Press, 1980.

Spade, Rupert. *Eero Saarinen.* New York: Simon and Schuster, 1971.

Spencer, Brian A. *The Prairie School Tradition.*

New York: Whitney Library of Design, 1979.

Stone, Edward D. "Frank Lloyd Wright: a tribute to a personal hero," *Pacific Architect and Builder* LXVI (March 1960), p. 20.

Storrer, William Allin. *The Architecture of Frank Lloyd Wright: A Complete Catalogue.* 2nd ed. Cambridge, Mass.: MIT Press, 1979.

"Story Behind the Book: An Autobiography," *Publishers Weekly*, July 25, 1977, p. 55.

Tafel, Edgar. *Apprentice to Genius: Years with Frank Lloyd Wright.* New York: McGraw-Hill, 1979.

Temko, Allan. *Eero Saarinen.* New York: George Braziller, 1962.

Twombly, Robert C. *Frank Lloyd Wright: His Life and His Architecture.* New York: John Wiley & Sons, 1979.

Vaughan, Rev. Jos., S.J. "A Priest Tells of Wright," *Capital Times* (Madison, Wis.), May 4, 1959.

von Eckardt, Wolf. *Eric Mendelsohn.* New York: George Braziller, 1960.

"Weiner and Wright," *Inland Architect* XIV (May 1970), p. 19.

Woodward, Christopher. *Skidmore, Owings, & Merrill.* New York: Simon and Schuster, 1970.

Wright, Frank Lloyd. *An Autobiography.* Rev. ed. New York: Horizon Press, 1977.

_____. *Ausgeführte Bauten und Entwürfe von Frank Lloyd Wright.* Berlin: Ernst Wasmuth, 1910.

_____. "Frank Lloyd Wright," *Architectural Forum* 88, no. 1 (January 1948), p. 116.

_____. *Frank Lloyd Wright: Ausgeführte Bauten.* Berlin: Ernst Wasmuth, 1911.

_____. "In the Cause of Architecture," *Architectural Record* 23 (March 1908), pp. 155–221.

_____. *The Living City.* New York: Horizon Press, 1958.

_____. *The Natural House.* New York: Horizon Press, 1954.

_____. "The Shape of the City." In the American Municipal Association's *Proceedings*, 1956, pp. 30–34.

_____. *The Story of the Tower: The Tree That Escaped the Crowded Forest.* New York: Horizon Press, 1956.

_____. "Straight Talk About Miami Architecture," *Miami Herald*, April 1, 1984, pp. 1E and 4E.

Wright, John Lloyd. *My Father Who Is On Earth.* New York: G. P. Putman's Sons, 1946.

Wright, Olgivanna Lloyd. *Our House.* New York: Horizon Press, 1959.

Wright, Robert Llewellyn. "A Son as Client," *The Frank Lloyd Wright Newsletter* 3, no. 2 (Second Quarter 1980), p. 7.

Zeckendorf, William. *The Autobiography of William Zeckendorf.* New York: Holt, Rinehart and Winston, 1970.

Ziegelman, Robert L., FAIA. "Letter on Frank Lloyd Wright's Visit in October 1957," *Portico* 5, no. 3 (Spring 1989), p. 19.

INDEX

Numbers in *italics* refer to illustrations and captions.

academic world, 230
Academy of Arts (Berlin, Germany), 44, 199
Adler and Sullivan, 53, 183, 228
Adler, Dankmar, 53, 183, 228
Affleck, Elizabeth, 95
Affleck, Gregor, residence (Bloomfield Hills, Mich.), 91, 92
Alabama State College, 148
All About Eve, 240
Allegheny River (Pittsburgh), 206
America. *See* United States
American
    family, 6
    people, character of, 20
American Institute of Architects (AIA), 24, 35, 112, 163, 180, 245
American Municipal Association, 2
"An American Architecture: Its Roots, Growth, and Horizons" conference, 34, 117, 218
An Autobiography (by Frank Lloyd Wright), 68, 69, 137, 159, 184, 193–95
Anderson, Sherwood, 201
Angel on My Shoulder, 240
Angkor Wat, 240
Ann Arbor, Mich., 95, 117
Annunciation Greek Orthodox Church (Wauwatosa, Wis.), 119, 184
Antioch College, 136
Apprentice to Genius: Years with Frank Lloyd Wright (by Edgar Tafel), 42
apprenticeship systems, 152
Architects Collaborative, The, 42
architectural design, team approach to, 42, 47, 120
Architectural Forum, 70, 104
architectural grammar, 228, 229
Architectural Record, 34, 112
Architectural Review, 48
architecture
    American, 52, 119, 182
    ancient forms of, 191, 122
    as blind spot of America, 24
    as the basis of a culture, 10
    commissions for, 28
    Greek, 52
    indigenous, 58
    Japanese, 52, 182
    Mayan, 48, 52
    Renaissance, 52, 229
    See also Art Deco, Beaux Arts, International Style, modern architecture, Prarie architecture
Arizona, 166
    desert of, 126, 147, 216
Arizona State Capitol "Oasis" project (Phoenix, Ariz.), 15
Arizona State University, College of Architecture and Department of Planning, 164
Arkansas Times, 163
Art Deco, 202
Art Institute of Chicago, 188
atom bomb, 6
Atomic Energy Commission, 204
Auer, James, 213–17
Ausgeführte Bauten und Entwürfe von Frank Lloyd Wright, 34. *See also* Wasmuth portfolio
Autobiography (by Olgivanna Lloyd Wright), 217
Autobiography of William Zeckendorf, 2
automobiles, design for, 5
Aztecs, 204

Bach, Johann Sebastian, 198
Balmoral Hotel (Miami), 8
Baltimore Building Department, 143
Barcelona (Spain) Pavilion, 54
Barcelona, Spain, 37
Barney, Maginel Wright, *118*, 231
Barnsdall, Aline, residence "Hollyhock" (Los Angeles), *179*
Bauhaus School, 42, 47
Baukunst, 37
Baxter, Anne, 240–44, *241*

on death of Frank Lloyd Wright, 243–44
    on last visit to Taliesin West, 243–44
Baxter, Catherine Dorothy Wright, 56, 231–34, *232*, 235, 237, 240, 242, 243
beauty, 9, 121, 192
Beaux Arts, 34
Becket, Welton, 23
bedroom design, 92
Beethoven, Ludwig von, 198, 229, 234, 243
Beharka, Robert, 237
Belluschi, Pietro, 23
Berger, Gloria, 109
Berger, Robert, 104–09
    on becoming interested in hiring Frank Lloyd Wright, 104
    on design of a doghouse, 108
    on design requirements for the house, 106
    on finishing the Frank Lloyd Wright–designed house, 107
    on hiring Frank Lloyd Wright, 106
    residence (San Anselmo, Calif.), *105*
Besinger, Curtis, 160
Beverly Hills, Calif., 79, 86
"Bicentennial Conference on Planning Man's Physical Environment" conference, 46
Blake, Peter, 53, 54
Bloomfield Hills, Mich., 90, 111
Bock, Richard, 224
Bordon Block (Chicago), 183, 184
Boston, 28
boxes, design of houses as, 157
Brandon, Henry, 66
Breuer, Marcel, 52, 118
Brierly, Cornelia, 184
Brigham, Peter Bent Hospital (Boston), 110
Broadacre City project, 7, 127, *128*, 187, 194
Buffalo, N.Y., 202
Burnham and Root, 53
Burnham, Daniel, 53
Butterfly Bridge project (Spring Green, Wis.), 15

California, 79, 80, 82, 144, 240
    homes in, 78
    southern, 84
Cape Cod style, 69
Capital Times (Madison, Wis.), 190
Capitol, U.S., 27
Cassanova, Frank Lloyd Wright's dog, 191
ceiling design, 92
Central Park (New York City), 6, 74
Cetto, Max, 46
Chadwick, Gordon O., 65, 71, 75, 76, 140–47
Chandler, Ariz., 196
Chekhov, Anton Pavlovich, 204
Cheney, Edwin H., residence (Oak Park, Ill.), 205
Cheney, Mamah Borthwick, 201, 206
Cherokee red paint, as used for Johnson Wax furniture, 120
Chicago, 5, 53, 84, 106, 112, 175, 197, 201, 207, 217, 224
    Academy of Fine Arts, 148
    elevated trains of, 228
    Institute of Design, 178
    south side of, 78
    World's Fair of 1933, 202
Christ, Jesus, 68, 75, 197, 221
Churchill, Winston, 218
cities
    American, 3
    as overgrown villages, 4
    decentralization of, 102
Civil War, 204
Colorado Springs, Colo., 15
Coonley, Mrs. Avery, 75
Corbusier, Le. *See* Le Corbusier
Crystal City project (Washington, D.C.), 71
culture, 120, 121

David (sculpture by Michelangelo), 226
deconstructivists, 120
Department of the Air Force, U.S., 16
Depression, 122
Donoian, John, 88, 90, 91

Douglas, Jim, 16
Drummond, William E., 226

Edinburgh, Scotland, 203
egalitarianism, U.S. drifting toward, 28
Eisenhower, Dwight, 6
Emerson, Ralph Waldo, 68, 75, 204, 206
England, dormitory towns of, 5
Eric Mendelsohn (by Wolf von Eckardt), 198
Euchtman, Joseph, residence (Baltimore), 140, *141*, 143
Europe, 54, 173, 218, 220
Europeans, 58
    domination of modern architectural design, 42
    western, 229
Evanston, Ill., 116, 122
Evening Star (Washington, D.C.), 70, 72
Evjue, William T., 190–92

Fagus Factory (Alfeld a. d. Leine, Germany), 44
Falls Church, Va., 140, 142
family. *See* American, family
Fascism, 52, 204
fashion, 230
Fayetteville, Ark., 162
Federal Bureau of Investigation, 204
Fisherman and the Genii (painting), 233
Florence, Italy
    Villa Fatuna, 226, *227*
Florida, 71
Florida Southern College (Lakeland, Fla.), 11, 12, *12*, 130, 151
Flour City Ornamental Iron Company (Minneapolis), 161
Ford Works Factory (Detroit), 173
form follows function concept, 75
Frank Lloyd Wright Day (Chicago), 165
    testimonial dinner, *165*
Frank Lloyd Wright Foundation, 107, 137, 164, 184, 194, 213
Frank Lloyd Wright Home and Studio (Oak Park, Ill.), 222, 238
    Christmas parties at, 233
    playroom of, 221, 223, *223*, 233
    studio, 218, 231, 232
Frank Lloyd Wright: Letters to Architects (by B. B. Pfeiffer), 200
freedom
    individual, 4
    meaning of, 10
Freeman, Samuel, 61–64
    on the design of his house, 62
    on working with Frank Lloyd Wright, 61
    on Frank Lloyd Wright the man, 63
    residence (Los Angeles), *62*
Froebel kindergarten toys, 221, 222
Frost, Robert, 204
Fuller, R. Buckminster, 39–41
functionalists, 50
furniture, design of, 169
Fyfe, William Beye, 136

Galt, Randolph, 243
Gaudi, Antonio, 37–38
Geddes, Patrick, 200, 203, 204
Geiger, John, 158–61
General Motors, 103
General Motors Technical Center (Warren, Mich.), 111
genius
    American, 4, 7
    Welsh definition of, 4
Germans, as technicians, 226
Germany, 221
glass, 23, 216
God, 13, 26, 90, 188, 189
Goff, Bruce, 34–38, *35*
    on Frank Lloyd Wright's architectural influence, 36
    on meeting Frank Lloyd Wright for first time, 36
Goldfinger, Erno, 174
Goodall, Robert, 136
Grand Rapids, Mich., 100
Green, Aaron G., 56, 107, 117, 148–57, *155*
Green Memories (by Lewis Mumford), 206
Gregorian chants, 242
Griffin, Marion Mahoney. *See* Mahoney, Marion
Griffin, Walter Burley, 116

Gropius, Ise, *43*
Gropius, Walter, 50, 52, 118, 42–47, *43*, 208
    on modern European architects, 45
    on Wright's individualism v. teamwork approach, 47
    residence (Lincoln, Mass.), 45
Guggenheim Museum (New York City), 57, 74, 106, 161, 181, 201, 206

Hanna, Paul R., residence "Honeycomb" (Stanford, Calif.), 157, *209*, 210
Harvard University, 42, 43, 45, 46, 68, 110
Hillside Home School (Spring Green, Wis.), 116, 122, *124*, 127, *127*, 130, 134, 184, 186, 187, 228
Hilton, Conrad, 74
Hiroshige, 180
Hitchcock, Henry-Russell, 205
Hitler, Adolf, 205
Hodiak, Katrina, 241, 242, 243
Hokusai, 180, 205
Hollywood, Calif., 83, 86
Hollywood Bowl, 218
    show people of, 167
Horizon Press, 193
House and Home, 161
House Beautiful, 70, 100
Houston, 163
Howe, John H., 93, 116–35, *117*, *118*, *125*
Hunt, Richard, 27

"I Remember Frank Lloyd Wright" panel discussion (Oak Park, Ill.), 117
Iannelli, Alfonso, 36, 224
Imperial Hotel (Tokyo, Japan), 69, 196, 220, 240, 241, *242*
"In the Realm of Ideas" exhibition, 74
Indiana, 113
International Style, 10, 42, 46, 48, 50, 51, 52, 180, 202

Jacobs, Herbert
    first residence (Madison, Wis.),42, 43, 90, 141, *142*
    second residence (Middleton, Wis.), *51*
Japanese culture, 221
Japanese prints, 129, 201, 229
Jenney, William Le Baron, 53
Johnson, Herbert F., residence "Wingspread" (Wind Point, Wis.), 130, *131*, 187
Johnson, Hoyt, 164–69
Johnson, Philip, 54, 48–52
Johnson Wax Administration Building (Racine, Wis.), *49*, 52, 119, 126, 130, 163, 187, 206, 225, *120*
Jones, Fay, 162–63
Jones, Isabel Roberts, 226
Jones, Jenny [Jennie] Lloyd, 231
Jones, John Lloyd, 159
"Joy and Work Is Man's Desire" (hymn of the Taliesin Fellowship), 134

Kant, Immanuel, 217
Kaufmann, Edgar J. Sr., residence "Fallingwater" (Ohiopyle, Pa.), 70, 80, 129, 130, *131*, 184, 187
Kaufmann, Edgar Jr., 184, 222
Keats, John, 68, 75
Kennedy, John F., Center for the Performing Arts (Washington, D.C.), 31
Klimt, Gustav, 36
Kovass, Steve, 94
Kunin, Larry, 92, 94

Lakeland, Fla. *See* Florida Southern College.
Larkin Company Administration Building (Buffalo, N.Y.), 44, *46*, 202
Laughton, Charles, 84, 85
Le Corbusier, 48, 50, 51, 52, 154, 206
Lee, Gerald Stanley, 11
Leighey, Marjorie, 65, 66, 74
Leighey, Robert and Marjorie, 65
Lescaze, William, 50
Lever Building (New York City), 23
Lewis Mumford: Toward a Human Architecture, 156
Lilien, Marya de Czarnecka, 139
Lloyd-Jones family, 68, 116, 135
Lockhart, Kenneth, 159
London, England, 174
Longman's, Green (publishers), 193

Los Angeles, 14, 83, 85, 98, 202, 224
    Exhibition Pavilion, 178, *179*
Los Banos, Calif., 237

Madison, Wis., 42, 106, 183, 185, 188, 190
Mahoney, Marion, 226
Maine, 73
mansions, Georgian and Elizabethan, 52
Marin County, Calif., 107
    Administration Building, *57*, 148, 153, 155,
    Amphitheater project, 15
    Children's Pavilion project, 15
    Civic Center, 15, 56–58
    Fair Pavilion, 15
    Health and Services Building, 15
    officials of, 56
    people of, 58
    Post Office, 15
Masieri Memorial project (Venice, Italy), 129
Masselink, Eugene, 56, 100, 106, 113, 122, 165, 166,
    172, 174, 175, 184
materials, 55, 68, 216
Mayans, 182, 204
Mayo Clinic, 110
Mayo, Dr. C. W., 110
McBride, Mary Margaret, 193
McCarthy, Charlie, 163
McCoy, Jerry, 75
Melville, Herman, 204
Mendelsohn, Eric, 50, 198–99, *199*
Mendelsohn, Louise, 198–99
Meredith Press, 194
Merrill, John Ogden, 23
metaphysics, 217
Mexico City, Mexico, 46
Miami, 8–14
Michigan, northern, 100
Midway Gardens (Chicago), 202, 224, *203*
Mies van der Rohe (by Philip Johnson), 54
Mies van der Rohe, Ludwig, 50, 51, 53–54, 118, 154,
    206
Mile-High Illinois Skyscraper project (Chicago), 2, 5, 207,
    207
Milianov, Duke Marco, 213
Milwaukee, Wisconsin, 34, 117, 218
    Art Institute, 184
Minneapolis, 132, 202
Missouri, 2, 6
Massachusetts Institute of Technology (MIT), 23, 34
mobocracy, 6
modern architecture, 15, 18, 19, 20, 42, 48, 52, 55, 182
    principles of, 58
Mondrian, Piet, 52
Monona Terrace Civic Center project (Madison, Wis.),
    15, 190
Monongahela River (Pittsburgh), 206
Montenegro, 213, 217
Morgan, Charlie, 116
Moser, Werner M., 198
Moses, Robert, 5, 207
Mount Vernon, Va., 66, 71
Mozart, Wolfgang Amadeus, 188, 234
Mumford, Lewis, 157, 200–10, 221
Mumford, Sophia, 205
Municipal Center (Los Angeles), 178
Museum of Modern Art (New York City), 52
    exhibition of 1932, 50
    exhibition of 1940, 151
    exhibition of 1947, 53
Mussolini, Benito, 52
My Father Who Is On Earth (by John Lloyd Wright), 224

Nakoma Country Club project (Madison, Wis.), 190, 191
Nakoma Golf Course (Madison, Wis.), 190
National Cultural Center (Washington, D.C.), 15, 31
National Trust for Historic Preservation, 66, 70, 74, 140
nature, 3, 6, 9, 25, 40, 50, 52, 55, 68, 75, 90, 214, 216
    principles of, 190, 191
    study of, 121, 162, 216
Nazism, 52, 204, 205
Neils, Henry J., residence (Minneapolis), 158–61, *159*
Nestingen, Mayor Ivan, *165*
Neutra, Richard, 50, 52, 198, 220

New Deal, 69, 70
New England, 43
New Mexico, 174
New World, 172
New York City, 4, 5, 11, 14, 19, 24, 57, 74, 80, 144,
    172, 180, 201
    critics, 83
    World's Fair of 1939, 202
New Yorker, The, 206
New York Telegram, 193
New York Times, 69, 73, 178
Nietzsche, Friedrich Wilhelm, 217
Nuclear Age, 205

Oak Park, Ill., 164, 218, 231, 239
Oboler, Arch, 76–87
    on death of Frank Lloyd Wright, 245
    on discovering and finding Wright, 83
    residence and gatehouse (Malibu, Calif.), *77, 78*
    retreat "Eaglefeather" (Malibu, Calif.), *78*
Ocatilla Desert Camp for Frank Lloyd Wright (Chandler,
    Ariz.), 140, 196
Olmsted, Frederick Law, 204
Olympus, 79
organic architecture, 20, 50, 52, 68, 111, 118, 119, 120,
    121, 126, 129, 162,   163, 200, 207
    as architecture of unity, 119
    meaning of word, 190–91
    philosophy of, 152
    principles of, 119, 121
Orr, Douglas William, 163
Ottawa, Canada, 196
Oud, J. J. P., 50
"Our House" (newspaper column by Olgivanna Lloyd
    Wright), 190
Owings, Nathaniel Alexander, 16
Oyakawa, Steve, 159, 161

Palmer, Mary, 95, 176
Palmer, William, 95, 176
    residence (Ann Arbor, Mich.), *95*
Palo Alto, Calif., 202
Panama Canal, 80
Paradise Valley (Scottsdale, Ariz.), 106, 241
Park Avenue (New York City), 31
Parker, Alfred Browning, 8
Pearce, John N., 140, 142, 143, 144, 146, 147
Pentagon, 204
Peters, William Wesley, 56, 102, 113, 130, 136–38, 143,
    158, 184
Pfeiffer, Bruce Brooks, 200
Philadelphia, 28
Phoenix, Arizona, 86, 174. *See also* Arizona State Capitol
    "Oasis" project
Pittsburgh Point Park project, 206
Pittsfield (Mass.) Defense Plant project, 15
Plaza Hotel (New York City), 194, 201
pollution, air and water, 6
Polytechnic Institute of Lwow, Poland, 139
Pope-Leighey House (Mount Vernon, Va.), 66, *67*
Pope, Loren B., 65–75
    residence (Falls Church and Mount Vernon, Va.),
    67, 140–47, *145*
post-modernists, 120
Potomac River (Washington, D.C.), 31
Prairie architecture, 48, 191
prefabricated houses, 201
Price Tower (Bartlesville, Okla.), 40, *41*
Princeton University, 71
profit system, 11
proportion, 121
Publishers Weekly, 193

Radde, Bruce, 61, 63, 109
Raeburn, Ben, 193–95
railroads, 7
Ray Hubbard Associates, Inc., 156
Reiach, Alan, 172–75
Rice University, 162
Richards, John Noble, 245
Richardson, H. H., 48
Richland Center, Wis., 214, 225
Rickert, Howard, 70, 143, 144
Robie, Frederick G., residence (Chicago), 44, *45,* 83

Robinson, Carol, 243
Rochester, Minn., 113
Rocky Mountains (Colorado), 17, 29
Rodin, Auguste, 180
Romeo and Juliet Windmill (Spring Green, Wis.), 185, *186*
Root, John Wellborn, 53
Rosenbaum, Stanley, residence (Florence, Ala.), *151*
Round the World on a Penny, 185
Rowan, Edward, 70, 69
Royal Institute of British Architects (RIBA), 174, 182

Saarinen, Aline B., 55, 178–82
Saarinen, Eero, 23, 55, 111, 136, 178
Saarinen, Eliel, 23, 55
Saltzstein, Joan W., 183–87
San Antonio (Tex.) Transit project, 15
San Francisco Bridge project, 15
San Francisco, 98, 117, 132, 148, 234, 243
San Marcos in the Desert project (Chandler, Ariz.), 196
Sandburg, Carl, 53
Santa Monica, Calif., 218
Santa Monica Mountains, 84
Santayana, George, 217
San Raphael, Calif. *See* Marin County, Calif.
Schindler and Neutra, office of, 220
Schindler, Rudolph M., 220
schools, 219
Schopenhauer, Arthur, 217
Schubert, Franz Peter, 228
sculpture, 122
Seagram Building (New York City), 5
Seattle, 28
Shamrock Hotel (Houston), 163
Sheraton Bal Harbour Hotel (Miami), 8
Silsbee, Joseph Lyman, 135
"Sixty Years of Living Architecture" exhibition, 158, 161
    in Florence, 205
    in New York City, 201, 206
    Pavilion (Los Angeles), *179*
Skidmore, Louis, 16
Skidmore, Owings and Merrill (SOM), 17, 20, 23
Sky Lines (articles in *The New Yorker* by Lewis Mumford), 206
Smith, Melvyn Maxwell, residence (Bloomfield Hills, Mich.), 96, 88–96, *89*, *94*, 158
Smith, Sarah, 88–96
Smithsonian Institution (Washington, D.C.), 74
snobocracy, 6
socialism, 3
Southern Conference on Hospital Planning (Biloxi, Miss.), 98
sovereignty of the individual, 4, 42
specifications, construction, 129
Sports Pavilion at Belmont Project (Long Island, N.Y.), 74
Spring Green, Wis., 89, 91, 106
    post office, 15
    train station, 172
St. Francis Xavier Church (Phoenix, Ariz.), 196
St. Louis, Mo., 2, 6
    Gateway Arch, 111
St. Mark's in the Bouwerie Towers project (New York City), *40*
St. Peter's Cathedral, Renaissance dome of, 57
Stalinism, 204
steel, as a modern material, 23
Stein, Gertrude, 36
Steinway piano, 129, 144
stencilists, 50
Sticks and Stones (by Lewis Mumford), 201
Stone, Edward Durell, 31, 56–58
Stonorov, Oskar, 50
suburbia, 7, 9
Sulgrave Manor Lectures of 1939 at RIBA, 174
Sullivan, Francis C., 196–97
Sullivan, Louis, 34, 35, 37–38, 53, 119, 142, 183, 225, 229
    as Frank Lloyd Wright's "lieber Meister," 227
    his definition of a "highbrow," 13
Swaback, Vernon D., 164–69
Swedenborg Memorial Wayfarer's Chapel (Rancho Palos Verdes, Calif.), 218, *220*, 221

Tafel, Edgar, 42, 44, 184
Taliesin (Spring Green, Wis.), 42, 47, 53, *64*, 71, 89, 91, 93, 100, 101, 103, 110, 113, 117, 118, 119, *123*, 132, 133, 142, 150, 159, 161, 164, 165, 166, 167, 168, 172, 174, 178, 182, 183, 185, 187, 188, 189, 196, 198, 202, 215, 217, 238, 243
    as "shining brow," 178, 241
    as returning to Mecca for apprentices, 216
    carriage house of, 185
    Chinese temple bell of, 180, *180*
    chorus of, 134
    Council, 164
    Taliesin Associated Architects, 117, 137, 148
    dams of, 129, 133
    drafting room of, 132, 191, 130
    Fellows of, 74, *118*, 130, 190
    hill garden of, 130
    living room of, *181*
    pianos at, 144
    picnics at, 187
    studio of, 126
    Wright's bedroom at, *123*, *173*
Taliesin Fellowship, 40, 47, 85, 86, 91, 116, 125, 148, 158, 161, 162, 164, 165, 167, 178, 183, 184, 184, 202, 213, 230, 242
    charter membership, 122
    chorus rehearsals of, 130
Taliesin Fellowship Complex (Spring Green, Wis.), *124*, 130, 186, 187, *189*
    construction of, 129
    drafting studio of, *124*, *125*
    theater of, 181, *182*, 185
    movies of, 185
    music as part of lives, 132
    String Quartet of, 184, 185
    Sunday picnics of, 185
    tuition of, 184
Taliesin-style, 74
Taliesin West (Scottsdale, Ariz.), 40, 86, 101, 102, 135, 139, *139*, *149*, *150*, 166, 174, 175, 190, 202, 216, 224, 241, 243
    construction of, 150
    drafting rooms of, 132
    entrance sign, *244*
    purchase of property, 139
Tao, 68, 75
taste, 4, 121, 162
Taylor, Elizabeth, 167
Texas, 103
The Golden Day (by Lewis Mumford), 209
The Razor's Edge (by Somerset Maugham), 240
The Spaces in Between: An Architect's Journey (by Nathaniel Owings), 16
The Ten Commandments, 240
Thoreau, David Henry, 204
Time, 86
Tip-Top Inn (Chicago), 225
Todd, Mike, 167
Tolstoy, Count Lev Nikolaevich, 204
transcendentalism, 221, 223
Tulane University, 88
Turczyn, Peter, *94*
Two-Zone House project, 127

U.S. Air Force Academy (Colorado Springs, Colo.), 15–31, *17*, *18*
U.S. Capitol, 21
U.S. Central Intelligence Agency, 204
U.S. Department of the Interior, 66
U.S. Embassy (London, England), 111
U.S. Embassy (Tokyo, Japan), 15
U.S. Mint (San Francisco), 98
U.S. Senate Committee on Appropriations, 27
United States, 4, 20, 174, 219
    government of, 31
    people of, 30
    West Coast of, 175, 220, 224
Unity Chapel (Spring Green, Wis.), 134, *135*, 159
Unity Church (Oak Park, Ill.), 117
University of Arkansas, 162, 163
University of Chicago, 83, 112, 183
University of Illinois, 165, 167, 166
University of Michigan, 176
University of Oklahoma, 35

University of Pennsylvania, 208
University of Wisconsin-Madison, 226
Usonian Exhibition House and Pavilion (New York City), 161, 206
Usonian houses, 88, 140, 142, 143
   furniture for, 144
   standard detail sheet for, 141, 143

Vaughan, Rev. Joseph A., S.J., 196–97
Venice, Italy, 129
Vienna, Austria, 36
Virginia, 73
   practice of democracy in, 69
von Eckardt, Wolf, 198

Wagner, Robert F., 2, 7
Walters, Carl, 110
war, 6, 190
Washington, D.C., 28, 30, 31
Washington Post, 236
Wasmuth portfolio, 34, 36, 42, 44, 45, 48, 218, 226
Watergate, 219
Wayne State University, 88
Webb & Knapp, 2
Weese, Harry, 112
Weiner, Egon, 188–89
Wendigen (by Henric Wijdeveld), 201
White, E. B., 73
Whitman, Walt, 204
Wijdeveld, Henric, 200, 201, 202
Willey, Malcolm E., residence (Minneapolis), *127*
Winged Victory (statue), 233, 206
Wisconsin, 98, 126, 174
Wisconsin Dells, Wis., 89
Wisconsin River (near Spring Green, Wis.), 198
   bridge near Taliesin, 159
Woodlawn Plantation (Mount Vernon, Va.), 66, 72, 74, 147
Woods, George, 94
Woolley, Taylor, 218, 226
World Trade Center (New York City), 207
World War II, 88, 90, 157, 204, 205
Wright, Anna [Hannah] Lloyd-Jones, 4, 225
Wright, Catherine Dorothy. *See* Baxter, Catherine Dorothy Wright
Wright, Catherine Lee Clark Tobin, 225, 228
Wright, David, 144, 235, 242
   residence (Phoenix, Ariz.), 237–238, *237, 239*
Wright, Eric Lloyd, 56, 218, 224, 226
Wright, Frances, 235
Wright, Frank Lloyd, *ii, x, 3, 16*
   abhorrence of the machine, 2
   affection for beautiful things, 86, 228
   approach to education, 47, 138
   architectural grammar of, 228, 229
   as a dramatic, 80, 231, 234
   as a genius, 54, 137, 218, 226, 230, 24
   as an individualist, 7, 47, 52, 137, 213, 218
   as an old master, 57, 83, 86
   as a piano player, 129, 228, 233–34
   as a teacher, 229–30
   at Bauhaus Exhibition at Museum of Modern Art in 1938, *43*
   at home of the Neils, *160*
   at Taliesin (Spring Green, Wis.), *64*
   at temporary office at Taliesin West, *151*
   birthday celebrations, 185
   birthplace of, 214
   Capehart photograph, 187
   concept of God, 191
   contributions to architecture, 36, 99, 157, 230
   Cord car of, 117
   creativity of, 50, 153, 209, 243
   delight in working with foreign students, 129
   dismissal of other historic epochs, 203
   eccentricities of, 138
   ego of, 46, 64, 95, 138
   European fame of, 44, 69, 199
   fallacy of the legends, 156
   family of, 68, 133, 221, 229–30
   favorite plant material in Wisconsin, 147
   first marriage to Catherine Lee Clark Tobin, 232
   gold medals, 24, 35, 163, 182, 205

government-related designs of, 6, 15
impressions of the Welsh, 175
in Marin County, Calif., *154*
in the drafting room, 133
jealousy of young followers as rivals, 203
lectures, 39, 116
Malacca cane, 81
on Antonio Gaudi, 37
on architects and architecture as a profession, 30, 173, 178, 180, 203
on art and religion, 13
on attending architecture school, 34
on form follows function, 181
on his death, 87
on imitation, 215
on Lewis Mumford, 157
on nature study, 121
on plan factories, 180
on the design of the New York cab, 102
patience of in making drawings, 129
pictured with Bruce Goff and students, *35*
presenting Mile-High Illinois Skyscraper project at Chicago, *207*
principles of, 215
public acclaim in U.S., 183
reaction to new building materials, 216
sculptured bust of by Egon Weiner, *189*
signature block of, 96, 130, 229, 236
standards for his students, 155
talking with students at University of Michigan, *177*
treatment of apprentices, 138
treatment of clients, 237
trip to Boston in 1940, 45
visit to University of California-Berkeley, 155
visit to Wales, 175
visit to Walter Gropius residence in 1940, 45
way of walking, 203
with Aaron Green, 155
with Eric Mendelsohn at Taliesin (Spring Green, Wis.), *199*
with his clients, 133
with John H. Howe, *117*
with Mayor Richard J. Daley and Mayor Ivan Nestingen, *165*
with Robert L. Ziegelman at the University of Michigan, *177*
with Taliesin Fellows and family at Taliesin (Spring Green, Wis.), *118*
with Walter and Ise Gropius, *43*
with wife Olgivanna Lloyd Wright, *212*
work as principle, 169
work of as a new classical order, 168
Wright, Frank Lloyd, Home and Studio. *See* Frank Lloyd Wright Home and Studio
Wright, Harold Bell, 69
Wright, Iovanna Lloyd, 56, 183, 187, 213
Wright, John Lloyd, 224, 231, 235
Wright, Lloyd, 56, 98, 218–30, *219, 220,* 231, 235, *241, 242*
   as draftsman in father's office, 225, 226
   on his apprenticeship training under his father, 223
Wright, Olgivanna Lloyd, 47, 56, 86, 101, *118,* 125, 132, 134, 135, 137, 180, 183, 184, 187, 190, 194, 201, *212,* 213–17, *214,* 242
   as a mystic, 217
   childhood in Europe, 217
   on meeting Frank Lloyd Wright, 217
   on students, 215
Wright, Robert Llewellyn, 144, 235–38, *235*
   residence (Bethesda, Md.), *236*
Wright, Svetlana Hinzenberg, 137, 183, 184, 187

Yale University School of Architecture, 136
Yosemite National Park, 15
Yugoslavia, 213

Zeckendorf, William, 2, 5, 6, 7, 183, 184, 187
Ziegelman, Robert L., 176–77, *177*
Zimmerman, Isadore J., residence (Manchester, N.H.), 158